The ASTD Reference Guide to

PROFESSIONAL TRAINING ROLES

& —

COMPETENCIES

Vol. I

Henry J. Sredl & William J. Rothwell

Human Resource Development Press

HRD Press, Inc. / Amherst, Massachusetts

First Edition

98765432

Copyright © 1987 by Henry J. Sredl and William J. Rothwell.

Library of Congress Cataloging in Publication Data
Sredl, Henry J., 1935–
    The ASTD reference guide to professional
training roles and competencies.

    Includes bibliographies and indexes.
    1. Employees, Training of—Handbooks, manuals,
etc. 2. Personnel management—Handbooks, manuals,
etc. I. Rothwell, William J., 1951– . II. American
Society for Training and Development. III. Title.
HF5549.5.T7S657   1987   658.3'124   86–26006

ISBN 0-87425-083-8 (v. 1)
ISBN 0-87425-084-6 (v. 2)

Preface

Since the ASTD's publication of *Models for Excellence* (Patricia McLagan, Volunteer Study Director) in 1983 Human Resources Development practitioners have been discussing it, debating it, and using it. Our book is intended to be a companion to *Models* and to expand on its significant contributions to the profession of Human Resources Development.

More than a few people we know have commented on the technical difficulties of this undertaking. They have pointed out that the format of *Models* does not lend itself easily to treatment in book form. Because the 15 roles of the HRD professional in *Models* overlap, we faced a serious problem in trying to treat each one separately. The same is true of the 31 competencies in *Models*.

We knew then from the beginning of this project that we could not simply use *Models* as a rough outline for a book. Instead, we have taken the approach of translating each role and its corresponding work outputs and competencies into a step-by-step process.* We do not consider this publication "finished" because it is in print; rather, we offer it as a comprehensive resource of current knowledge on the roles and competencies of HRD professionals, and as a base on which to build as the world in which we live and work undergoes changes.

About our authorship: If it were possible to list our names without implying a senior or junior author, we would do so. *We are entirely co-equal authors*. Each complements the other with his perception of life and its opportunities and challenges for HRD practitioners and those

This book does not represent the official position of the ASTD nor are the opinions expressed in this book necessarily those of the authors' employer.

they serve. This guide would not have been possible without both of us. We deserve equal credit—or blame—for the final product.

The days of authors as lonely scribes are gone. In this age of group efforts and technological advances, this publication would never have been completed without "our team," and they deserve recognition. Dee Safley, owner and manager of Modern Office Management Systems, Corvallis, Oregon, was responsible for the most difficult operation of producing the final manuscript on a word processor. Her insightful reflections and unending support throughout this process enabled us to meet crucial deadlines. Stephanie Gallagher typed and proofed the embryonic stage of this book and sent it into the outside world for review; she then continued to be most helpful throughout with her eye for copy detail and conceptual thought. Glenda Collier devoted her technical talents to the original presentation of the publication's many figures. The friends and staff members at the American Society for Training and Development and at Random House encouraged and supported the authors with a look to the future. And most important, our wives—Rowena Sredl and Marcelina Rothwell—not only gave up their spouses for three years, but encouraged them during those many times when this lengthy undertaking seemed beyond the possibility of completion.

This work is dedicated to all humans, the most precious resource on this planet—and beyond.

HENRY J. SREDL   **WILLIAM J. ROTHWELL**
Corvallis, Oregon   *Springfield, Illinois*

March, 1986

Contents

PART SIX: The HRD Program— How Learning Is Planned   311

Figures

Chapter 2

Chapter 3

Chapter 4

Chapter 5

Chapter 6

Chapter 7

Chapter 8

Chapter 9

Chapter 10

Chapter 11

Chapter 12

Chapter 13

Overview

Human Resources Development (HRD)—usually considered to mean in-house employee training and development—is an enormous but hidden industry:

- A 1982 survey by *Training* revealed that there are over 200,000 full-time and 700,000 part-time trainers in the U.S., not including those in the military. A 1983 update showed an increase of full-time trainers to nearly 250,000.

- U.S. organizations spend roughly $30 billion per year on formal training for their employees and another $180 billion on informal training. When you compare these sums with governmental spending on formal education (see Figure 1), it is easy to see that the total amount spent by employers on training for mainstream employees each year is about the same as that spent by government to support formal education.[1]

What accounts for this enormous investment in formal and informal training by employers?

The answer is simple enough: since 1929, economic data have clearly shown that human beings—not machines—have accounted for the greatest growth in national product (see Figure 2). People who receive even informal training on the job, as opposed to off-the-job programs, increase their earning potential and productivity by as much as 13 percent for the college-educated and 19 percent for those who did not attend college.[2]

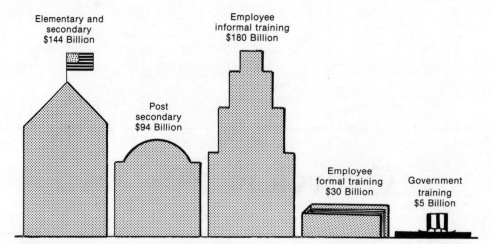

Figure 1 The learning enterprise *(Source: "The Learning Enterprise," by A. Carnevale. Training and Development Journal, 1986. Reprinted with permission.)*

Employers have acted in their own best interest by providing instruction in how to do the work. In-house training helps new employees in the socialization process, facilitating their mastery of how to apply what they know in a unique organizational context. In-house education keeps employees up to date as their occupations change and helps prepare them for movement into new jobs.

However, not all organizations provide the same amount of training to all age groups and occupational categories. As Figure 3 shows, employers in the service industry spend the most on training in the aggregate, while government employers spend the most per employee. Highly regulated and specialized industries tend to spend more on training than those not so regulated or specialized. HRD efforts also tend to be directed at areas within an organization that are most crucial for dealing with changes wrought by outside forces. As Figure 4 illustrates, employees under age 45 receive the most in-house instruction, while Figure 5 shows that white-collar workers receive substantially more instruction than other groups.

Growing technological change and turbulent economic conditions will probably make human resources development a growth field for some time to come. The Bureau of Labor Statistics predicts growing occupational demand for human resources specialists. Already more than 200 colleges and universities offer degrees in HRD and related fields.[3]

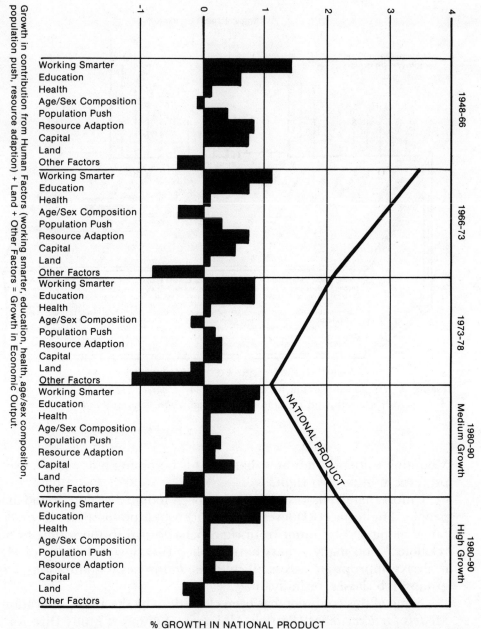

Figure 2 Components of growth in economic output 1948–1978 and projected Through 1990 (*Source:* Human Capital: A High Yield Corporate Investment (*Executive Summary*), *by A. Carnevale. American Society for Training and Development, 1982. Reprinted with permission.*)

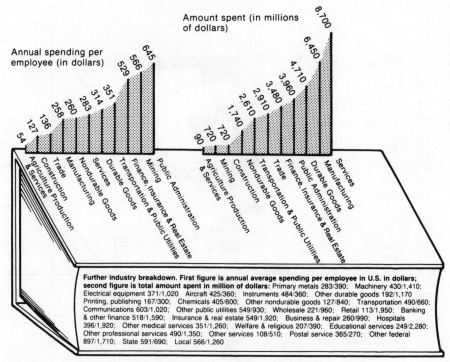

Total average spent per employee in the U.S. on training—$283.

Figure 3 Employee training by industry, 1984 *(Source: "The Learning Enterprise," by A. Carnevale, Training and Development Journal, 1986. Reprinted with permission.)*

Mounting evidence indicates that HRD is becoming a discipline, even a profession, in its own right.

Unfortunately, however, HRD has been too many things to too many people. The term HRD loses significance when philosophies of practice range along a continuum from rigid behaviorism to the softest human relations.[4] Too many writers have implied that one philosophy of HRD is always appropriate across all cultures, industries, organizations, work groups, job classes, or individuals.

Some of this confusion has been cleared up by the 1983 publication of *Models for Excellence* (Patricia McLagan, Volunteer Study Director), a massive study about what HRD practitioners actually do and which identifies 15 practitioner roles, 31 competencies and 102 outputs of HRD work.

The *ASTD Guide to Professional Training Roles and Competencies* is in-

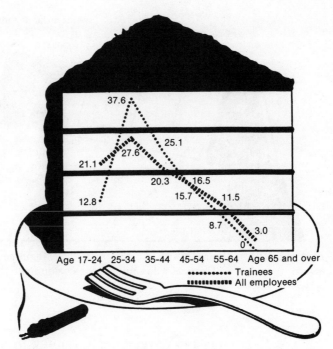

Figure 4 Trainees and all employees by age, 1981 (*Source: "The Learning Enterprise," by A. Carnevale,* Training and Development Journal, *1986, Reprinted with permission.*)

tended to update, build on, and expand on the aims of *Models for Excellence.* Our purpose is to provide a guide and reference work for HRD professionals, those planning to enter the HRD field, and serve as a text or source-book in formal college degree programs in HRD. Specifically, this guide is useful to HRD managers and specialists:

- As an aid to identifying the breadth of the T&D [Training and Development] department's activities.
- As a starting point for identifying strategic assumptions that will affect T&D priorities.
- As a guide to use in organization and job design.
- As an aid in incumbent performance appraisal.
- As an aid to selection of new staff and promotion/career pathing of existing staff.

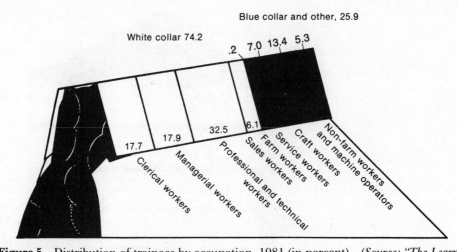

Figure 5   Distribution of trainees by occupation, 1981 (in percent)   (*Source: "The Learning Enterprise," by A. Carnevale,* Training and Development Journal, *1986. Reprinted with permission.*)

- With guidance in developing a training program for staff.
- As an aid in career counseling.
- To assemble a project team that balances needed roles and competencies.
- As an aid in communicating with management about the positioning, mission, and goals of the Training and Development unit.
- As an aid to strengthening the manager's own performance.
- As a framework for profiling the current job.
- As a framework for self-assessment.
- As an aid to deciding directions for job expansion.
- As a career planning tool.
- As a framework for development planning.
- As a language for communicating with management about personal strengths, career goals, job redesign ideas, development priorities.
- As an aid in describing what T&D work is when people outside the field ask, "What do you do?

It serves people aspiring to HRD careers:

- By helping them understand what it is like to do T&D work.
- As an aid to understanding what the field encompasses.
- As the basis for a checklist to help identify their transferable competencies.
- As an aid in determining the roles to pursue.
- As a language to use in resumés and as a framework for identifying the requirements of specific jobs during a job interview.
- As a framework for identifying development priorities.

It also serves members of the academic community:

- As a guide for assessing current program/service focuses and priorities.
- As material to include in courses that survey the T&D field.
- As a student assessment framework.
- To help identify departments within the institution whose programs and expertise can/should be drawn on for a T&D Curriculum.
- As a language to use across departments and among colleges and universities across the country about the T&D field and its educational/curriculum needs.
- As a framework for identifying research projects and topics for graduate and post-graduate theses.
- To assist student counseling for careers in the T&D field.
- As aids in selecting and developing faculty.
- To help justify programs, curricula, and budget requests to central administration and within colleges. (*Models for Excellence,* p. 105)

The author of any book makes a value statement, implicitly or explicitly, about his or her view of the world. We are no different. Philosophically, we believe that:

- *HRD is (and should be) eclectic.* For this reason, we draw on theories from many disciplines.
- *HRD approaches should depend, in part, on the environment in which they are applied and on the values of those who use them.* We do not

espouse any particular philosophy of learning or instruction. Instead, we prefer to describe four different philosophies of instruction. At the same time, we also believe that each practitioner develops a personal philosophy of HRD that guides his or her behavior. For this reason, we try to help the reader clarify his or her own values and beliefs regarding human nature, learning, and other issues.

• *HRD should be viewed holistically and strategically.* Professionals in any field are prone to magnify their own importance, as if what they do is an end in itself. We try to avoid this tendency by stressing repeatedly that HRD is only the means to ends such as fulfilling organizational strategic plans and individual career plans. Since both personal and organizational development occur over time, we focus our attention primarily on the long-term organizational curriculum rather than on short-term, one-shot learning experiences, courses, workshops, or programs.

To achieve these aims, we have structured the book into 12 parts.

The first volume contains Parts One through Six and focuses on relationships between HRD and its setting; the second volume contains Parts Seven through Twelve and focuses on specific activities of HRD practitioners. However, since each chapter is self-contained, there is no need to read them in the order presented.

References

1. Carnevale, A. "The Learning Enterprise." *Training and Development Journal* 40 (1986) 1: pp. 18–26.

2. Ibid.

3. *Directory of Academic Programs in T&D/HRD.* Washington, D.C.: American Society for Training and Development, 1982.

4. Zemke, R. "In Search of a Training Philosophy." *Training,* 22(1985) 10: pp. 93–94, 96, 98.

Henry J. Sredl
William J. Rothwell

1

Human resources development— its background and setting.

What is human resources development (HRD)? What are some of its major ideas, and where did they come from? What are the factors that affect HRD—that is, the context in which it must function—and why are they crucially important?

Part One addresses these questions and others. It thus establishes a general perspective from which to view HRD.

CHAPTER 1

The roots of human resources development.

This chapter defines Human Resources Development (HRD), describes its forerunners, and summarizes its basic assumptions. ■

What is HRD?

HRD does not have a single definition on which all writers agree. Some use the term for government-sponsored educational or training programs aimed to help the disadvantaged; others use it for any form of education or training; still others use it to refer to training or education sponsored by an employer and imbued with a humanistic philosophy.

In this book HRD refers to *organized learning experiences sponsored by an employer and designed and/or conducted for the purpose of improving work performance while emphasizing the betterment of the human condition through integration of organizational goals and individual needs.* To elaborate on this definition:

- *Organized learning experiences*—HRD activities are planned experiences. While learning can take place spontaneously, HRD activities usually have outcomes specified in advance.

- *Sponsored by an employer*—HRD activities are supported by the employer and geared to meet the unique needs of the organization. In most cases, colleges and universities can provide general knowledge of a profession or discipline but cannot provide—as HRD does—specific guidance on how to apply that knowledge in the unique context and culture of a specific organization.

- *Designed and/or conducted for the purpose of improving work performance*—the goal of HRD efforts is not centered on the general enlightenment of the individual, as is education, but rather on improving how well the individual can do his or her work, now and in the future. The environment and culture of the organization are of major importance in designing learning experiences and using them to influence work performance.

- *While emphasizing the betterment of the human condition*—HRD efforts are based in humanism, which is characterized by: 1) faith in human rationality; 2) a belief that people are capable of continuous learning and growth throughout their lives; and 3) emphasis on the importance and dignity of individuals as human beings with needs, feelings, and desires.

- *Through integration of organizational goals and individual needs*—HRD efforts do not stress, to the exclusion of the individual, what the organization needs from its employees to achieve its future goals. Instead, managers within the organization recognize that what the individual visualizes as his or her future career goals can be compatible with organizational goals. Only by making a genuine attempt to respect (and even aid) employees in achieving their goals can an organization gain commitment and thereby increase productivity.

HRD has been affected by philosophical trends and ideas from several fields.

Forerunners of HRD

Many beliefs commonly shared by HRD professionals stem from a much broader human resources philosophy. That accounts for some confusion about the term. Indeed, economists and management theorists were referring to "human resources" as early as 1958, but "human resources development" was not coined by Leonard Nadler until ten years later.

Initially, Nadler equated HRD with any group of planned activities intended to result in behavioral change. He later revised his thinking—with a telling shift of emphasis—to equate it with "an organized *learning* experience within a given period of time with the *possibility* of *performance* change." Some writers have been even more free with the term, linking it to any activity associated with training or education.

Several attempts have been made to define HRD by distinguishing it from related fields. Nadler distinguishes it from two others: Human Resource Utilization (HRU) and the Human Resource Environment (HRE). HRU encompasses all duties traditionally handled by personnel departments, while HRE encompasses all efforts to change the interaction of work groups or allocation of work duties across jobs. Some distinguish HRD (individually-oriented change efforts) from Organization Development (organization-wide change efforts) and Human Resources Management (the use of existing human resources). Others have virtually given up trying to define the term.

Whatever wording is used, there are clearly some similarities across definitions. Most writers agree that HRD deals with human learning, more often than not in an organizational setting outside an educational institution. Most also agree that the assumptions of HRD are normative, philosophical ideals, and that applications vary widely. Taken together, these assumptions are the culmination and fusion of separate developments in several disciplines.

No field of study is immune from change. In the *Structure of Scientific Revolutions*, Thomas Kuhn [1] characterized the development of science itself as involving problem-solving activities carried out within the framework of shared theories or viewpoints. A scientific revolution is a change in theory which, in turn, results in different ways of looking at problems. Kuhn believes that even nonscientific fields experience such revolutions.

Nowhere is Kuhn's rather controversial theory perhaps more appropriate than in charting the progress of such proto-sciences as economics, psychology, communication, management, and education. In each case the pendulum of thought has swung from a generally negative to a more positive view of human nature. These changes laid the foundation for a broad human resources philosophy (see Figure 1.1).

To show the general direction of these changes, we shall describe them briefly in the next section.

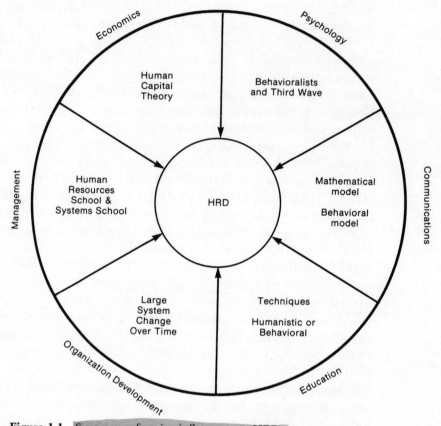

Figure 1.1   Summary of major influences on HRD

Economics

Adam Smith's *Wealth of Nations* (1776) is generally considered the first statement of a comprehensive economic theory. From earlier writers Smith accepted the belief that production is dependent on three key factors: land, labor, and capital. Smith likewise accepted the belief, known as the Labor Theory of Value, that labor is the pre-eminent factor in production. The key to a nation's prosperity can be found in "the skill, dexterity, and judgment with which its labor is generally applied." After all, it is only through the application of labor that land or capital is rendered useful. Some later economists, most notably Karl Marx and David Ricardo, accepted but modified this theory.

The early 19th-century economist J. B. Say successfully attacked the

Labor Theory of Value. He maintained that "productive agencies," in combination, produced goods.

> Instead of seeing the process of production as a series of human exertions
> . . . Say asserted the existence of different "productive agencies" that com-
> bined together to produce goods. What these productive agencies were ulti-
> mately producing was 'utility' . . .[2]

Later 19th-century economists refined this view, called the Utility Theory of Value. For example, J. S. Mill felt that capital investment and accumulation were the force behind employment and increased productivity. Mainstream 20th-century economic theory generally assumes that capital is the pre-eminent factor in production. Two key thinkers in this tradition have emerged: John Maynard Keynes and Milton Friedman.

Keynes argued that spending by government is essentially the cornerstone of full employment and that the supply of labor has nothing to do with demand. Unlike Adam Smith and J. B. Say, who believed that markets are self-adjusting, Keynes believed that widespread unemployment could persist indefinitely. To counteract unemployment, government should tax and spend in such a way as to influence business activity. In short, fiscal policy (government spending) can be used to stimulate employment or retard inflation.

Milton Friedman's views contradict those of Keynes. To Friedman, interest rates and the growth of the total amount of money available in the economy are the keys to productivity and employment. Governmental attempts to stimulate or retard the business cycle do not serve the best interest of long-term economic prosperity, Friedman believes. Instead, wild swings in governmental spending merely worsen economic conditions, because it is the total amount of money available in the economy that determines conditions for prosperity. Government's role should be to establish a uniform, predictable monthly increase in the total amount of money available in the economy. Since the Federal Reserve Board controls money supply in the U.S., Friedman sees the Board's actions in setting interest rates as central to national economic health.

Beginning in the late 1950s, critics of mainstream economic theory began to question the assumptions of writers like Keynes and Friedman.[3] Forerunners of what was later to be called the Human Capital school, these critics began to ask whether demand for labor is really a function of monetary or fiscal policy. They suggested that it is possible to consider labor a form of capital, not a factor of production separate from (and driven by) it. This view has gained increasing support in the wake of perceived failures in the application of mainstream economic theory since 1964.[4] The Human Capital school has spawned the notion that labor is a human resource connoting the abilities and potential of people to contribute to their work not only their talents and skills but also their creativity.[5]

The human capacity for creating new ideas and disseminating or processing information—not the traditional economic view of labor as synonymous with physical exertion—underlies this revolutionary view of the importance of people in the production process.[6] National economic well-being is not a function of monetary or fiscal policy; rather, it results from long-term investment in human capital through education and training. As proof of this assertion, economists point to the coincident increase in the U.S. Gross National Product (GNP) and aggregate investments in education and training between 1919 and 1957.[7] Human capital has been a major force in the growth of GNP, advocates of this theory assert.

Summing up, economics has thus evolved from Smith's 18th-century emphasis on labor to a 19th- and early 20th-century emphasis on capital as pre-eminent in the production process. Until 1958, labor was largely considered synonymous with physical exertion. National economic well-being was considered a function of the manipulation of money through government spending or through steady growth of the money supply. With the failure of mainstream economic theory since 1964, there has been growing interest in a radically different view of labor as a form of capital, an asset and not an expense. While the Human Capital theory remains controversial, some economists believe that people are human resources that can be developed through investment in education and training.

Psychology

Psychology is the study of the human mind, generally emphasizing treatment of individual mental aberrations. As in economics, management, and education, any psychological theory is essentially based on a view of human nature. From that view stems a theory of how to change people. The history of psychology, like that of many other disciplines, is essentially a history of changes in views about human nature.

Sigmund Freud is generally acknowledged to be the first modern psychological theorist. He believed that human nature is determined by unconscious drives and psychosexual occurrences during the first few years of life. Human beings are energy systems consisting of three parts: 1) the id, which serves as the repository of instincts; 2) the ego, which deals with the outside world and focuses on the practical; 3) the superego, which serves as the internalized voice of societal norms and thus focuses on the moralistic. Personality is largely determined in early childhood through such developmental stages as the oral, anal, and phallic. For Freud, psychological health is achieved by making the unconscious manifest and by strengthening the ego to withstand instinctual urges.

Freud's theory was challenged by a second wave of psychologists, known as behaviorists. Led by B. F. Skinner and other writers, the behaviorists asserted that human nature is determined by the environment, not (as Freud believed) by unconscious drives. People are passive agents molded by their surroundings. Freud thought that psychological problems could be solved largely by consciously recognizing them. He thus assumed that attitudes and beliefs guide behavior. In contrast, the behaviorists assumed that behavior guides attitudes and beliefs. As a result, therapeutic psychological change comes about through alterations in the environment and through acting out behavior consistent with desired change.

Beginning in the late 1950s and the early 1960s, a third wave of psychological theorists challenged the views of behaviorism. Known as person-centered psychology and led by such writers as Carl Rogers and Abraham Maslow, this movement maintained that human nature is neither entirely determined by the unconscious or by environment. People are not passive agents, as both Freudians and behaviorists implied; rather, human nature encompasses a proactive as well as a reactive side. People have a deep need to grow and realize their potential. Hence, therapeutic change results from self-awareness and self-acceptance. The psychologist serves as a mirror for clients, stimulating insight that in turn prompts change.

Rogers' person-centered psychology is humanistic. His view of human nature is optimistic, with a deep faith in human perfectability. When applied to education or training, it places responsibility for learning squarely on the student or trainee—not on the instructor. It requires learners to experience themselves as people in the present rather than in the future. Learners must trust in themselves, substitute self-approval for instructor approval, and be willing to grow over time rather than expect to cease learning at some point.

Figure 1.2 How three major psychological theories differ

	Freudian	*Skinnerian*	*Rogerian*
Theory Name	Psycholoanalysis	Behaviorism	Person-centered therapy
View of Human Nature	Passionistic	Pessimistic	Optimistic
Determinants of Human Nature	Unconscious drives and early childhood experience	Environmental conditions	The individual's need to grow
Nature of Therapeutic Change	Make the unconscious conscious; strengthen the ego	Change attitudes and beliefs through behavior	Evoke greater self-awareness

Twentieth-century psychology has evolved from a view of people as passive agents of their unconscious or their environment to active agents capable of influencing their unconscious and their environment. Figure 1.2 summarizes basic assumptions of Freudian, Skinnerian, and Rogerian psychology.

Management

Management is an activity aimed at acquiring, allocating, and using human and physical resources to achieve a goal or series of goals. A management theory is essentially a unified way of looking at the nature of people, work, and organizations. The evolution of management thought, like that of economics and psychology, has led to a new view of these three elements that is consistent with the human resources philosophy.

Although management as an activity is as old as civilization, management theory is relatively new. Frederick Taylor (1856–1915) is generally considered to be the first to conceptualize a view of management coupled with a philosophical framework. Taylor's major work, *The Principles of Modern Management* (1911), was based on his work at Bethlehem Steel in the early 1900s. To summarize his contributions:

• Taylor believed that management's job was to analyze every task done by workers to determine the most efficient work methods.

- Taylor recognized that different people have different talents. Managers should select workers carefully to ensure that each job is filled by a person uniquely suited for it.
- Workers should be sufficiently trained and educated so that they know what they are expected to do and how they can best do it.
- Managers and workers should cooperate and should not inherently be in conflict.
- Employees should be compensated according to how much they produce.

Taylor's work has had a profound and lasting impact on management thinking. Subsequent writers have criticized Taylor for a theory that, in effect if not by intent, fostered the assumption that people are basically lazy. Others have claimed that the glowing research reports Taylor used to justify his theory were largely prefabricated lies.[8]

Writing in Europe at the same time Taylor was writing in America, Henri Fayol (1841–1925) concentrated on organizational theory. He contributed 14 famous principles that are still considered in day-to-day management. They are:

1. *Division of labor.* To increase efficiency, workers should specialize in tasks for which they are best suited.
2. *Authority.* Managers should have authority, the right to issue orders. With authority comes responsibility for ensuring that the work is done.
3. *Discipline.* The organization should expect obedience from its employees, and in turn employees should expect to be treated with dignity by their employers.
4. *Unity of command.* Each employee should report to only one supervisor.
5. *Unity of direction.* Each activity in an organization should have one leader and one plan.
6. *Subordination of personal interests.* Management must ensure that decisions are made from a rational standpoint and not solely to placate self-interested individuals or groups.
7. *Remuneration.* People should be paid in order to motivate them.

8. *Centralization.* The issuing of orders creates a degree of centralization in all organizations. However, it is possible to increase employee autonomy (decentralization) or decrease it (centralization).

9. *The Scalar Chain.* Authority is hierarchical and must be made explicit. In other words, it must be clear who reports to whom.

10. *Order.* All materials and all activities should be kept where they are appropriate.

11. *Equity.* Employees should be treated justly.

12. *Stability of tenure.* People resources should be planned for.

13. *Initiative.* Employees should be encouraged to be enthusiastic about their work.

14. *Esprit de corps.* Management should encourage harmony and discourage destructive conflict within the organization.

Fayol's views supplement those of Taylor. However, a second wave of management theorists challenged the theories of both Taylor and Fayol. From a series of experiments conducted at the Hawthorne, Illinois, facility of Western Electric between 1924 and 1932, such writers as Elton Mayo and F. J. Roethlisberger concluded that:

- People are more interested in social relations than in making money.
- People are more responsive to the feelings of their work group than to management attempts to control them.
- Work is heavily influenced by social relationships, not so much by the logic of making money.
- Organizations are influenced as much by human feelings as by efficiency.

From these assumptions, Human Relations theorists concluded that managers are effective to the extent that they help workers feel accepted by their work groups, persuade employees to accept their decisions, and listen for feelings as well as for facts from their subordinates.

Critics of Human Relations theory have pointed out that it is based on management merely appearing to be interested in employee concerns. Workers are only made to *feel* good and useful, not to *be* good and useful. Later researchers have seriously questioned the way the Hawthorne studies were conducted. Some critics have suggested that the conclusions were inaccurate or even fallacious.

Two theories of management have dominated since the early 1960s: the systems and the human resources views.

Ludwig von Bertalanffy is commonly considered the first person to use the term General Systems Theory (GST), in 1937. Subsequent writers, including Kenneth Boulding and Norbert Wiener, refined the theory. Early behavioral scientists, basing their work on the assumptions of human relations, concluded that organizations are social *systems* composed of interacting, interrelated, and interdependent parts. *Closed systems* do not depend on their surroundings for vital supplies or other resources; *open systems* depend entirely on their surroundings.

Katz and Kahn have noted ten common characteristics of open systems:

1. *Importation of energy.* Open systems import energy from the environment. For example, organizations depend on their environment for such resources/inputs as people, supplies, finances, and information.

2. *Throughput.* Open systems transform inputs through some work process or method.

3. *Output.* Open systems expel the transformed inputs into the environment surrounding them.

4. *Cycles of events.* Exchanges between the environment and the organization have a pattern.

5. *Negative entropy.* Open systems must reverse the natural tendency of organizations to disintegrate or to lose energy.

6. *Information input, negative feedback, and the coding process.* Open systems receive information in the form of inputs, regulate their operations, and code the information received based on signals to which they are attuned.

7. *The steady state and dynamic homeostasis.* The rate of exchange—that is, the general amount of energy expended in receiving inputs, transforming them, and expelling them as outputs—remains relatively constant, in a steady state. The result is dynamic homeostasis, meaning that an even level of activity is attained and preserved in an organization.

8. *Differentiation.* Open systems are characterized by a movement from general to more specialized functions.

9. *Integration and coordination.* Open systems are characterized by integrative forces that counter differentiation to achieve unity. Coordination assures uniform functioning within the system.

10. *Equifinality.* Open systems are capable of reaching the same final state through many different ways.[9]

According to open systems theory, organizations are totally dependent on the larger environment in which they operate. The manager is in charge of a subsystem, a part within the organizational system. The system is, in turn, a part of a larger suprasystem, such as the industry of which the organization is a part, the national or international economy, or the nation's culture. Work is viewed as a transformation process that is largely value-neutral, meaning that in itself it is neither good nor bad. Individuals in the system take *roles,* and indeed the organization is a *system of roles* that regulates behavior. Organizational roles, the parts played by people, result from a complex interplay of environmental and organizational factors, role expectations established and sent by others, personal attributes, work group relations, and interpretations of the role made by the person in it.

Figure 1.3 depicts the organization as an open system.

While the systems view has exerted an important influence on current thinking about management, another school has also had a major impact. Highly philosophical, the Human Resources view gained prominence during the recession of 1957–1958.[10] It extended key assumptions of the Human Relations view.

From the work of such writers as Argyris, McGregor, Maslow and others, the Human Resources school holds that:

• Individuals are by nature creative and deserve greater self-direction and responsibility.

• Individuals are capable of much greater usefulness to their work groups and co-workers than is recognized or taken advantage of.

• Work is as natural as play. People want to work, because it is a vehicle for self-expression and creativity.

• Leadership consists of making employee potential manifest. The manager's job is to unlock employee talents and nourish them.

• Organizational structures too often interfere with employee creativity. Despite job descriptions and other trappings of bureaucracy,

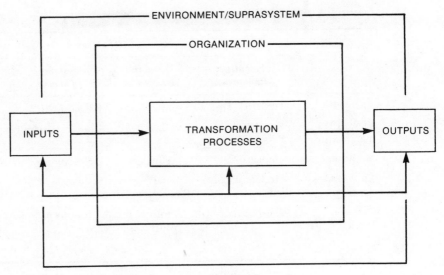

Figure 1.3 The organization as an open system

employees should be encouraged to make suggestions and be creative.

- Power in organizations should consist more of influencing employees than exacting obedience through rewards or punishments. Above all, the manager should exemplify the qualities most prized by the organization.

- Organizational goals and individual needs are capable of integration and are not inherently at odds.

Critics have attacked both the General Systems and Human Resources theories for promising more than they have delivered—or, indeed, could deliver. GST is accused of making organizations appear mechanistic; Human Resources theory is accused of providing norms but no guidelines for applying them. However, the Human Resources view has had an important influence on HRD.

Figure 1.4 summarizes the four major management theories.

Organization Development

Organization Development (OD) is a long-range attempt to increase collaboration and interpersonal trust in an organization, particularly in work

Figure 1.4 Key points of four major management theories

	Theories			
	Scientific Management	*Human Relations*	*Systems Theory*	*Human Resources*
Theorist	Frederick Taylor	Elton Mayo	Katz & Kahn	Chris Argyris
View of Human Nature	Economic/ Pessimistic	Social	Dramatic (Roles)	Creative
Motivation	Money	Feelings	Expectations	Needs
View of Organizations	Mechanistic (like machines)	Social	Systems	Restrictive to individuals
Nature of Work	A necessary evil	A forum for group relations	A transformation process	A vehicle for self expression and creativity

groups, with the help of an outside consultant who draws on the theories and applications of the behavioral sciences.[11] As a precursor of HRD and as a related field, OD deserves attention. While we cannot treat it in detail here, we will describe the field, summarize its key concepts, and discuss its historical emergence.

OD can be viewed as a continuation of the Human Relations school fused with open systems theory and the work of certain industrial psychologists and sociologists. From human relations, OD takes its heavy emphasis on the use of work teams, not individuals, to improve the level of interpersonal trust and cooperation in organizations. Its focus is primarily, though not exclusively, on the nature and impact of individual feelings within and between groups in an organizational setting. From open systems theory, OD takes its emphasis on the interrelatedness of organizational parts.

OD has grown from three major historical elements.[12] The first is laboratory research based on unstructured small-group sessions where participants learn about themselves, others, and the nature of group processes. From a 1946 workshop led by such important people as Kurt Lewin, Kenneth Benne, and Ronald Lippitt, researchers found that learning about group functioning appeared to take place more readily through feedback to members of the group than through lectures. In 1947, several of the original researchers held the first T-group session ("T" stands for "training"). It was the precursor of modern T-group training in which strangers meet for about one week in a series of lectures and small, unstructured sessions to explore group dynamics. In the late 1950s, several attempts were made to apply T-group methods in settings where participants knew one another.

The second major element of OD is survey-guided development, using attitude-survey results to produce an impetus for organizational change. In particular, the work of Rensis Likert figured prominently. He discovered that attitude surveys were a waste unless managers and subordinates used the results in joint planning of organizational improvement.

The third major element of OD is *action research,* a model for problem-solving and change. Though the term was coined by John Collier, Kurt Lewin was the first to use it in an organizational change effort. Sometimes called the basis of OD, it consists of a clearly identifiable sequence of activities:

1. *Diagnosis,* in which problems are identified.
2. *Data gathering,* in which information about problems is collected.
3. *Feedback,* in which information collected through data gathering is fed back to participants.
4. *Data analysis,* in which participants examine information collected about problems.
5. *Planning,* in which participants establish plans for solving problems.
6. *Action,* in which plans are implemented.
7. *Evaluation,* in which results of implementation are compared with problems and plans.

Each activity in this long-term cycle may include, in miniature, the other activities. For example, the diagnosis phase may include such activities as diagnosis, data gathering, and feedback.

OD makes certain important assumptions. These include beliefs that people want to belong to a work group, that individual feelings affect group performance as much as facts, that leaders cannot see to the needs of everyone in a group all the time, that openness and interpersonal trust are essential to group performance, that most groups function far less effectively than they are capable of, and that a willingness to see others as creative and useful can be a self-fulfilling prophecy.[13]

Many different kinds of OD applications have been documented, all based on the action research model. Some of the best known include team building, in which groups become less prone to destructive conflict; process consultation, in which the change agent observes behavior as it happens and provides feedback about it; and survey-guided development, in which results of attitude surveys are fed back to managers and their subordinates as a catalyst to produce joint planning to solve problems or act on issues.

Organizational Communication

Communication has to do with sharing information and emotions. Organizational communication occurs within an organizational structure. It is the basic process from which all management and learning functions stem. HRD can be viewed as a part of organizational communication.[14]

In every school of management thought, key assumptions are made about the communication process. Scientific Management emphasized the role of manager as an information link between employees and higher-level supervisors. Fayol believed that the Scalar Chain, referring to differing levels of authority in organizations, should be preserved by allowing workers to communicate only with immediate superiors, unless they were specifically granted permission to communicate with higher authority. The Human Relations school first recognized the important effect that feelings, interpersonal trust, and openness can have on the reception of information from superiors and co-workers. The Human Resources school recognizes that employees, as well as managers, are potentially important sources of information. As a result, it stresses two-way communication. Finally, Open Systems theory stresses the value of information as a vital input for organizations.

Organizational communication experts use certain special terms, including:

- *Upward communication:* messages directed up the Scalar Chain.
- *Downward communication:* messages or orders directed down the Scalar Chain.
- *Lateral communication:* messages directed to those of equal authority.
- *The sender:* the source of a message.
- *The medium:* the way by which a message is sent.
- *Transmission:* the process of sending a message.

- *Noise:* anything that distorts the sending, transmission, or reception of a message.
- *The receiver:* the receiver of a message.
- *Feedback:* the process of determining whether the message was received.
- *Formal communication:* information that travels along steps in the Scalar Chain.
- *Informal communication:* information that travels along friendship channels, including gossip and rumors spread via the grapevine.
- *The communication audit:* a way of tracking the quality and quantity of communication in an organization.
- *Communication model:* a simplified depiction of the communication process.

There are three major schools of communication theory: mathematical (or cybernetic), behavioral, and transactional.[15] Advocates of the first theory see the communication process as mechanical, resembling the relationship between a radio transmitter and receiver. Shannon and Weaver's model (see top of Figure 1.5) is the best-known of this type. Messages are encoded from a source, sent through a medium, and decoded by a receiver. Noise is what distorts a message, just as static affects radio reception.

In contrast, advocates of the second theory regard communication as a process indistinguishable from determinants of behavior. Berlo's model (see middle, Figure 1.5) represents this theory. The sender is affected by his or her skills of expression, attitudes about the message and receiver, personal knowledge, and the social system. The message consists of content and medium, while the channel may be a stimulus to any of the five senses. The receiver is affected by communication skills, attitudes about the message and the sender, personal knowledge, and the social system.

Advocates of the third theory stress the interactive nature of the communication process, which they call transactional. Both sender and receiver have three ego states: parent, adult, and child. The parent ego state represents the internalized values of a person's parents and is moralistic; the adult state is highly rational; the child state represents a person's childhood and is spontaneous, impulsive, creative, and manipulative. For transactional analysis, communication is effective when the same or complementary ego states of a sender and a receiver speak to each other;

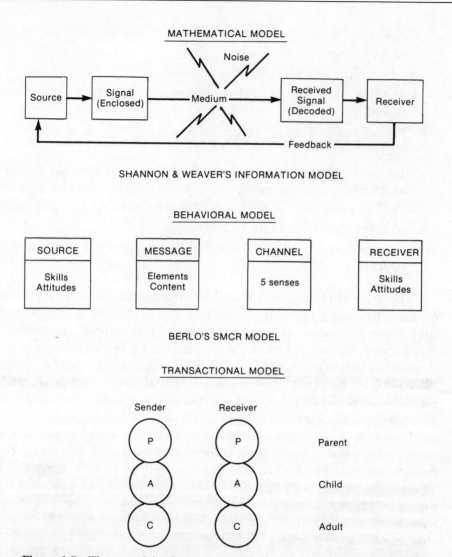

Figure 1.5 Three models of communication

communication is ineffective when a message directed to one ego state is answered with a message directed to an incompatible ego state. For example, the comment "If I were you, I'd go to school" is moralistic in tone and is thus the kind of statement made by the parent ego state to the receiver's child ego state. An appropriate response from the message receiver would be a comment from the child ego state, such as "I wanted to do something else." An inappropriate response would be a remark directed to the wrong ego state, like "What do you care what I do?" ("What" indicates the adult ego). Transactional communication emphasizes the importance of feelings and the interactive nature of meaning within a social context.

Communication theory has thus evolved from a rather limited—even mechanistic—view to one that stresses the importance of interaction. Other contributions of communication theory, such as the nature of communication in small groups, will be discussed later in the book.

Adult Education and Job Training

Two final forerunners of HRD are adult education and job training. They have provided many of the techniques used to carry out HRD activities in work settings. While a complete history of these two activities is beyond the scope of this book, we will sketch their emergence briefly.

The history of adult education and job training is inextricably linked to the history of education in general. The early Greeks and Romans viewed education as a means of awakening the human spirit. Philosophy was the highest order of priority, because it taught the contemplation of truth and beauty, which were considered the greatest goods. Education, for the Greeks, was not equated with preparation for a career. Indeed, the Greeks considered work distasteful, a matter best left to slaves. The purpose of education was to instill appreciation for the arts and teach skills of governance. During the Middle Ages and the Renaissance, universities were created and the thinking of the ancients on educational matters was formalized in Europe. Of course, agriculture was the dominant industry, so relatively few people achieved literacy at all. Those who did were almost entirely men.

Essentially, three forms of educational preparation emerged. A child's schooling was dependent on social station. First-born males of aristocratic birth were schooled as gentlemen, and many attended universities. To obtain a baccalaureate degree, students devoted four years to the study of the classical *trivium*, consisting of Latin grammar, logic, and rhetoric. An advanced degree required an additional three years devoted to the study of the classical *quadrivium*, consisting of arithmetic, geometry, astronomy, and music. Males of aristocratic birth, but not first-born, were apprenticed to study the "professions": medicine, law, or the military. Males of nonaristocratic birth, but whose families had more money than peasants, were apprenticed to such trades as weaving and metalworking. With the dawn of the Industrial Revolution in the 18th century, the need for unskilled labor increased. Peasants migrated from the country to the cities. The remnants of feudal society gradually crumbled, giving way to a new class of wealthy industrialists who modeled the schooling of their children on the earlier practices of the aristocracy. Success was seen to be the result of hard work and proper morals. Education became a means of instilling proper morality in undisciplined youth.

Early in the 20th century, many industrial nations instituted mandatory education of some kind. In the United States, the campaign for public schools was led by reformers but funded by business. Education was stressed as a means of socializing young people so as to instill values that would subsequently make them docile, morally disciplined workers.[16]

Steinmetz [17] and Nadler [18] have sketched the history of job training in the U.S., and Cohen [19] has described the history of federal labor policies. As industry developed, the old apprenticeship system proved increasingly inadequate to train workers, so it was gradually replaced by factory schools that were essentially early training centers intended to teach skilled trades. Hoe and Company established one of the first in 1872 and several others were founded over the next 20 years.

Coupled with the rise of the factory school were two other developments: the YMCA began to offer trade training as early as 1892, and the first efforts to establish cooperative education began early in the 20th century. In cooperative education, students alternate between school and work, thus combining theory with practical experience. During the same period, legislation created the nation's system of Land Grant colleges, later a source of college-trained labor.

Relatively little was done about employee training during the early years of the 20th century, despite widespread acceptance of Frederick Taylor's Scientific Management, which emphasized its importance. Even severe shortages of skilled labor during World War I did little to stimulate interest, and the Depression years made it easy for employers to pick and choose among experienced workers as an alternative to training the inexperienced.

It was World War II that stimulated new interest in training. Indeed, initiatives begun during and immediately after that war have had a profound impact on today's workforce. Three major initiatives were begun:

1. The "J programs" were introduced. The first, Job Instruction Training (JIT), not only gave first- and second-line supervisors instruction in how to train, but also emphasized human relations.

JIT was so successful that it was followed by a series of other programs: Job Methods Training (JMT), Job Safety Training (JST), and Program Development Training (PDT).

2. The Engineering, Science and Management War Training program (ESMWT) was introduced to meet the need for college-trained workers for technical and managerial work.

3. The GI Bill (post-World War II) stimulated the development of higher education by providing funds for war veterans to attend college.[20]

Since the 19th century, education has been touted as the key to upward social mobility in the U.S. The Horatio Alger myth—that poor people can get rich in America through hard work—came to mean the poor can get rich or become successful by educating themselves appropriately. Since there is a correlation between the amount of education and the inclination to seek more, the increasing average level of education found in the labor force after World War II may have contributed to the growth of organizational training. The reason: Employer-sponsored training, perhaps even more than formal education, facilitates promotion and occupational mobility.

In the 1960s, researchers began to study adult teaching and learning as a discipline distinct from the study of children's learning. Stimulated by Third Wave Psychology and the Human Resources School of management thought, writers such as Houle[21] and Tough[22] suggested that adults simply learn in ways different from children. A new term—*andragogy*, meaning those activities intended to help adults learn—was coined. It differed from *pedagogy*, meaning activities intended to help children learn. Figure 1.6 summarizes some of the major differences between them.[23]

Stimulated by the Systems school of management thought and new behavioristic psychology, writers such as Gilbert[24] have emphasized that training is rightfully an outgrowth of performance engineering, sometimes called *teleonomics*. It is a method for examining and improving human performance by focusing on results and using some process or technique to achieve them. Employee training is only one of many such processes or techniques. Theorists in this tradition focus on the tangible outputs of jobs, their monetary impact on the organization, and the various environments that affect performance.

Figure 1.6 How pedagogy and andragogy differ

Topic	Pedagogy	Andragogy
The learner	Dependent	Independent
Role of learner experience	Unimportant; a nuisance	Essential, because learning occurs through the pooling of learner experiences
Motivation to learn	External to the learner; dictated by society	Internal to the learner; dictated by personal/career needs
Orientation to learn	Subject-matter arranged logically	Process-oriented; oriented around problems and arranged psychologically

How HRD Relates to Training, Education, and Development

HRD concerns ways to improve employee performance in an organizational context. The term overlaps with such others as employee training, education, and development. The reason: HRD deals philosophically with *how* individually-oriented change should be handled, not with *what to do* to create that change.

Training is one of several methods used to stimulate individual change. Its focus is short-term and is solely directed at furnishing necessary knowledge or skill for carrying out present work duties efficiently and effectively.[25] When employee performance suffers because people do not know what to do or how to do it, training may be an effective solution.

Education is another method used to stimulate individual change. Its focus is intermediate-term and is aimed at preparing people for promotion, transfer, or other anticipated future progress. It may also be used to give a person new insights or to upgrade skills prior to technological or other changes in the job, occupation, industry, or organization. When the organization suffers because the right kind of people with the right skills are not available when needed, employee education may be an effective solution.

Development is a third method used to stimulate individual change.

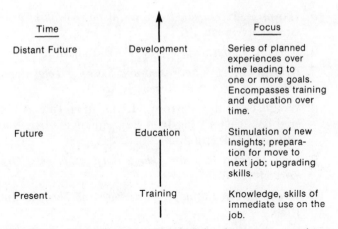

Figure 1.7 Training, education, and development: a continuum

Its focus is long-term, sometimes spanning three years or more. In most cases it is intended to groom people for positions or equip them with experience and skills needed years in the future. When an individual is systematically rotated through a series of jobs in an organization with some goal in mind, it is a process of development. For each job, the person may receive training in specific knowledge and skills; over time the person may be educated for subsequent growth. However, the real emphasis is on some longer-term aim.

Training, education, and development form a continuum by virtue of their respective time-frames (see Figure 1.7). Each refers to a specific kind of individual change effort.

References

1. Kuhn, T. S. *The Structure of Scientific Revolutions.* Chicago: University of Chicago, 1962.

2. Hunt, E. *The History of Economic Thought: A Critical Perspective.* Belmont, CA: Wadsworth, 1979.

3. Ginzberg, E. *Human Resources: The Wealth of a Nation.* New York: Simon & Schuster, 1958.

4. Carnevale, A. *Human Capital: A High Yield Corporate Investment.* Washington: American Society of Training and Development, 1982.

5. Harbison, F. *Human Resources as the Wealth of Nations.* New York: Oxford University Press, 1973.

6. Naisbitt, J. *Megatrends.* New York: Ballantine, 1983.

7. Kendrick, J. *The Formation and Stocks of Total Capital.* New York: National Bureau of Economic Research, 1976.

8. Wrege, C., and A. Perroni. "Taylor's Pig-Tale: A Historical Analysis of Frederick W. Taylor's Pig-Iron Experiments." *American Management Journal* 17 (March, 1974): pp. 6–27.

9. Katz, D., and R. Kahn. *The Social Psychology of Organizations,* 2nd ed. New York: John Wiley, 1978.

10. Wren, D. *The Evolution of Management Thought,* 2nd ed. New York: Wiley, 1979.

11. French, W., and C. H. Bell, Jr. *Organization Development: Behavioral Science Interventions for Organization Improvement,* 3rd ed. Englewood Cliffs, NJ: Prentice-Hall, 1984.

12. Ibid.

13. Ibid.

14. Pace, R. *Organizational Communication: Foundations of Human Resource Development.* Englewood Cliffs, NJ: Prentice-Hall, 1983.

15. Lewis, P. *Organizational Communication,* 2nd ed. Columbus, OH: Grid, 1980.

16. Nasaw, D. *Schooled to Order: A Social History of Public Schooling in the United States.* New York: Oxford University Press, 1979.

17. Steinmetz, C. "The History of Training." In *Training and Development Handbook,* 2nd ed., R. Craig, ed. New York: McGraw-Hill, 1976.

18. Nadler, L. *Developing Human Resources,* 2nd ed. Austin, TX: Learning Concepts, 1979.

19. Cohen, S. *Labor in the U.S.,* 5th ed. Columbus, OH: Merrill, 1980.

20. Steinmetz, C. "The History of Training." In *Training and Development Handbook,* 2nd ed., R. Craig, ed. New York: McGraw-Hill, 1976.

21. Houle, C. *The Design of Education.* San Francisco: Jossey-Bass, 1972.

22. Tough, A. *The Adult's Learning Projects,* 2nd ed. Toronto: Ontario Institute for Studies in Education, 1979.

23. Knowles, M. *The Modern Practice of Adult Education,* Revised Edition. New York: Association Press, 1980.

24. Gilbert, T. *Human Competence.* New York: McGraw-Hill, 1978.

25. Nadler, L. *Corporate Human Resources Development.* New York: Van Nostrand Reinhold, 1980.

For More Information

Beer, M. *Organization Change and Development.* Santa Monica, CA: Goodyear, 1980.

Burke, W. *Organization Development: Principles and Practices.* Boston: Little, Brown & Company, 1982.

Cavanagh, G. F. *American Business Values in Transition,* 2nd ed. Englewood Cliffs, NJ: Prentice-Hall, 1984.

Corey, G. *Theory and Practice of Counseling and Psychotherapy,* 2nd ed. Monterey, CA: Brooks/Cole, 1982.

Deutsch, A. *The Human Resources Revolution.* New York: McGraw-Hill, 1979.

Francis, G. *Organization Development: A Practical Approach.* Reston, VA: Reston Publishing, 1982.

Giddens, A. *A History of Sociological Analysis.* New York: Basic Books, 1978.

Goldhaber, G. *Organizational Communication,* 3rd ed. Dubuque, IA: William C. Brown, 1983.

Goldhaber, G., and D. Rogers. *Auditing Organizational Communication Systems.* Dubuque, IA: Kendall/Hunt, 1979.

Grattan, C. *In Quest of Knowledge: A Historical Perspective on Adult Education.* Salem, NH: Ayer Company, 1971.

Harvey, C., and D. Brown. (1982). *An Experiential Approach to Organization Development,* 2nd ed. Englewood Cliffs, NJ: Prentice-Hall, 1982.

Huse, E., and T. Cummings. (1985). *Organization Development and Change,* 3rd ed. St. Paul, MN: West, 1985.

Jones, L. *Great Expectations: America and the Baby Boom Generation.* New York: Ballantine, 1980.

Koehler, J., K. Anatol, and R. Applebaum. *Organizational Communication: Behavioral Perspectives,* 2nd ed. New York: Holt Rinehart and Winston, 1981.

Kundu, C. *Adult Education: Principles, Practice and Prospects.* New York: Apt Books, 1984.

Levitan, S., G. Mangum, and R. Marshall. *Human Resources and Labor Markets,* 3rd ed. New York: Harper & Row, 1981.

Marshall, F., V. Briggs, Jr., and A. King. *Labor Economics: Wages, Employment, Trade Unionism, and Public Policy,* 5th ed. Homewood, IL: Richard D. Irwin, 1984.

Neilsen, E. *Becoming an OD Practitioner.* Englewood Cliffs, NJ: Prentice-Hall, 1984.

Patterson, C. *Theories of Counseling and Psychotherapy,* 3rd ed. New York: Harper & Row, 1980.

Reed, P. "Human Resource Development: Vital Element in Corporate Renewal." *Directors and Boards,* Summer, 1976: pp. 20–26.

Reynolds, L. *Labor Economics and Labor Relations,* 8th ed. Englewood Cliffs, NJ: Prentice-Hall, 1982.

Sredl, H. J., J. S. Everett, and W. J. Rothwell. "What is Human Resource Development?" Unpublished manuscript, 1979.

CHAPTER 2

The complex world of HRD.

This chapter summarizes factors that can influence human resources development efforts. They include: the organization's external environment, the environment within the organization, the work group, the individual, and relationships between job performance and satisfaction. Some of these factors are more fully treated in later chapters; this chapter serves as an overview.

Human Resources Development efforts are affected by their context—that is, by factors existing where HRD occurs. Unlike university courses, HRD efforts are set in organizations that do not exist solely for the purposes of training, education, or development. Hence, HRD is rarely the chief priority of the organization. Moreover, each organization faces its own unique problems, resulting in part from the influence of the world outside it and the philosophies and values of management. To add to this complexity, work groups and individuals differ in their willingness to apply new information acquired through learning. These factors, along with others, affect HRD's role and methods in any specific setting. ■

Factors That Influence HRD

The context of HRD refers to everything that can influence it in an organization including: (1) the broad environment outside the organization; (2) the more limited environment outside the organization that is especially pertinent to its operations; (3) the internal climate and culture of the organization itself; (4) the norms and status hierarchy of work groups to which trainees are assigned; and (5) individual differences between people. Figure 2.1 illustrates this context.

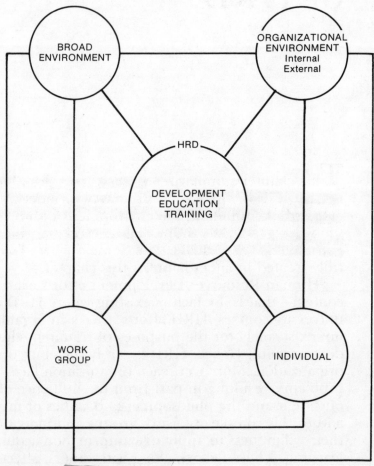

Figure 2.1 The context of HRD

The Broad Environment

All organizations and individuals are affected by general conditions in the world, whether they presently exist or are only anticipated. The broad environment refers to international and national:

- Economic conditions
- Markets
- Resource supplies
- Politics
- Technological developments

Any change in these conditions can affect an organization's ability to make or sell its products or deliver its services. Further, change can affect individuals by influencing the willingness of employers to hire or retain workers with certain kinds of skills.

The impact of the broad environment on HRD efforts is profound. Employers facing unfavorable conditions are likely to save money by reducing HRD efforts—or eliminating them entirely. Hence, the more favorable general environmental conditions, the more favorable conditions for HRD. By the same token, the more HRD efforts are perceived as furnishing ideas and methods needed for dealing with environmental conditions, the more likely they are to be perceived as essential to organizational success.

The Organizational Environment

Although all organizations are affected by the broad environment, not all are affected in the same ways or to the same extent. Each organization faces its own unique environment resulting from:

- The definition of what business it is in.
- Its philosophy of doing business and serving customers.
- Its goals for the future.
- The kinds of people or markets it serves.
- Its past, present, and anticipated financial status.
- Its special resource needs for making products or delivering services.
- Its relative position and size in its industry.

- The geographical scope of its operations.
- Its access to needed supplies, production methods, or markets.
- Governmental regulations or laws affecting the organization's industry.

A local grocery store obviously faces an environment quite different from those faced by International Business Machines, the Mayo Medical Clinic, or the Internal Revenue Service.

Changes in the external environment will lead to adaptive adjustments within the organization. The more adaptable an organization, the greater the likelihood that it can survive and prosper. HRD efforts can narrow the gap between what people presently know and do and what, because of external environmental change, they should know and do. Thus, training, education, and development can help an organization meet the challenges of changing external conditions.

Each organization is also characterized by an *internal* environment, which includes:

- Processes, such as patterns of communication, decision-making practices, and methods of gathering information about the environment.
- Technology, or the way in which work is conducted.
- Structure, referring to authority relationships and the means by which job duties are divided.
- Culture, defined as the relatively enduring pattern of beliefs, norms, and values internalized by employees and managers.
- The dominant coalition, which consists of major decision-makers.

HRD efforts can be used to:

- Assimilate new employees into an organization so that they may function effectively in its unique culture. In this sense, HRD becomes a rite of passage, an initiation.
- Institutionalize and streamline organizational policies and procedures. In this respect, HRD increases efficiency by familiarizing people with appropriate work methods.
- Generate new ideas about how to do the work. In this way, HRD can help to produce better results from the resources used.

• Meet learning needs resulting from any changes in organizational structure, leadership, technology, or other internal processes.

The influence of the organizational environment on HRD efforts is substantial (see Figure 2.2). Any change that takes place inside or outside an organization can create a learning need. The role of HRD can range along a continuum from purely maintenance-oriented instruction designed to increase efficiency and streamline existing work methods to adaptive-oriented instruction intended to increase effectiveness and equip people with the skills they need to cope with environmental demands.

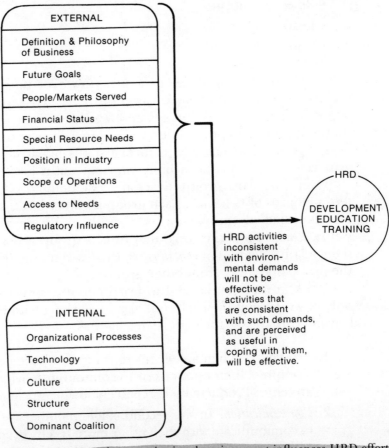

Figure 2.2 How the organizational environment influences HRD efforts

The Work Group

The work group refers to organizationally-created associations of people. There are two kinds:

The command group, which consists of employees reporting to the same immediate supervisor.

The task group, which consists of employees who must work together to complete a job process, a product, or a project.[1]

Work groups are crucial for both individual and organizational performance. They are characterized by certain common features, including:

- Structure
- Roles and norms
- Leadership
- Cohesiveness

Each work group develops a structure over time. Group members are accorded a *status* or *rank,* based on perceived expertise, power, and aggressiveness. Formal status is endowed by official action (such as promotion); informal status is endowed unofficially over time by group members. A supervisor has a high formal status by virtue of position; a 40-year veteran usually has a high informal status because of experience.

Over time, work groups develop *norms,* defined as beliefs and unwritten standards of behavior. Each group member has a *role,* a set of behaviors expected of the person as a result of his or her job duties and status. *Leadership* is the force that directs group action. Groups vary in their relative degrees of *cohesiveness,* the force that pulls members toward the group and away from other groups.

Work groups can be said to learn because individuals gain skill not only in working at their jobs but also in working with each other. Group learning progresses through such stages as:

1. *Acceptance.* When a new group is formed, members are less willing to express their opinions or to communicate with others than they are later. Productivity is relatively low.

2. *Communication.* In the second stage, members of the group begin to communicate with each other more freely. Productivity increases with improved interpersonal relations.

3. *Productivity.* In the third stage, group members direct their efforts to group goals rather than goals arising from their respective jobs. Productivity is highest.

4. *Control.* A fully-formed group regulates behavior of its members through shared norms. A change effort imposed from outside the group is resisted when perceived to be inconsistent with these norms; a change effort proposed from within the group is resisted when the person who suggests it is low in status, leadership is lacking, or the group is low in cohesiveness.[2]

Relationships between work groups depend to a large extent on:

1. *The relative compatibility of their goals.* Every member of an organization has a perspective based on his or her position in it. In many cases, goals conflict. For example, a production manager is more likely to value efforts perceived as increasing production. A training manager, on the other hand, is more likely to value efforts leading to efficient and effective training of employees. The production manager who thinks that a training program will take time away from production without any benefits can be expected to oppose it, while the training manager can be expected to favor it.

2. *The relative compatibility of their education.* Given the specialization of labor, people are typically hired according to their specific entry qualifications. Specialists in each field acquire their own jargon and set of ideas, based in part on education and supplemented by experience. Education serves to socialize people to a certain kind of work and work group. Accountants are prepared to work with other accountants; lawyers with other lawyers; and marketing specialists with others in marketing. With this variety of backgrounds, different groups may very well conflict.

3. *Relationships between leaders.* Conflict between leaders of two or more groups will affect the behavior of their respective group members. When attacked from outside, groups tend to close ranks behind their leaders.

4. *Relationships based on structure.* Some work groups depend on others; some must cooperate to accomplish a single task; some have few, if any, dealings with others. The greater the dependence of one group on another, the more likely that conflict will develop.

Intragroup and intergroup relationships affect job performance by setting parameters for behavior. By themselves, training and employee education are rarely effective solutions to group performance problems, because training and education are usually directed to individual change rather than to group or organizational change. Organization Development, a sister discipline to HRD, is more appropriate for dealing with group learning. Its focus is on long-term interpersonal and structural change.

The work group exerts a powerful influence on HRD efforts by affecting the environment in which an individual is expected to apply newly learned skills (see Figure 2.3). The learning of one person will not necessarily be encouraged in work groups where group norms and status influence behavior and departures from norms may result in an individual being ridiculed or ostracized by co-workers. In fact, the transfer of

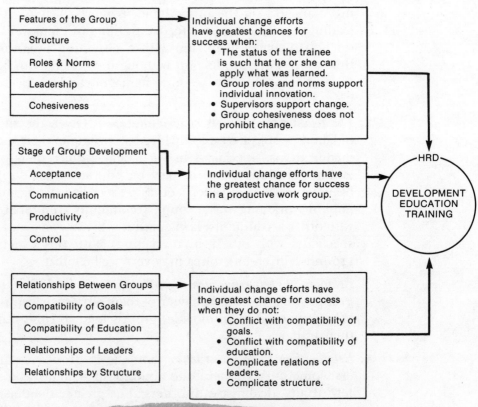

Figure 2.3 How the work group influences HRD efforts

learning from a classroom to the job may depend heavily on such factors as discretion in work procedures (how much freedom does the worker have to use new methods?); supervision (how much and what kind of feedback does the supervisor provide about the use of new methods?); group norms (how willing are co-workers to accept new methods?); group status (is the individual of high or low status?); and surroundings (how does placement of the work group affect its interaction with other groups and interaction between group members?).

The Individual

In HRD terms, the individual is one who occupies a role in the organization. Individuals are distinguished by:

- *Physiological variables,* such as physical and mental abilities.
- *Psychological variables,* such as perception, attitudes, personality, learning, and motivation.
- *Environmental variables,* such as family, culture, and social class.
- *Motivational variables,* such as values associated with various types of rewards.[3]

See Figure 2.4 for a summary of how these variables influence HRD. Individuals differ in their physical and mental attributes, and these physiological variables create both limitations and opportunities. To the extent that an HRD effort is geared to develop latent talent or to avoid calling on skills that an individual does not possess, it is likely to be successful.

Individuals also vary psychologically. They may differ in:

- *Perception,* how they understand events, issues, situations, and other people.
- *Attitudes,* what they think.
- *Personality,* the traits and behaviors that collectively identify them.
- *Learning,* their prior education, experience, and style of acquiring knowledge about the world.
- *Motivation,* their goals and level of goal-directed activity.

Obviously, an HRD effort is likely to be successful to the extent that it remains consistent with these characteristics and even capitalizes on them.

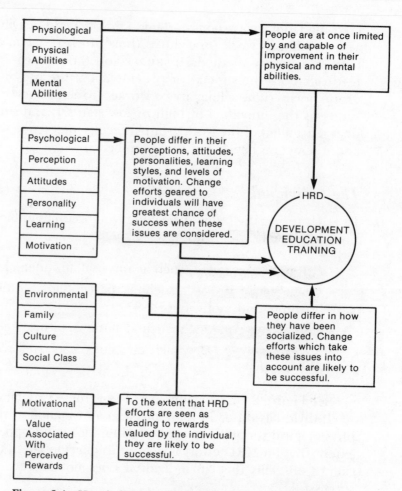

Figure 2.4 How individual differences influence HRD efforts

Environmental variables relate to the individual's upbringing and to beliefs arising from family and social programming. They are perhaps most elusive of all to identify and use. However, they can influence how a person learns.

Finally, motivational variables concern individual goals and aspirations. People are inclined to do that which they value or view as helping them to achieve what they value. The more that an HRD effort is perceived as leading to a reward, the greater the motivation to learn.

How Does Performance Relate to Satisfaction?

Performance refers to the outcomes of behavior and consists of three levels: organizational, group, and individual. *Satisfaction* refers to feelings both about outcomes and about methods used in achieving them. Individuals experience satisfaction or dissatisfaction, but groups and organizations are said to have high or low morale. *Productivity,* a measure of performance, is simply output (e.g., dollars or products) divided by input (work hours in a given time).

The relationship between performance and satisfaction—or between productivity and morale—is complex and has provoked a long-standing debate in human resources circles. For HRD practitioners, the relationship is important, especially if HRD efforts are to serve "the purpose of improving work performance while emphasizing the betterment of the human condition through the integration of organizational goals and individual needs." Of course, high performance and morale, viewed separately, are each desirable goals. The real question is whether they are related.

As early as the 1950s, research demonstrated that satisfied workers are not necessarily productive workers. Nor are relationships between employees and supervisors or co-workers of paramount importance in productivity.[4] Victor Vroom compared the results of 20 research studies on relationships between morale and productivity. He found a low but generally positive correlation between them.[5]

The issue is complicated because both job performance and satisfaction are complex concepts affected by many variables. Performance can be influenced by such factors as job design, supervision, co-workers, compensation and reward practices, working conditions, training, evaluation and feedback, individual ability, and motivation.[6] Satisfaction can also be affected by these factors. Some are beyond the control of the individual, who is the traditional focus of HRD efforts. For this reason, not all performance or morale problems can be remedied through HRD efforts.

The highest correlation between morale/satisfaction and performance/productivity occurs when individuals have the greatest discretion in how they do their work. If performance is dependent on an individual or work group and tasks cannot be routinized or automated, there is a link between satisfaction and productivity.[7] Changes in job or work group designs are more likely the key to improving the performance of those with limited freedom in how they conduct their work. In contrast, the productivity and satisfaction of white-collar employees—whose performance is tied to motivation—can be increased by management leadership that stimulates such motivation.

In the simplest sense, performance is dependent on:

- The opportunity to perform.
- The knowledge and skills that the individual possesses or can be taught.
- The nature of the performance required.
- The outcomes associated with performance.
- Feedback on the outcomes.

HRD efforts are likely to have the greatest impact on performance when:

- Individuals have difficulty identifying opportunities to perform, but identification is possible.
- Individuals lack the skills or knowledge to perform.
- The nature of the required performance is unclear but can be clarified.

HRD efforts are likely to be ineffective when:

- Opportunities to perform are difficult to identify, even for experienced employees.
- Individuals lack ability or motivation to be taught how to perform.
- The nature of required performance varies sharply by situation or according to the supervisor.
- Employees are unable to predict the outcome of their performance, are not rewarded or are inadequately rewarded for their performance, or do not value the rewards associated with performance.
- Employees do not get concrete and timely feedback on how well their efforts match job/task demands or supervisory expectations.
- Individuals face a conflict—whether real or only perceived—between required or expected performance and:
  a. their own physical and mental abilities, attitudes, aspirations, and values.

   b. their perceived role (i.e., behaviors associated with a specific job in a specific organization).
   c. work group norms.
   d. organizational culture.

   Under these circumstances, HRD efforts are likely to be less effective than longer-term Organization Development interventions or other change strategies.

References

1. Gibson J., J. Ivancevich, and J. Donnelly, Jr. *Organizations: Behavior, Structure, Processes,* 5th ed. Plano, TX: Business Publications, 1985.
2. Ibid.
3. Ibid.
4. Wren, D. *The Evolution of Management Thought,* 2nd ed. New York: Wiley, 1979.
5. Vroom, V. *Work and Motivation.* New York: Wiley, 1964.
6. *Productivity Research in the Behavioral and Social Sciences,* A. Brief, ed. New York: Praeger, 1984.
7. Beach, D. *Personnel: The Management of People at Work,* 4th ed. New York: Macmillan, 1980.

For More Information

Argyris, C., and D. Schön. *Organizational Learning.* Reading, MA: Addison-Wesley, 1978.

Bailey, R. *Human Performance Engineering.* Englewood Cliffs, NJ: Prentice-Hall, 1982.

Bedeian, A. *Organizations: Theory and Analysis,* 2nd ed. Chicago: The Dryden Press, 1984.

Cummings, L., and D. Schwab. *Performance in Organizations: Determinants and Appraisal.* Glenview, IL: Scott-Foresman, 1973.

Kotter, J. *Organizational Dynamics: Diagnosis and Intervention.* Reading, MA: Addison-Wesley, 1978.

Robbins, S. *Organizational Behavior: Concepts, Controversies, and Applications,* 3rd ed. Englewood Cliffs, NJ: Prentice-Hall, 1986.

2

HRD as a profession and career.

What are values? What is a personal philosophy of HRD practice? What is the range of potential roles that can be played by HRD practitioners in organizational settings? How do you plan a career in HRD?

Part Two addresses these questions. It focuses on the importance of clarifying one's own philosophy of HRD, describes generally what HRD practitioners do or *can do,* and identifies important issues in planning an HRD career.

CHAPTER 3

Values and professionalism in HRD.

This chapter tells why norms and values are vitally important for HRD professionals. In the simplest sense, a *norm* is a rule of conduct, and a *value* is a principle that is freely selected among a range of alternatives. *Ethics*, created from the Greek word for character, is the science of values; it is sometimes called moral philosophy.

Theorists have defined values in various ways. Regardless of these conflicting definitions, values are important because they guide actions and perceptions. HRD practitioners should be aware of their values and those of their employers, because learning events can only be successfully applied in a work setting if they are consistent with an individual's or organization's values. ■

The Importance of Norms

A norm is a rule of conduct. There are two kinds: explicit and implicit. An explicit norm is a formal policy or procedure, while an implicit norm arises informally among individuals. Violating an explicit norm may result in a reprimand, suspension without pay, or discharge. Violating an implicit norm may result in ostracism or ridicule by co-workers.

An example of an explicit norm is a company policy against horseplay. If an employee is caught fooling around with company equipment—like playing catch with a lug wrench or drag racing on a forklift—the result is reprimand, suspension, or often immediate discharge.

To illustrate an implicit norm, suppose an hourly worker on a production line runs to get a foreman when she sees co-workers engaged in horseplay. While she is justified from the standpoint of an explicit norm, there may be an unwritten rule among her co-workers that nobody tattles to a supervisor under any circumstances. As a result of her action, her co-workers stop speaking to her. Somebody slashes the tires of her car in the parking lot. She has violated an implicit norm and is punished for it by her co-workers.

Norms serve to regulate individual behavior. For the HRD professional they are important because the way that instruction is designed and delivered must be consistent with them. It is, after all, pointless to teach people things they are formally or informally prohibited from doing. In fact, to do so would only lead to confusion and create frustration or resentment. Trying to change norms or organization culture goes beyond HRD, and is more properly a function of Organization Development.

Individual and Organizational Values

Writers have defined values in various ways. Rokeach[1] has called them persistent beliefs that one way of behaving or one goal is preferable to an opposite way of behaving or another goal. He distinguishes between two types: instrumental values, which are beliefs about how to achieve goals, and terminal values, which are beliefs about goals themselves.

Regardless of different definitions, most writers would agree with Raths, Harmin and Simon[2] that a value is:

Selected: 1. By choice.
             2. Among alternatives.
             3. After consideration.

Cherished:	1. By virtue of satisfaction.
	2. By public affirmation.
Used:	1. As a guide for choosing.
	2. More than once.

These yardsticks can be used to determine whether an individual actually values an idea, an object, a behavior, or some belief.

Thought of in this way, it is clear that values are not abstract concepts of little practical use. Indeed, what we value can guide:

- Decision-making among alternatives.
- Interpersonal relations.
- Efforts to influence or persuade others.
- Evaluations of ideas, concepts, or people.

They are thus standards by which to make judgments and guide behavior.

The issue of values is, however, complicated in that individual values come from different sources than organizational values. Individual values come from such sources as:

- Early programming by parents and peers.
- Educational experiences.
- Religious beliefs and attitudes.
- Electronic media.

As Wordsworth said, the child is the father of the man. Early experiences are internalized as a value system, a set of beliefs about what is good or bad, right or wrong.[3] These beliefs help individuals evaluate—a word meaning the process of valuing—the world around them.

Organizational values, on the other hand, stem from such sources as:

1. *The individual values of the chief power brokers and decision-makers.* What top managers have wanted in the past and desire in the future often exerts a powerful influence on decision-making, interpersonal relations, and evaluations of people and ideas.

2. *Experiences of the organization.* The results of past actions are retained in an institutional memory, often manifested in job descriptions, procedure manuals, and other relics of tradition. They demonstrate to a watchful eye where resources are really devoted and thus what activities are valued.

3. *The nature of the business.* Some industries carry with them an entire value system of their own, arising from the kind of services they deliver. Perhaps one of the strongest is in health care, where the nature of the service leads to a firm belief in the sanctity of life and the dignity of human beings.

Institutionalized and preserved over time, these values are synonymous with an organization's culture.

Value theory—essentially the study of ethics—has exerted a profound influence on primary and secondary education recently. Educators now realize that value clarification, the process of helping children identify what they value and how it influences their behavior, is central to the development of the self-directed individual. The same idea has been echoed in the business community, especially after major scandals in which the names of prominent people or respected businesses are sullied because of illegal, immoral, unethical, or otherwise shady activities.

Generally, managers as a group:

- Admire responsibility and honesty in themselves and others.
- Are less certain of their subordinates' values the higher up in the chain of command they progress.
- Believe that effectiveness—the ability to get things done right—is the most important organizational value.[4]

The Values and Ethics of HRD Professionals

Although individuals and organizations can be said to have value systems that govern their conduct, evidence also suggests that people in the same profession or occupation are likely to share similar values.[5] Nor is this surprising: people in the same profession do similar work and thereby acquire similar beliefs, though individual and organizational differences may cause some variation.

But is HRD a profession? There are three general definitions of a profession: the trait, the institutional, and the legal.[6]

For trait theorists, a profession has core elements different from those of other occupations. To practice, a professional requires a high level of training, specialized knowledge, techniques capable of being taught to others, representation by an association of peers, ethical standards, and a sense of purpose.

For institutional theorists, professions are identifiable by their stages of development. These stages include: the development of a professional association, a change in name, the acceptance of a code of ethics, gradual recognition by the public, and finally the advent of special facilities for the training and anticipatory socialization of members.[7]

For legal theorists, a profession is simply an occupation requiring State licensure to practice.

Although HRD is not yet a profession according to the legal definition, and some continue to debate the core of knowledge unique to it, it does meet most of the criteria of a profession listed by trait and institutional theorists. For example, the practice of HRD requires:

- *A high level of training.* HRD practitioners are increasingly required to have graduate degrees and exercise a wide range of skills in their work.

- *Specialized knowledge.* HRD practitioners must know how to analyze performance problems, design learning experiences, select and use delivery methods suitable for meeting a learning need, evaluate the effectiveness of learning, and gauge the extent of its application on the job.

- *Techniques capable of being taught to others.* HRD practitioners can teach others how to analyze performance problems or assess opportunities for improving performance.

- *Self-organization and the emergence of a professional society.* HRD practitioners in the U.S. are represented by one major professional society and several smaller ones. The major society is the American Society for Training and Development (ASTD), with a national membership of approximately 25,000 and local membership another 25,000, out of an estimated 200,000 training professionals. Another society—the American Society for Personnel Administration (ASPA)—primarily represents personnel professionals in the U.S. The National Society for Performance and Instruction (NSPI) is smaller than ASTD and represents a viewpoint best described as behavioral. The Society for Applied Learning Technology (SALT) focuses on the use of modern technology in learning. Several other organizations—such as the Organization Development Institute (ODI), the Organization Development Network (ODN), and subdivisions of the Academy of Management and the American Psychological Association—have some members whose main interest is HRD. Small, highly specialized HRD associations also exist within certain professions, industries, and occupations.

- *A change in name.* HRD was once called training and development.

- *Gradual recognition by the public.* Every large news magazine has run articles on the growth of organizational training and related learning events.

- *A sense of purpose.* HRD is a means to the end of "improving work performance while emphasizing the betterment of the human condition through the integration of organizational goals and individual needs."

- *The growth of facilities for training and socializing members.* With the appearance of the *ASTD Directory of Academic Programs in Human Resource Development/Training and Development,* it is obvious that more colleges and universities are offering formal degree programs in HRD.

- *The acceptance of a code of ethics.* HRD professionals adhere to the Code of Ethics published by ASTD (see Appendix A at end of this chapter).

Like any other profession, HRD has its own

- *Specialties and subspecialties.* There are those who specialize in types of training (e.g., management or clerical), types of delivery (e.g., computer-based or classroom), and specific HRD issues (e.g., brain research or the development of training policy).

Figure 3.1 Components of an HRD philosophy

Issue	Description of the Issue	A Normative Position of HRD	What Are Your Personal Assumptions?
Human Nature	What are the basic characteristics of human beings?	People should be considered self-actualizing.	What do you think about pepole? Why?
Individual-Organizational Relationship	To what extent are individuals free to exercise initiative in organizations?	The relationship between organization and individual can be mutually beneficial.	What do you think about the relationship between organization and individual?
Goals of Learning	What should learning goals be in an organization?	Ranges from educating the individual to improving job performance to meeting organizational needs.	What do you believe learning goals should be? Why?
Functions(s) and Role(s) of HRD Practitioners	How do HRD practitioners facilitate learning in organizations?	Described by the competency study *Models for Excellence* (1983).	To what extent do you see the primary allegiance of the HRD practitioner to the profession? Why?
Nature of Learning in Organizations	How do people learn in an organizational context?	Learning occurs best when it is geared to individual needs and managers encourage application of training.	How do you believe people learn in an organization?
Trainer-Trainee Relationship	What should be the relationship between HRD practitioners and the group they serve?	Varies by situation, but HRD generally favors humanistic, I-thou relationship.	What do you believe should be the relationship between the practitioner and those served?
Means of Motivating Learning	How are people best motivated to learn?	People are best motivated to learn through intrinsic rewards, but it may vary by individual.	How do you believe people are best motivated to learn? Why?
Conditions When the Theory Will Not Work	In what kind of organization will one's personal theory not work? For what reasons?	Varies by type of organization. Self-actualization is not easy in authoritarian organizations.	When will your theory not work? Why?
Example of the Theory as It Is Applied	How is the theory applied? What are some guidelines for applications?	Purest expressions by Malcolm Knowles and Leonard Nadler.	How can your theory be applied?

- *Schools of thought and theory.* As Chapter 12 will explain, there are different theories about the nature of human learning and of instructing. As a result, there are different schools of thought about HRD practices.
- *Variations among practitioners.* No two doctors or lawyers apply their professions in exactly the same way or have exactly the same personal philosophy about their professions. So it is with HRD practitioners.

As with any profession, the values, experiences, and personal attributes of the HRD professional will lead to a personal philosophy about HRD and its practice. This process begins with personal assessment and clarification of values concerning such issues as human nature, the relationship between the individual and organization, the goals of learning experiences, the function and role of the HRD professional in facilitating such experiences, the nature of appropriate trainer-trainee relationships, methods of motivating people to learn, and other issues (see Figure 3.1). When these assumptions and values are made explicit, the prospective HRD practitioner has taken the first step in developing a personal philosophy of HRD to guide subsequent practice. Though this philosophy is likely to change as the practitioner gains experience and undergoes socialization in different organizational contexts, it is an important guide to decision-making.

To further explore the subject of professional values, see the For More Information section at the end of this chapter.

APPENDIX A: ASTD Code of Ethics *

The ASTD Code of Ethics provides guidance to members to be self-managed human resource development professionals. Clients and employers should expect from ASTD members the highest possible standards of personal integrity, professional competence, sound judgment and discretion. Developed by the profession for the profession, the ASTD

---

* Source: *ASTD Who's Who Membership Directory 1986.* American Society for Training and Development, 1986.

Code of Ethics is the Society's public declaration of its members' obligations to themselves, their profession and society.
I strive to . . .

- Recognize the rights and dignities of each individual.
- Develop human potential.
- Provide my employer, clients and learners with the highest level quality education, training and development.
- Be a good citizen and to comply with the laws and regulations governing my position.
- Keep informed of pertinent knowledge and competence in the human resource field.
- Maintain confidentiality and integrity in the practice of my profession.
- Support my peers and to avoid conduct which impedes their practicing their profession.
- Conduct myself in an ethical and honest manner.
- Improve the public understanding of human resource development and management.
- Fairly and accurately represent my human resource development/ human resource management credentials, qualifications, experience and ability.
- Contribute to the continuing growth of the Society and its members.

References

1. Rokeach, M. *The Nature of Human Values*. New York: The Free Press, 1973.
2. Raths, L., M. Harmin, and S. Simon. *Values of Teaching*. Columbus, OH: Charles E. Merrill, 1966.
3. Massey, M. *The People Puzzle*. Reston, VA: Reston Publishing, 1979.
4. Schmidt, W., and B. Posner. *Managerial Values and Expectations: The Silent Power in Personal and Organizational Life*. New York: American Management Associations, 1982.
5. Flowers, V., C. Hughes, M. Myers, and S. Myers. *Managerial Values for Working*. New York: Amacom, 1975.

6. Lansbury, R. *Professionals and Management.* St. Lucia, Queensland: University of Queensland Press, 1978.

7. Caplow, T. *The Sociology of Work.* New York: McGraw-Hill, 1964.

For More Information

Argyris, C. *Personality and Organization.* New York: Harper and Row, 1957.

Beauchamp, T., and N. Bowie. *Ethical Theory and Business,* 2nd ed. Englewood Cliffs, NJ: Prentice-Hall, 1983.

Blau, P., and W. Scott. *Formal Organizations: A Comparative Approach.* London: Routledge and Kegan Paul, 1969.

Drucker, P. "Management of the Professional Employee." *Harvard Business Review* 30 (1952) 3: pp. 86–96.

England, G., O. Dhingra, and N. Agarwal. "The Manager and the Man—A Cross-Cultural Study of Personal Values." *Organization and Administration Sciences* 5 (1974) 2: pp. 1–97.

Gouldner, A. "Cosmopolitans and Locals: Towards an Analysis of Latent Social Roles." *Administrative Science Quarterly* 2 (1957) 2: pp. 281–306.

Graves, C. "Levels of Existence: An Open System Theory of Values." *Journal of Humanistic Psychology* 10 (1970) 2: pp. 131–155.

Hall, B. *Value Clarification as a Learning Process: A Guidebook.* New York: Paulist Press, 1973.

Hall, B., and M. Smith. *Value Clarification as a Learning Process: A Handbook.* New York: Paulist Press, 1973.

Hawley, R., and I. Hawley. *Human Values in the Classroom: A Handbook for Teachers.* New York: Hart Publishing, 1973.

Kirschenbaum, H. *Advanced Value Clarification.* La Jolla, CA: University Associates, 1977.

Kornhauser, W. *Scientists and Industry: Conflict and Accommodation.* Berkeley, CA: University of California Press, 1964.

Marvick, D. *Career Perspectives in a Bureaucratic Setting.* Ann Arbor, MI: Institute of Public Administration, University of Michigan, 1954.

Maslow, A. *The Farther Reaches of Human Nature.* New York: The Viking Press, 1971.

Massey, M. *The People Puzzle.* Reston, VA: Reston Publishing, 1979.

Merton, R. *Social Theory and Social Structure,* rev. ed. New York: The Free Press, 1957.

Peterson, R. "A Cross-Cultural Perspective of Supervisory Values." *Academy of Management Journal* (March, 1972): pp. 105–117.

Rogers, C. *Freedom to Learn.* Columbus, OH: Charles E. Merrill, 1969.

Simon, S., L. Howe, and H. Kirschenbaum. *Values Clarification: A Handbook of Practical Strategies for Teachers and Students.* New York: Hart Publishing, 1972.

Smith, M. *A Practical Guide to Value Clarification.* La Jolla, CA: University Associates, 1977.

Wren, D. *The Evolution of Management Thought,* 2nd ed. New York: Wiley, 1979.

Zenger, J. "Managers' Perceptions of Subordinates' Competence as a Function of Personal Value Orientations." *Academy of Management Journal* (December, 1971): pp. 415–424.

CHAPTER 4

The many roles of HRD professionals.

H RD professionals play various *roles* depending in part on their jobs, the organization, and themselves. *Work outputs* are the observable results of role behaviors, while *competencies* are the skills needed to achieve those results.

This chapter provides an overview of 15 major roles, 31 competencies, and 102 outputs associated with the professional practice of HRD. ∎

Understanding Roles

People are hired into jobs or positions. Often, a written job description outlines what they are to do. A written job specification describes the kind of education, experience, or other qualifications associated with necessary entry-level skills. Employee performance appraisals measure, over some definite time period, how well an individual is performing job duties.

But how people approach their jobs is a question of role, the part played by an individual in the context of the environment, organization, and work group. Roles are thus behaviors associated with a job. Values guide what roles are accepted and, in part, how they are carried out.

See Figure 4.1 for a model that represents the nature of a role. In this model:

- The environment is everything outside the organization.
- The organization is a system of roles. Each person in it plays multiple parts.
- Role senders are those people who deal with someone filling a role. They have expectations about the role and behavior appropriate for it.
- The role receiver is the person who is cast in a role.
- Individual variables are based on physiological, psychological, environmental, and motivational factors.
- Work group/interpersonal relations concern small group contexts in which a role is enacted.

Though the model may appear complicated, it is really quite simple. Anybody working in an organization is both role sender and receiver. Individual behavior in a role is influenced by:

1. The environment, which creates demands on the organization and may create demands on roles within it. For example, if a new

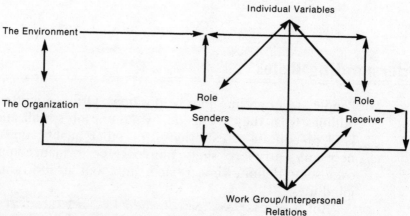

Figure 4.1 A model for understanding roles   *(Adapted from:* The Social Psychology of Organizations *by D. Katz and R. Kahn. Copyright © 1978, John Wiley and Sons, Inc. Reprinted by permission of John Wiley and Sons, Inc.)*

law is passed regulating an industry, it may result in special pressures on legal staff (who interpret it) and on those directly affected by it. Court decisions on affirmative action may create special pressures on personnel managers and those who make hiring decisions.

2. The organization, which has its own culture, norms, and values. In one organization, people might have one idea about the role of accountant, for example. People in other organizations might have different ideas about this role.

3. Role senders, who send messages to role receivers. They expect certain kinds of behavior from someone occupying a position and do not expect other kinds of behavior. Expectations may stem from past dealings with people occupying similar positions. A production manager may have a set of expectations about the role of HRD specialist, for example. When an HRD specialist acts consistently with those expectations, the production manager is satisfied. If behavior differs from expectation, the manager may comment on appropriate role behavior and thus send a message about it.

4. Role receivers, who occupy roles. They receive messages from others about how they should behave. Their actions—that is, role behaviors—are messages that show how they perceive their role and interpret role messages from others.

5. Individual variables that influence both role senders and receivers. For example, differences in innate talents cause people to differ in how they enact a role.

6. Work group and interpersonal relations that also affect both role senders and receivers. An individual's status and interpersonal skills may influence how well a role can be enacted. Similarly, relationships between groups may influence role perceptions.

This model is useful in clarifying how and why people act in an organizational setting.

Because of the many roles in organizations, it is not unusual to find role conflict—that is, inconsistency between expected and actual behavior. There are several kinds of role conflict:

- *Intrapersonal role conflict.* When an individual's role calls for behavior inconsistent with personal values, it produces intrapersonal role conflict. For example, if an HRD practitioner is asked to train people to do work that is illegal, he or she may experience conflict of this kind.

- *Intrarole conflict.* When several role senders have different expectations and convey contradictory role messages, the result is intrarole conflict. The person enacting the role cannot satisfy all the demands. If top managers have one set of expectations for a training program, middle managers have a different set, foremen a third, and trainers a fourth, the HRD professional experiences intrarole conflict.
- *Interrole conflict.* Individuals play more than one role in most organizations. For example, supervisors play the role of management agent but may also serve as spokespersons and advocates for their work units with higher management. When there is a conflict between the wishes of higher management and those of the work group, the supervisor may experience interrole conflict as a result of the contradictory demands.[1]

To resolve such conflicts, it may be necessary to replace or try to change the person in the role, try to gain consensus on expectations, or minimize multiple roles.

Role theory occupies a central place in the social sciences and has influenced sociology, psychology, and anthropology. It has been applied in Organization Development and other fields. Though it has been criticized for promising much while delivering little, it does provide a starting point for understanding organizational behavior.

The Roles, Competencies, and Work Outputs of HRD Professionals

Despite the shortcomings of role theory and the variations in roles that may occur across organizations, there have been many efforts to identify the roles of HRD practitioners and the competencies associated with successful performance of those roles.[*] The goal of these efforts was to make the training of HRD practitioners easier and to increase the stature of HRD as a profession calling for similar skills across organizations.

The most ambitious attempt to identify the roles and competencies

---

[*]Some of these efforts have been: Competency Analysis;[2] EDS Curriculum Plan;[3] Pinto and Walker;[4] A Self-Development Process;[5] and Varney.[6] See also Neilsen[7] and Standards.[8]

to identify roles

of HRD was sponsored by the American Society for Training and Development (ASTD). The 1983 report based on this study, *Models for Excellence,* was also the most sophisticated ever done on this topic. It identifies 15 possible roles for HRD practitioners. They are listed and defined in Figure 4.2, along with the chapters in this book that deal with them.

Each role is associated with certain outputs (see Figure 4.3) and competencies (see Figure 4.4).

Some competencies are more important or widely used than others, as shown in Figure 4.5.

To provide better understanding of the 31 competencies, *Models for Excellence* includes concrete examples of each one as it would be applied by an HRD professional at three different levels of expertise: basic, intermediate, and advanced. These examples follow in Figure 4.6.

There are four distinct clusters of related roles that share many of the same competencies, while three roles are unrelated to others.

The Leadership Cluster

The leadership cluster includes two related roles: manager of training and development and strategist.

The *manager of training and development* role consists of "planning, organizing, staffing, [and] controlling training and development operations or training and development projects, and of linking training and development operations with other organizational units." It produces such outputs as:

1. "Training and development department or project operating objectives."
2. "Training and development budgets developed and monitored."
3. "[A] positive work climate in the training and development function or project group."
4. "Department/project staffing."
5. "Training and development standards, policies and procedures."
6. "Outside suppliers/consultants selected."
7. "Solutions to department/project problems."
8. "Training and development actions congruent with other HR and organization actions."

Figure 4.2 The 15 roles of HRD professionals and the chapters that deal with them

Roles	Corresponding Chapters
EVALUATOR . . . The role of identifying the extent of a program, service or product's impact.	23, 24
GROUP FACILITATOR . . . The role of managing group discussions and group process so that individuals learn and group members feel the experience is positive.	22
INDIVIDUAL DEVELOPMENT COUNSELOR . . . The role of helping an individual assess personal competencies, values, goals and identify and plan development and career actions.	9
INSTRUCTIONAL WRITER . . . The role of preparing written learning and instructional materials.	20
INSTRUCTOR . . . The role of presenting information and directing structured learning experiences so that individuals learn.	21
MANAGER OF TRAINING AND DEVELOPMENT . . . The role of planning, organizing, staffing, controlling training and development operations or training and development projects and of linking training and development operations with other organization units.	11
MARKETER . . . The role of selling Training and Development viewpoints, learning packages, programs and services to target audiences outside one's own work unit.	19
MEDIA SPECIALIST . . . The role of producing software for and using audio, visual, computer and other hardware-based technologies for training and development.	18
NEEDS ANALYST . . . The role of defining gaps between ideal and actual performance and specifying the cause of the gaps.	14, 15
PROGRAM ADMINISTRATOR . . . The role of ensuring that the facilities, equipment, materials, participants and other components of a learning event are present and that program logistics run smoothly.	19
PROGRAM DESIGNER . . . The role of preparing objectives, defining content, selecting and sequencing activities for a specific program.	16, 17
STRATEGIST . . . The role of developing long-range plans for what the training and development structure, organization, direction, policies, programs, services, and practices will be in order to accomplish the training and development mission.	10
TASK ANALYST . . . Identifying activities, tasks, sub-tasks, human resource and support requirements necessary to accomplish specific results in a job or organization.	14, 15
THEORETICIAN . . . The role of developing and testing theories of learning, training and development.	12
TRANSFER AGENT . . . The role of helping individuals apply learning after the learning experience.	25, 26

Source: *Models for Excellence.* Washington, D.C.: American Society for Training and Development, 1983.

Figure 4.3 Outputs associated with each role

The Critical Outputs for the Training and Development Field

The following are the outputs which study respondents said are critical now and/or in five years. Some outputs are produced for internal use by the training and development functions. Others describe end products which go to the user (learners or client organizations).

Evaluator:
1. Instruments to assess individual change in knowledge, skill, attitude, behavior, results.
2. Instruments to assess program and instructional quality.
3. Reports (written and oral) of program impact on individuals.
4. Reports (written and oral) of program impact on an organization.
5. Evaluation and validation designs and plans (written and oral).
6. Written instruments to collect and interpret data.

Group Facilitator:
7. Group discussions in which issues and needs are constructively assessed.
8. Group decisions where individuals all feel committed to action.
9. Cohesive teams.
10. Enhanced awareness of group process, self and others.

Individual Development Counselor:
11. Individual career development plans.
12. Enhanced skills on the part of an individual to identify and carry out his/her own department needs/goals.
13. Referrals to professional counseling.
14. Increased knowledge by the individual about where to get development support.
15. Tools, resources needed in career development.
16. Tools for managers to facilitate employees' career development.
17. An individual who initiates feedback, monitors and manages career plans.

Instructional Writer:
18. Exercises, workbooks, worksheets.
19. Teaching guides.
20. Scripts (for video, film, audio).
21. Manuals and job aids.
22. Computer software.
23. Tests and evaluation forms.
24. Written role plays, simulations, games.
25. Written case studies.

Instructor:
26. Video tapes, films, audio tapes, computer-aided instruction and other AV materials facilitated.
27. Case studies, role plays, games, tests and other structured learning events directed.
28. Lectures, presentations, stories delivered.
29. Examinations administered and feedback given.

Figure 4.3 (Continued)

The Critical Outputs for the Training and Development Field

30. Students' needs addressed.
31. An individual with new knowledge, skills, attitudes or behavior in his/her repertoire.

Manager of Training and Development:

32. T&D department or project operating objectives.
33. T&D budgets developed and monitored.
34. Positive work climate in the T&D function or project group.
35. Department/project staffed.
36. T&D standards, policies and procedures.
37. Outside suppliers/consultants selected.
38. Solutions to department/project problems.
39. T&D actions congruent with other HR and organization actions.
40. Relevant information exchanged with clients/departments (internal and external).
41. Staff evaluated.
42. Staff developed.

Marketer:

43. Promotional materials for T&D programs and curricula.
44. Sales presentations.
45. Program overviews.
46. Leads.
47. Contracts with T&D clients (internal and external) negotiated.
48. Marketing plan (developed and implemented).
49. T&D programs/services visible to target markets.

Media Specialist:

50. T&D computer software.
51. Lists (written and oral) of recommended instructional hardware.
52. Graphics.
53. Video-based material.
54. Audio tapes.
55. Computer hardware in working order.
56. AV equipment in working order.
57. Media users advised/counseled.
58. Production plans.
59. Purchasing specifications/recommendations for instructional/training software.
60. Purchasing specifications/recommendations for instructional/training hardware.

Needs Analyst:

61. Performance problems and discrepancies identified and reported (written/oral)
62. Knowledge, skill, attitude problems and discrepancies identified and reported (written/oral).
63. Tools to assess the knowledge, skill, attitude and performance level of individuals and organizations.
64. Needs analysis strategies.
65. Causes of discrepancies inferred.

Figure 4.3 (Continued)

The Critical Outputs for the Training and Development Field

Program Administrator:

66. Facilities and equipment selected and scheduled.
67. Participant attendance secured, recorded.
68. Hotel/conference center staff managed.
69. Faculty scheduled.
70. Course material distributed (on-site, pre-course, post-course).
71. Contingency plans for back-ups, emergencies.
72. Physical environment maintained.
73. Program follow-up accomplished.

Program Designer:

74. Lists of learning objectives.
75. Written program plans/designs.
76. Specifications and priorities of training content, activities, materials and methods.
77. Sequencing plans for training content, activities, materials, and methods.
78. Instructional contingency plans and implementation strategies.

Strategist:

79. T&D long-range plans included in the broad human resource strategy of the client organization.
80. Identification (written/oral) of long-range T&D strengths, weaknesses, opportunities, threats.
81. Descriptions of the T&D function and its outputs in the future.
82. Identification of forces/trends (technical, social, economic, etc.) impacting T&D.
83. Guidelines/plans for implementing long-range goals.
84. Alternative directions for T&D.
85. Cost/benefit analyses of the impact of T&D on the organization.

Task Analyst:

86. Lists of key job/unit outputs.
87. Lists of key job/unit tasks.
88. Lists of knowledge/skill/attitude requirements of a job/unit.
89. Descriptions of the performance levels required in a job/unit.
90. Job design, enlargement, enrichment implications/alternatives identified.
91. Sub-tasks, tasks, and jobs clustered.
92. Conditions described under which jobs/tasks are performed.

Theoretician:

93. New concepts and theories of learning and behavior change.
94. Articles on T&D issues/theories for scientific journals and trade publications.
95. Research designs.
96. Research reports.
97. Training models and applications of theory.
98. Existing learning/training theories and concepts evaluated.

Figure 4.3 (Continued)

The Critical Outputs for the Training and Development Field

Transfer Agent:

99. Individual action plans for on-the-job/real world application.
100. Plans (written/oral) for the support of transfer of learning in and around the application environment.
101. Job aids to support performance and learning.
102. On-the-job environment modified to support learning.

Source: *Models for Excellence.* Washington, D.C.: American Society for Training and Development, 1983.

Figure 4.4 HRD competencies

There are thirty-one (31) competencies in this model:

1. *Adult-Learning Understanding* . . . Knowing how adults acquire and use knowledge, skills, attitudes. Understanding individual differences in learning.
2. *A/V Skill* . . . Selecting and using audio/visual hardware and software.
3. *Career-Development Knowledge* . . . Understanding the personal and organizational issues and practices relevant to individual careers.
4. *Competency-Identification Skill* . . . Identifying the knowledge and skill requirements of jobs, tasks, roles.
5. *Computer Competence* . . . Understanding and being able to use computers.
6. *Cost-Benefit-Analysis Skill* . . . Assessing alternatives in terms of their financial, psychological, and strategic advantages and disadvantages.
7. *Counseling Skill* . . . Helping individuals recognize and understand personal needs, values, problems, alternatives and goals.
8. *Data-Reduction Skill* . . . Scanning, synthesizing, and drawing conclusions from data.
9. *Delegation Skill* . . . Assigning task responsibility and authority to others.
10. *Facilities Skill* . . . Planning and coordinating logistics in an efficient and cost-effective manner.
11. *Feedback Skill* . . . Communicating opinions, observations and conclusions such that they are understood.
12. *Futuring Skill* . . . Projecting trends and visualizing possible and probable futures and their implications.
13. *Group-Process Skill* . . . Influencing groups to both accomplish tasks and fulfill the needs of their members.
14. *Industry Understanding* . . . Knowing the key concepts and variables that define an industry or sector (e.g., critical issues, economic vulnerabilities, measurements, distribution channels, inputs, outputs, information sources).
15. *Intellectual Versatility* . . . Recognizing, exploring and using a broad range of ideas and practices. Thinking logically and creatively without undue influence from personal biases.
16. *Library Skill* . . . Gathering information from printed and other recorded sources. Identifying and using information specialists and reference services and aids.
17. *Model-Building Skill* . . . Developing theoretical and practical frameworks which describe complex ideas in understandable, usable ways.
18. *Negotiation Skill* . . . Securing win-win agreements while successfully representing a special interest in a decision situation.
19. *Objectives-Preparation Skill* . . . Preparing clear statements which describe desired outputs.
20. *Organization-Behavior Understanding* . . . Seeing organizations as dynamic, political, economic,

Figure 4.4 (Continued)

and social systems which have multiple goals; using this larger perspective as a framework for understanding and influencing events and change.

21. *Organization Understanding* . . . Knowing the strategy, structure, power networks, financial position, systems of a SPECIFIC organization.

22. *Performance-Observation Skill* . . . Tracking and describing behaviors and their effects.

23. *Personnel/HR-Field Understanding* . . . Understanding issues and practices in other HR areas (Organization Development, Organization Job Design, Human Resource Planning, Selection and Staffing, Personnel Research and Information Systems, Compensation and Benefits, Employee Assistance, Union/Labor Relations).

24. *Presentation Skill* . . . Verbally presenting information such that the intended purpose is achieved.

25. *Questioning Skill* . . . Gathering information from and stimulating insight in individuals and groups through the use of interviews, questionnaires and other probing methods.

26. *Records-Management Skill* . . . Storing data in easily retrievable form.

27. *Relationship Versatility* . . . Adjusting behavior in order to establish relationships across a broad range of people and groups.

28. *Research Skill* . . . Selecting, developing and using methodologies, statistical and data collection techniques for a formal inquiry.

29. *Training-and-Development-Field Understanding* . . . Knowing the technological, social, economic, professional, and regulatory issues in the field; understanding the role T&D plays in helping individuals learn for current and future jobs.

30. *Training-and-Development-Techniques Understanding* . . . Knowing the techniques and methods used in training; understanding their appropriate uses.

31. *Writing Skill* . . . Preparing written material which follows generally accepted rules of style and form, is appropriate for the audience, creative, and accomplishes its intended purposes.

Source: *Models for Excellence.* Washington, D.C.: American Society for Training and Development, 1983.

9. "Related information exchanged with clients/departments (internal/external)."

10. "Staff evaluated."

11. "Staff developed."

These outputs are listed in Figure 4.3 and are treated later in this book.

The manager of training and development role requires these competencies:

#1. Adult-Learning Understanding

#3. Career-Development Knowledge

#5. Computer Competency

#6. Cost/Benefit-Analysis Skill

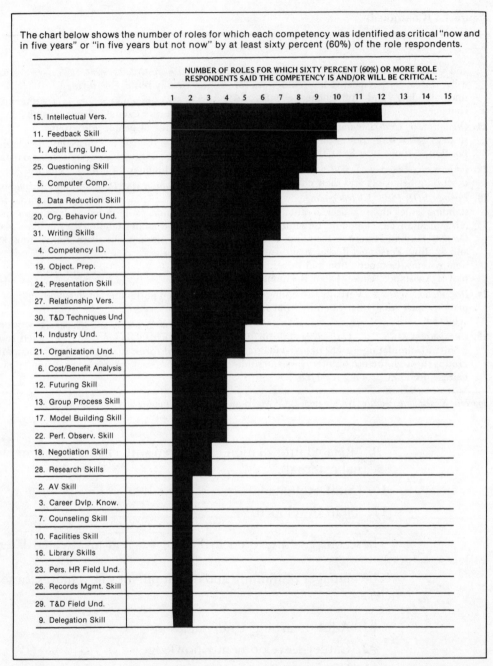

The chart below shows the number of roles for which each competency was identified as critical "now and in five years" or "in five years but not now" by at least sixty percent (60%) of the role respondents.

NUMBER OF ROLES FOR WHICH SIXTY PERCENT (60%) OR MORE ROLE RESPONDENTS SAID THE COMPETENCY IS AND/OR WILL BE CRITICAL:

15. Intellectual Vers.
11. Feedback Skill
1. Adult Lrng. Und.
25. Questioning Skill
5. Computer Comp.
8. Data Reduction Skill
20. Org. Behavior Und.
31. Writing Skills
4. Competency ID.
19. Object. Prep.
24. Presentation Skill
27. Relationship Vers.
30. T&D Techniques Und
14. Industry Und.
21. Organization Und.
6. Cost/Benefit Analysis
12. Futuring Skill
13. Group Process Skill
17. Model Building Skill
22. Perf. Observ. Skill
18. Negotiation Skill
28. Research Skills
2. AV Skill
3. Career Dvlp. Know.
7. Counseling Skill
10. Facilities Skill
16. Library Skills
23. Pers. HR Field Und.
26. Records Mgmt. Skill
29. T&D Field Und.
9. Delegation Skill

Figure 4.5 How HRD competencies rank in importance (*Source: Models for Excellence,* p. 125.)

Figure 4.6 Sample behaviors illustrating levels of expertise

The Competency Model for the T&D Field

The Competency:	Example Behaviors Illustrating Levels of Expertise		
	Basic:	*Intermediate:*	*Advanced:*
1. *Adult-Learning Understanding . . .* Knowing how adults acquire and use knowledge, skills, attitudes. Understanding individual differences in learning.	• When preparing visuals for a presentation, the T&D specialist assures that there are *no more than five to seven points on each slide.* • Knowing that support and review are important after a learning experience, the T&D specialist implements a series of *follow-up brochures which review key points and application ideas* from a course. • Etc.	• In order to assure that the managers participating in a management development program get the most out of their learning, the T&D specialist develops a half-day module on *how to self manage their learning process.* The module is designed to *be highly participative* and presents the latest findings about *how adults learn.* • When asked to develop a career development program, the T&D specialist develops a program which *uses participative methods, learning contracts, and continuing learning plans.* • A writer preparing a self-study manual for experienced nurses includes action planning modules at the end of each section to *assure that the nurses have a formal opportunity to relate the theories to their own practices.* • Etc.	• Microcomputer customers complain that the written instruction and information provided by local company reps is too confusing. The learning specialist reviews the manuals, interviews customers, observes local reps. He then *develops a workshop entitled "How to teach adults about microcomputers,"* complete with a set of job aids for interpreting the manuals. The course is given to all company reps. • A T&D specialist interested in exploring the applications of a broad range of learning theories to the training and development field, invites *ten leading learning theorists* to be featured at a one-day colloquium. The T&D specialist *identifies the issues to be addressed and moderates and provides commentary on discussions during the meeting.* • Etc.
2. *A/V Skill . . .* Selecting and using audio/visual hardware and software.	• When asked to provide media support for a product information course, the T&D specialist selects *overhead transparencies and flip charts* as the major visual	• Given a request for television support and an outline for a new three lesson course on operating a tire retreading machine, the T&D specialist *pre-*	• When asked to develop a media/presentation strategy for a sales training program which will be sold to companies across the country, the T&D specialist de-

Figure 4.6 (Continued)

The Competency Model for the T&D Field

Example Behaviors Illustrating Levels of Expertise

The Competency:	Basic:	Intermediate:	Advanced:
	aids because the content will be frequently revised and delivery sites are only equipped with overhead projectors and easels.	pares a shooting plan for the shows and makes suggestions for added visual material to improve the shows.	termines content for visual aids, designs and constructs a video feedback process, prepares scripts and supervises the shooting and taping of a 35mm slide-tape support program.
	• A modification is made in the power supply of a small computer necessitating a change in the manager training course. From information supplied by the engineering department, the T&D specialist makes the appropriate changes to the overhead masters used in the computer repair training courses, and has new overhead materials produced and distributed to all instructors.	• When a new two-projector programming device is purchased, the T&D specialist retrays and reprograms all current single projector shows, making minor soundtrack and slide changes as needed to revise the shows to the new format.	• Faced with the need to simultaneously introduce a new major product to the annual sales convention and to overseas distributors, the T&D specialist sets communications goals, supervises concept and script development of a multi-projector presentation and videotapes in three languages, arranges and monitors production, and then arranges logistics of each presentation.
	• Etc.	• After a new company takes over a smaller one, the T&D specialist of the acquiring company designs and produces a four-projector show which portrays the acquiring company's capabilities and history.	• A manager selects A/V equipment for a large new training center so that the center is capable of supporting teleconferencing, interactive video, computer-aided instruction and a variety of film, slide, and multi-media needs. He assures that the layout, engineering and loading capability of the facility will support advanced equipment.
		• Etc.	• Etc.
3. *Career-Development Knowledge . . .*		• The T&D specialist develops a simple one page aid to help in-	• Management has previously given no support to an existing
			The organization has adopted upward mobility policies. The

Understanding the personal and organizational issues and practices relevant to individual careers.	dividuals *identify their personal skills, values, and career goals.* • A management trainee has trouble defining a career path. The T&D specialist helps her see that it is at least as important *to be able to describe the criteria for selecting jobs as it is to know the career moves to plan for in the future.* • Etc.	T&D specialist works with groups of clerical people *to help them analyze skills, life values, goals and to identify possible career paths.* • After a major reorganization, the T&D specialist changes the *company career information booklet* to reflect the changes. She also notes the *potential impact of the changes on career opportunities* in the company. • The T&D manager *discusses career issues with individuals in her department at their request.* She provides feedback on how she sees their skills, style and visibility; guides them through self-assessment and goal setting; recommends resources to use for information or development; and provides various kinds of development support. • Etc.	career development program and actively resists participating. The T&D specialist *evaluates the current program against several state-of-the-art programs, incorporates new career development methods and techniques, and implements a plan which is accepted at all levels of management.* • Management requests a career development strategy proposal which will allow people to move laterally and vertically. The T&D specialist identifies the key competency requirements of all departments and management levels and recommends a *competency-based promotion strategy which will enable people to move across divisions.* • In a growing organization, goals are established for succession planning to achieve management continuity. As part of this effort, the T&D specialist develops an assessment center program which helps assess core management skills and which also includes a *career planning module which among other things, helps participants consider whether or not they really want to move up in the organization, make lateral moves, stay in their current job, or take other career steps.* • Etc.
4. *Competency-Identification Skill* . . .	• When writing a course on interpersonal skills for ticket	• Given a list of competency requirements for marketing peo-	• When asked to help design a career development system for the

Figure 4.6 (Continued)

The Competency Model for the T&D Field

Example Behaviors Illustrating Levels of Expertise

The Competency:	Basic:	Intermediate:	Advanced:
Identifying the knowledge and skill requirements of jobs, tasks, roles.	agents, the T&D specialist *breaks the skills identified in the needs analysis into smaller units so* they will be easier to present and understand. • When asked to help develop a program to develop the math skills relevant to maintaining a computer, the T&D specialist first reviews the operations manual and *identifies those activities which require math skills.* • Etc.	ple in a large retail organization, the T&D specialist *develops behavioral examples of excellent performance that reliably and validly demonstrate* various levels of each competency. • After she reviews the list of tasks an airline pilot must perform, the T&D specialist points out *the skill and knowledge themes which cut across tasks.* • When a series of new accounting procedures is introduced to an auditing firm, the T&D specialist reviews the processes and works with an audit partner to *identify the knowledge and skills* which the audit training program must address to support the change. • Etc.	marketing function, the T&D specialist works with management and marketing experts to define what performance will characterize marketing excellence in the future. He then *helps identify the knowledges and skills which underlie excellent performance.* These become the basis for subsequent decisions about the career program. • A large department which is anticipating heavy management turnover from retirement asks the T&D department to propose a strategy for developing managers internally. The T&D specialists assigned to the task interview current managers, review the department's long- and short-range plans, study the successful managers who are most thought to be models for tomorrow, and *recommend the ten competencies which will be most valuable to the organization in the future.* • When a large sales department is decentralized and asked to add service to its responsibilities, the T&D specialist is asked to *help identify the new knowledges and skills which will be needed.* Since there are no models to study in

5. *Computer Competency* . . . Understanding and being able to use computers.

- After participating in a short training course about the computer, the instructor *teaches two people how to enter and edit data.*
- After she has completed a course in the use of the computer in adult education, the writer *selects existing software to help her use the computer to provide drill and practice* in a course module.
- Etc.

- When the media specialist is asked to convert a traditional classroom course to a *computer-aided course* suitable for individual instruction, she prepares *steps and a flow chart for writers to use* in preparing the program.
- When she is told that the computer analysis of a set of data is incorrect, the instructor *debugs the program* and teaches the learner *how to interpret error messages* and thus save time in the future.
- When a T&D manager is asked to help identify the potential uses of computers in the department, he discusses the long-run costs and benefits of *computer aided instruction, interactive computer video, and computer managed instruction* compared to the other learning modes his department would use if the computer were not available.
- Etc.

the existing organization, *she studies several other companies whose sales organizations have similar challenges, and develops a competency model* which is successfully used to hire and develop new sales reps.
- Etc.

- When management requests a computer assisted program to teach strategic planning to executives, the program designer designs an *interactive video program where the computer-assisted learning components* access the company's marketing and finance data base.
- When a new computer is made available to the training department, a program designer *builds a relational data base of existing instructional material* and develops a set of production *guidelines which can be followed in the future to easily incorporate new modules into the system.*
- When asked to evaluate a computer-based training program to train foremen across the country in supervising a new manufacturing process, the evaluator develops *computer-aided testing modules* to incorporate in the program and selects and sets up the use of a *statistical software package to process the data.*
- Etc.

Figure 4.6 (Continued)

The Competency Model for the T&D Field

Example Behaviors Illustrating Levels of Expertise

The Competency:	Basic:	Intermediate:	Advanced:
6. *Cost/Benefit-Analysis Skill . . .* Assessing alternatives in terms of their financial, psychological, and strategic advantages and disadvantages.	• When asked to compare the costs and benefits of an expensive in-house training program with the costs and benefits of a new commercially available program, the T&D specialist notes *the similarities and differences in objectives of the course and calculates the per person costs of each.* • When the training manager reviews a program, budget and financial report, he *identifies the areas where costs must be controlled.* • A media specialist estimates the cost of producing a 30-minute program on video. She then recommends film because *even though it will be more expensive to produce, it will be usable on existing equipment.* • Etc.	• During a critical stage of a needs analysis, the T&D specialist asks a cross-section of managers and technical experts to identify the areas where technical performance is weakest and to identify the costs to the organization of those weaknesses. Then she *compiles the results and uses them as a basis for recommending areas where training can have the most impact.* • When asked to advise whether a program should be cancelled or continued, a T&D specialist reviews financial and evaluation reports, assesses the extent it is achieving its objectives, and *compares the costs with performance on objectives.* • In a major presentation of a new instructional system, the marketer talks with his audience about the *pricing of the program in light of the benefits which other companies in their industry have experienced from earlier versions of the program.* • Etc.	• As part of her annual report to management about the effectiveness of the T&D department, the manager works with the department's accountant to *compute the direct and indirect costs of department-sponsored activities.* She then reviews the data on program impact which her evaluators have collected during and after each program, *quantifies that impact based on existing assumptions about the value of different kinds of behavior/attitude change to the company, and draws conclusions about the department's overall contributions.* • A T&D manager who must help quote a price for developing a new six module course for production supervisors, analyzes the costs associated with preparing a design, developing materials, piloting the program, packaging it, training the trainers, and conducting on-going evaluation. He *compares these costs with savings estimates from improved productivity and proposes a course price.* • Etc.

| 7. *Counseling Skill* . . .

Helping individuals recognize and understand personal needs, values, problems, alternatives and goals. | • The T&D specialist uses a career planning kit as an aid in helping an individual who has sought career assistance. She *empathizes with the employee's quandry* and, based on the data from interest questionnaires, *helps the employee explore a variety* of suitable new career directions.

• When helping a non-exempt employee who has voluntarily sought career counseling and eagerly taken a brief assessment inventory, the T&D specialist *refers to the interpretation grid accompanying the inventory and helps the employee interpret her scores.*

• Etc. | • A participant in a leadership program is befuddled by survey feedback he has gotten from people he asked to assess his leadership style before the program. The program facilitator notices him puzzling over his data, asks if she can help, *listens to and acknowledges his concerns, and helps him interpret the* results and decide on a course of action.

• During a series of discussions with the training director of a large department, the consultant *finds out the director's concerns about the organization and helps her* explore several options for training department direction.

• When counseling with an individual exploring potential career options, the T&D specialist *puts him through a guided imagery exercise as a way of gathering data* about the individual's career preferences.

• Etc. | • When asked to help an angry, shocked fifty year old ex-executive who has just been fired, the T&D specialist *gives him time to vent his feelings and concerns,* and then *helps channel his energy* into self-assessment, opportunity search.

• When helping a manager who has reluctantly asked his subordinates to complete a feedback questionnaire on his management practices, the T&D specialist first helps him *analyze and overcome his fears and resistance to the feedback.* Then he reviews the feedback—*helping the manager understand and internalize* it by asking him to think of critical events which the feedback seems to relate to.

• A T&D specialist works with an executive who has just completed an assessment center to help her develop action plans for improving skills and modifying style. The executive is sensitive about the assessment results. The T&D specialist takes time helping her air her concerns and goals, asks for her interpretation of the results, and helps set long- and short-term goals which the executive *feels she can and wants to achieve.*

• Etc. |
| 8. *Data-Reduction Skill* . . .

Scanning, synthesizing, and drawing conclusions from data. | • A program designer reviews the subject matter available for inclusion in a course on negotiating. He *selects the material* | • In order to assess the effectiveness of a new computer technology course, the T&D specialist *interprets test results* using stan- | • In order to prepare the strategic plan for training and development, the manager reviews a 2,000-page summary of ten year |

Figure 4.6 (Continued)

The Competency Model for the T&D Field

Example Behaviors Illustrating Levels of Expertise

The Competency:	Basic:	Intermediate:	Advanced:
	which is most relevant to the course objectives and purpose.	dardized data provided for a comparable population.	projections. He then *identifies the ten major new development issues which most of the agency's divisions will face.*
	• When asked to develop improvements to an existing program, the instructional writer *reads a program evaluation report, and develops clear conclusions about what needs to be changed.*	• Given data from a follow-up evaluation study of a management development program, the evaluator *scans the interview and observation data and separates the changes which are most likely due to the influence of the program from those which were probably caused by other factors.*	• When she is asked to interpret the raw data from an ill-designed three-year study of the effects of entry level training on performance, the evaluator reviews factor analyses, correlation data, turnover data and performance appraisal results, *identifies the key redesign areas* and makes recommendations for redesign of the program.
	• When asked to identify the best electronics course for the company's needs, the T&D specialist develops criteria for selecting a program, *reviews the two available programs against the criteria,* and recommends the course which is the best fit.	• A T&D specialist sets out to assess the effectiveness of a sales training program. He reviews *two years of data from the organization's files (reaction sheets, appraisals, development plans, productivity data from branch offices that have and have not participated in the training)* and uses this data to prepare a report.	• Etc.
	• Etc.	• Etc.	
9. Delegation Skill . . . Assigning task responsibility and authority to others.	• An evaluator prepares guidelines for pulling data from a computer printout and *asks her secretary to do the data by synthesis.*	• A manager who does not trust one of her staff's ability to coordinate and manage projects for the department identifies her reasons for feeling uncomfortable about delegating work to that person. She then directly discusses her concerns with the	• A manager who is known for her design contributions to the T&D field recognizes that she does all the most exciting design work herself—even though her job is to manage ten people. She decides to *bite the bullet and delegate an attractive design project to one*
	• The T&D administrator assigns *responsibility for conducting a* needs assessment survey for		

of her staff. Furthermore, she works with that person to develop a quality criteria and provide support but stays out of the day-to-day work even though the work style of the designer is quite different than hers.

- A manager whose three staff people have varying abilities to proactively manage their work develops a strategy for each whereby he delegates work and then provides the different levels of support appropriate for each person. His goal—and he tells them so—is to help them become progressively more able to make key decisions without his approval and review.

- The T&D manager delegates to a T&D specialist the responsiblity for reviewing, assessing and revising the training system for headquarters staff. This includes planning and scheduling courses, conducting needs assessment, recruiting and assigning instructors, marketing, logistics management and evaluation. She works with the specialist to develop clear goals and indicators to monitor and is direct about her performance expectations.

- Etc.

---

employee and works out an "if this . . . then that . . ." plan to progressively delegate greater levels of work autonomy.

- The T&D manager asks one of his technical instructors to manage a training project which includes planning, organizing, testing and monitoring the work of other technical instructors. He discusses the new project manager's fears and abilities and works with him to develop a support plan for the early stages of the project.

- A program administrator turns the responsibility for staging the general sessions of a conference over to a production company—but provides and negotiates very specific quality criteria.

- Etc.

---

the department's secretarial staff to her experienced clerical staff supervisor.

- The T&D specialist prepares materials and trains foremen to conduct a basic first aid course. Each foreman is delegated the responsibility for scheduling and teaching basic first aid to all people on their crews.

- Etc.

---

10. *Facilities Skill . . .*

Planning and coordinating logistics in an efficient and cost effective manner.

- Given a request to secure space for a workshop of forty people which will require four breakout rooms, the T&D specialist reviews the workshop's activities and determines the room sizes and equipment required.

- A conference coordinator collects lists of AV needs from speakers and then selects and manages an equipment vendor to provide all the equipment and technical support needed for a 300 person conference.

- Given a rough floor plan of four rooms in existing training facilities, the T&D specialist reviews projected training and related space needs. He then prepares a design for renovation of space which integrates AV, lighting, writing

Figure 4.6 (Continued)

The Competency Model for the T&D Field

The Competency:	Example Behaviors Illustrating Levels of Expertise		
	Basic:	*Intermediate:*	*Advanced:*
	• Knowing that the physical setting of a training room affects the learning environment, the facilitator *rearranges a room so that chairs, easels, window location* are more supportive of the informal, open mood she wants to establish. • The T&D specialist manages the ongoing relationship with a hotel whose space is under contract to be used weekly for the company's training. He reviews *space, equipment, power supplies and service available* to assure they meet each week's specifications. • Etc.	• Using an on-line airline information service, the training administrator *prepares master flight and ground transportation schedules* for 25 trainees from across the country who will attend a local workshop. The schedules assure both *efficient routing and discount pricing.* • In preparation for a two-week conference in a single location where the participants will be housed in various hotels away from the conference site, the T&D coordinator *arranges for the appropriate conference meeting space and hotel support.* He keeps prices within his budget and gets assurances of quality service. • Etc.	*boards and storage. The* plan meets budget and "learning atmosphere" requirements. • Faced with immediately adding 650 tech service reps to an already overloaded facility, the T&D specialist *rearranges load schedules, rents additional housing, and arranges meal service and transportation to permit smooth absorption of overload.* • While working with a major hotel which will be the site of a technical training conference, the T&D coordinator sets up the plan *for materials receiving and storage, power line changes, room setups to meet speaker specifications, meal and break logistics and special check-in procedures.* She also holds a special meeting for the hotel staff explaining who will be in the group and what quality of service they will expect. • A T&D manager is asked to help design and supervise the construction of a new training facility. He determines *how the facility will be used over time, and what equipment, learning approaches, and political issues the faculty must support. Then he coordinates budget,*

staff, architects, contractors, and vendors throughout the construction.

- Etc.

11. Feedback Skill . . .

Communicating opinions, observations and conclusions such that they are understood.

- After observing a trainee practice a series of manual operations, the T&D specialist *informs him that he has accomplished* each of the major activities listed on a testing checklist.
- A writer developing a programmed instruction module prepares several paragraphs which will *provide helpful feedback* to students selecting wrong answers to test questions.
- Etc.

- Six weeks after a training program, participants have reverted to their former practices. Realizing that management and work flow do not support the skills taught in the program, the T&D specialist *meets with management to communicate his observations of the situation.* They agree that a problem exists.
- A program designer, remembering experiences he has had in the past where he has not *communicated course objectives and content to those who will produce his program, meets regularly with the writer and media specialist who will develop his new program.* In those meetings he talks about his ideas and gets their *questions and ideas. By the time the program is ready, everyone is on the same wavelength.*
- Etc.

- When asked by the president of the organization to give feedback on his public speaking skills, the T&D specialist clarifies the criteria he will use. He then observes the president's next speeches and *communicates his observations—supported by concrete examples—of what the president did and said in his talks.*
- A middle manager exhibits skepticism and challenges assessment center data. The T&D specialist *provides specific, concrete examples from several assessment exercises and from her own observations outside the center to support the conclusions.*
- Etc.

12. Futuring Skill . . .

Projecting trends and visualizing possible and probable futures and their implications.

- Presented with an economic forecast for the next year, the T&D specialist roughly *predicts the impact on training needs in his own company.*
- The T&D specialist is invited to present a session on the future uses of computer aided in-

- The T&D specialist is asked to review the strategic plan and to recommend the number of executives who will need to be developed to meet the company's needs in the next five years. *The T&D specialist prepares projections based on succes-*

- The T&D manager has noticed that her organization has a history of being overly optimistic in its strategic planning and frequently has missed critical employee skill shortages and dramatic shifts in the general business environment. She *pre-*

Figure 4.6 (Continued)

The Competency Model for the T&D Field

Example Behaviors Illustrating Levels of Expertise

The Competency:	Basic:	Intermediate:	Advanced:
	struction. He *develops scenarios illustrating new applications of CAI.*	*sion planning information and on analysis of the human resource requirements implied in the strategic plan.* • As part of the Training Department's strategic planning process, the T&D specialist helps identify what changes in supervisory practices may occur in the next five years. Using a list of demographic changes as a starting point, he *develops two scenarios illustrating effective supervisory practices now and in five years.* • The T&D manager has been invited to be a member of a national advisory board for health care trainers and is asked to chair a sub-group on the future of health care training. *He prepares scenarios predicting changes needed in the competencies of health care trainers as a result of trends in health care techniques and health care organizations.* • Etc.	*pares scenarios of the HR problems the company will face if they continue to ignore labor projections and the potential impact of the changing business environment.* • The T&D specialist is asked to write a brief handout illustrating the implications of brain research for adult learning. She reviews the literature and writes a paper that *predicts several new directions that group learning will take because of findings from brain research.* • From a variety of forecasting and futuring sources, the T&D specialist *synthesizes a number of one, five and ten year scenarios for her company.* The scenarios accurately reflect probable trends and the critical forces facing the industry as a whole. • Etc.
13. *Group-Process Skill* . . . Influencing groups to both accomplish tasks and fulfill the needs of their members.	• A training group is hard at work in its second session when a new member arrives. The instructor stops the task work briefly; *provides for the introduction of the*	• A line manager asks the T&D specialist to work with her in planning and conducting better staff meetings. The T&D specialist observes one meet-	• When asked to help a new task force learn the skills they will need in order to work together effectively, the T&D specialist *reviews and models several approaches*

for exploring ideas, reaching consensus, and managing conflict in a group.

- Having completed the "get-acquainted" phase with a new group, the facilitator finds that work on the task is being frustrated by a battle for control by three group members who are accustomed to being group leaders. *Understanding what is happening, the facilitator stops the task work, helps the group identify what is going on, leads them to a resolution of the problem, and gets them back to the task with all parties feeling they have been heard and are committed to proceeding.*

- Etc.

ing, interviews a few staff members, and recommends *various means for increasing group participation which will fit the needs and styles of the group members and the typical nature of the tasks.*

- At the end of a training program, the T&D specialist senses a reluctance of the group to end the strong relationships built up. *She talks about this with the group and allows members to talk about what the group and individuals in it have meant to them and how they feel about leaving it.*

- In a continually disruptive classroom situation, the T&D specialist allows *the disruptive group to air their issues and then is honest about her expectations and their alternatives should they choose not to cooperate.* As a result, the general tension level in the group is reduced.

- Etc.

member to the group, and *vice versa; sets up a late informal get-together process; and quickly orients the new member to the on-going task.*

- In a large group meeting of people who have successfully worked together before, the facilitator conducts a series of group involvement exercises and negotiates a "group contract" for the direction and goals of the meeting.

- In a session where some different points of view are beginning to develop some negative feelings among group participants, the facilitator encourages the quiet participants to talk about their right to have a point of view. The discussion then returns to an open, highly participative one.

- Etc.

14. *Industry Understanding . . .*

Knowing the key concepts and variables that define an industry or sector (e.g., critical issues, economic vulnerabilities, measurements, distribution channels, inputs, outputs, information sources).

- A consultant develops a proposal to design a development strategy for coal mine supervisors. The proposal *reflects an indepth knowledge of the issues facing the energy industry in general and the coal industry in particular.* Recommendations focus on the coal mining industry's actions which most can improve management productivity measures.

- From a broad range of industry

- After reviewing analyses of and commentaries on recent legislation, the T&D specialist projects *the changes the legislation will cause in her company's industry.* After checking out her assumption with key managers in her organization, she identifies the effects the changes will have on skill requirements.

- Given the National Association of Broadcasters Code of Ethics

- The T&D specialist describes the *major types of services currently being offered by insurance companies in her area and reviews her own company's product training to see if it is up to date in product knowledge for these areas.*

- In a meeting with hospital administrators, the hospital training consultant *overviews trends in hospital equipment changes and*

Figure 4.6 (Continued)

The Competency Model for the T&D Field

Example Behaviors Illustrating Levels of Expertise

The Competency:	Basic:	Intermediate:	Advanced:
	points out their implications for training and development. • In a discussion with a potential client from the banking industry, the T&D specialist *describes the four key factors which influence the growth of savings and loan associations.* • Etc.	and a summary of current issues, the T&D specialist prepares a set of case studies for a broadcaster's counsel of ethics. The cases *reflect a broad range of situations facing people in that industry.* • A writer preparing an interactive video-based agency orientation program develops a module describing *the place of the agency in the governmental system and teaching people how public sector organizations are unique.* • Etc.	sources, the T&D specialist identifies five possible directions the industry could take. The scenarios *reflect many subtle forces facing the industry as a whole.* • Etc.
15. *Intellectual Versatility* . . . Recognizing, exploring and using a broad range of ideas and practices. Thinking logically and creatively, without undue influence from personal biases.	• After reviewing a *new research report* about audio-accompanied computer-based instruction, the T&D specialist *decides to rewrite* one of his training modules to better use the media. • When asked to develop a course in counseling skills for a client department, the T&D specialist *explores the potential applications of several approaches and then adopts* the best design even though it is the one she is least familiar with. • Etc.	• The T&D specialist recognizes that the changing demographics and values of his prime training audience will affect the impact of his programs. *Deducing that he must change his management development content* to emphasize more participative techniques, he incorporates them into his programs, *even though* his own management style and preferences remain primarily non-participative. • When presented with competing arguments by staff experts for the appropriate training	• During one week, a program designer works with subject matter experts to develop *program outlines for courses in auditing, counseling, and fork lift operating.* The course designer incorporates *very different kinds* of learning activities as appropriate for each course. • When a management development specialist is asked to prepare a development strategy for the company's engineers, she spends time with experts in the engineering field and *realizes that subject matter will require a different*

analysis and design approach than she has used for management development. She then works to *grasp the key principles in the field* and *explore* appropriate training options.

- Faced with client departments who have drastically cut back in expenses for training due to recession, the T&D director reassesses his manpower needs and *explores a broad range of other opportunities.* He decides to seek temporary assignments for training staff in line departments and to train line managers to deliver several basic but staff-consuming programs even though both decisions will reduce his department size.

- Etc.

- When asked to develop a way to access a broad range of courses, books, journals, and reports and training manuals, the T&D specialist *sets up an informational retrieval system* which uses the most up-to-date library *science coding systems.*

- A program designer is asked to develop a plan for continuous updating of a course to help scientists know state of the art genetic research. He asks the technical library to send copies of all articles and materials, scans an *on-line research data base* for current and projected issues; initiates and jointly develops an on-

---

methodology to use in a key engineering course, the T&D specialist *explores each position for its strengths and liabilities and tries to keep his own preferences for a* classroom based instruction *from biasing his decision.*

- Etc.

- A T&D specialist responsible for the continuing education of accountants in a large CPA firm, sits at his computer every month to personally identify new trends and their implications for training content. He *searches authors, subjects and resources without the help of a library expert.*

- In order to gather data for video-based case studies and simulations to be used in an executive development program, the T&D specialist realizes she needs information about how other companies are handling several key problems. She gives

---

- When asked to recommend a film for use in a conflict management course, the media specialist *calls her contacts at a major clearing house.*

- When preparing the annual update of a "References" section of a course on adult learning, the writer *asks the company information specialist to secure articles that appear relevant.*

- After being asked to prepare a resource list for an upcoming "Women in Management" course, the T&D specialist works with a library specialist to access a computer time-shar-

---

16. *Library Skill* . . .

Gathering information from printed and other recorded sources. Identifying and using information specialists and reference services and aids.

Figure 4.6 (Continued)

The Competency Model for the T&D Field

The Competency:	Example Behaviors Illustrating Levels of Expertise		
	Basic:	Intermediate:	Advanced:
	ing *file of articles, books, and research studies on the topic.* • Etc.	all the instructions a researcher needs for gathering *information from the Wall Street Journal Index, Abstracted Business Information Services,* and a number of other computer-aided search services. • Etc.	going *literature search plan* with the head information scientist. • When asked to do a needs analysis for a law firm, the T&D specialist interviews a cross section of lawyers in and outside the firm, formulates six key questions *to research in the literature,* and asks *a library specialist to gather articles, books, and computer generated abstracts* of recent articles related to the key questions. • Etc.
17. *Model-Building Skill* . . . Developing theoretical and practical frameworks which describe complex ideas in understandable, usable ways.	• When a writer is asked to prepare an article explaining how attitudes affect behavior, he *adopts a four-box flow chart* he saw in a psychology text—using it to help him *graphically* overview the data for the article. • When a writer is asked to prepare materials for an employee orientation program, *she creates a map* illustrating the major purposes of each department and how they support and interconnect with each other. • Etc.	• When she is asked to develop a training program for sales reps which will address needs and present content identified in a comprehensive needs analysis, the program designer *organizes the data into units that will make sense for the learners and develops a simple flow chart illustrating the course content.* The flow chart is easy to remember and use. • When the T&D specialist is asked to develop a process for introducing and supporting new T&D programs into the	• After a meeting with researchers who are investigating how to make computers more "friendly" to users, the T&D specialist notes that information and decision theorists are addressing some of the same problems that adult educators face. After a detailed exploration of that field, he proposes *a learning model which incorporates concepts* from information theory, adult learning theory, and other sources.) • After a review of many different models of engineering management, the program designer *cre-*

ates a new model which will enable participants in a course for new technical managers to quickly *see and understand* the major responsibilities of someone in an engineering management position.

- In order to present complex information about data-based information systems to a naive audience which will have to use it, the writer develops many charts, tables and well-organized outlines which *include all the important data but organize it in a comprehensive way.*

- Etc.

organization, she *builds a model depicting the process flow.*

- Etc.

18. *Negotiation Skill . . .*

Securing win-win agreements while successfully representing a special interest in a decision situation.

- A program designer meets with three busy subject matter specialists and *successfully secures agreement* to hold the next meeting within three days.

- A group facilitator who *wants a group to reduce* the number of items on its agenda *successfully helps a group prioritize its actions* for a meeting and *drop* several items from its list.

- Etc.

- In a program design review with management, management wants to reduce the length of a new program from five to two days. The T&D specialist probes their reasons for wanting to shorten it, reminds them of the needs the program has been designed to address, points out the advantages and disadvantages he sees on both sides and *gets support for the program length* if two of the days are designed as follow up and occur at least one month after the first three.

- When the company's executives decide to implement quality circles company wide, they hire an outside "expert" without consulting their training department. The director of training meets with several executives over lunch to discuss this issue and the

- On a large contract project where most of the program and implementation guides are complete, but the client has only paid one-third of the fees, the client becomes hostile about a slipped deadline and refuses further payment. The project manager *finds the key decision makers, convinces them that they share responsibility for the common goal, and gets approval to proceed.*

- When two T&D specialists vie for the same project, the manager suggests they *negotiate the decision.* They decide to each list the value of the project to them and its relationship to the other assignments. *They agree to use these criteria to assign the job to the person for whom it's the best fit.*

Figure 4.6 (Continued)

The Competency Model for the T&D Field

Example Behaviors Illustrating Levels of Expertise

The Competency:	Basic:	Intermediate:	Advanced:
		• A T&D manager has been asked by a VP who is also a personal friend to relax the promotion criteria for a particular position so that he can be promoted into the T&D department. The T&D manager tactfully explains why doing this would not be in the best interests of the company, the VP, or the nominee. *The VP is left agreeing with the manager's position and feeling that his confidentiality will be respected.* • Etc.	department's desire to work on this effort. After listing the department's *capabilities and describing the need for long-term support and customization of the program, management agrees to ask the expert to work with the Training Department.* • A manager tells the T&D specialist that she wants to use two case studies from one of the T&D department's management programs in a staff meeting. The T&D specialist *does not want to release the studies because they constitute a major portion of a key course.* He asks what the manager wants to achieve and then *recommends another approach. The alternative is accepted.* • Etc.
19. *Objectives-Preparation Skill . . .* Preparing clear statements which describe desired outputs.	• Asked by the Personnel office to "find a film and conduct a 90-minute meeting for heads of offices on working with unmotivated workers," the T&D specialist draws on her past experience with the topic and drafts a letter which includes *a list of what people will learn in* this session.	• A T&D specialist is asked to help develop guidelines for independent learning projects which will occur as follow-ups to a formal management development course. She develops designs which include *lists of learning objectives for each module. These objectives include indicators that managers can use on*	• A T&D specialist with little experience in the technical area is asked to prepare a training plan based on a 200-page needs analysis report of the training needs for a high technology group. She *develops detailed training objectives to pass the review of a technical advisory board.*

- As part of a development strategy for auditors in a public accounting firm, the T&D specialist must develop objectives to guide the developer of course modules. Realizing that many outputs of successful auditing work are subjective, she develops *objectives which list a variety of indicators which can be used to measure each objective.*

- A T&D specialist is asked to design a strategy for upgrading the skills of a decentralized staff in a rapidly changing, highly technical job. Working with subject matter experts and with people who know the company's strategy, the T&D specialist identifies the critical skills which must be developed and prepares *objectives for use in on-the-job training.*

- Etc.

- After a take-over merger, the training specialist is asked to set up a series of sessions to help orient the managers of the acquired company to the philosophy of the new organization. Through a series of interviews with top managers from both companies, the T&D specialist *identifies their fears, concerns, and hopes and develops a program that addresses each but still has the terminal goal of getting acceptance to the new philosophy.*

---

their own to assess their progress.

- A T&D specialist who has designed supervisory training programs before is asked to prepare a program to train new technical supervisors. He works with a taskforce of technical managers to identify special issues in technical supervision and *develops objectives for supervisory skills in the highly technical environment.*

- When given a list of clearly defined tasks, their skill requirements and a description of the typical audience for a new program to train new technicians, the T&D specialist *writes objectives with observable behaviors, measurable performance criteria, and a description of conditions under which performance will occur on the job.*

- Etc.

- When management asks for help in changing the organization culture from a reactive to a proactive mode, the T&D specialist helps identify the new knowledges, skills and attitudes required, but strongly *points out that management practices and promotion criteria must also change* to support new employee behaviors.

- An evaluator notes that although a series of electronic

- A T&D specialist receives a detailed task analysis and knowledge/skill list for one segment of a toy assembler's job. He rewrites the task statements using *the language of behavioral objectives prescribed in established guidelines.*

- Etc.

20. Organization-Behavior Understanding . . .

Seeing organizations as dynamic, political, economic, and social systems which have multiple goals; using this larger perspective as a framework for understanding and influencing events and change.

- A writer preparing a budgeting module for a middle management self-study program, ends the section with a guide to help participants plan how they will use and introduce the budget techniques on the job. She *offers suggestions for making changes acceptable and understood in the organization.*

- The T&D specialist is to develop a job aid to train people in the use of a new company-

Figure 4.6 (Continued)

The Competency Model for the T&D Field

Example Behaviors Illustrating Levels of Expertise

The Competency:	Basic:	Intermediate:	Advanced:
	wide expense voucher format. Knowing that this change will meet some resistance, he *builds in a rationale for the change which is likely to appeal to the needs of its primary users.* • Etc.	workshops is successfully helping production engineers *develop skills they need for incorporating microprocessors into new products, the number of products which use that technology has not significantly increased. She proposes that other groups in the company may be blocking the new technology and recommends the skills training program be dropped unless the system's problems are resolved.* • Etc.	• The T&D specialist is asked to develop a training program to improve productivity. *Rather than immediately developing a program, he convinces key managers that productivity improvement may require some major changes in how people work. He proposes to first identify productivity problems and then work with management to design a combined training and organization change program.* • Etc.
21. *Organization Understanding . . .* Knowing the strategy, structure, power networks, financial position, systems of a *specific* organization.	• Before submitting the department budget, the T&D manager *identifies other department managers who must review it.* He discusses the budget with them before he proposes it. • A program administrator schedules participation in a popular class to assure that each class contains supervisors *from a cross-section of company departments.* • Etc.	• When asked to identify future career options for professionals in the organization, the career specialist creates several scenarios of future work in the company. *These scenarios take the company's strategy, structure and culture into account.* • A T&D specialist works with representatives from Public Affairs, Public Relations and Employee Communication to develop a self-study *review of company structure, policies, and procedures.*	• The T&D specialist heads a study team to identify areas for productivity improvement in the company. Her study plan reflects an *indepth knowledge of where the greatest opportunities and leverage points are in the company.* • In a presentation of a costly proposal for executive development, the T&D specialist refers to a *broad range of data from the company's financial statements, budgets, and strategic plan.* • Etc.

- *Based on a thorough understanding of the company's direction and major current challenges,* the T&D manager lists ten major strategic challenges for the human resource development function.

- Etc.

- In preparation for designing a conflict management program for executives, the T&D specialist *observes merger negotiations between representatives of major corporations. She develops an observation recording system which reliably identifies each person's verbal and nonverbal activity* in terms of who talks to whom, about what, and the impact that it seems to have on the meeting and the individuals included.

- In a facilitated negotiation meeting with ten representatives from labor and management, the T&D specialist *identifies those who seem to accept the speaker's point of view, those who might accept the speaker's and those who may never accept the speaker's point of view.* He records the specific behaviors which have led to his conclusion and uses them as a basis for helping determine the reasons for each position.

- Before he prepares a report describing the strengths and development needs of an executive who has just completed a series of assessment center activities,

---

22. *Performance-Observation Skill* . . . .

Tracking and describing behaviors and their effects.

- At the request of the Personnel department, the T&D specialist *observes the performance of the* company's mail sorters and *develops a list of the major tasks in*volved in doing that job.

- While she is leading a fairly structured discussion of a modeling tape, the instructor *notices non-verbal signals* from one person that indicates he doesn't understand the concept being discussed. She stops the tape and asks further questions.

- In order to determine training needs, a needs analyst *watches* an assembler work, compares what he does to a time-phased description of the tasks and subtasks, and *identifies areas which are not being performed ac-*cording to standards.

- Etc.

- At a manager's request, the T&D specialist spends two days *watching the manager's team de-*velop a plan to upgrade the feed systems on the MX-11B widget stamper; the T&D specialist writes a report on the group's ability to function as a team and, using a standardized rating form, rates and critiques the interpersonal skills of each.

- When given a vague list of tasks which engineering consultants must perform, a specialist watches several superior performers work and then *defines and identifies observable and mea-*surable performance criteria and the variables which affect job performance.

- With the permission of a group undergoing a team building session, the T&D specialist *observes the group at work and com-*piles a chart showing frequency of *and lines of communication be-*tween various members.

- Etc.

Figure 4.6 (Continued)

The Competency Model for the T&D Field

Example Behaviors Illustrating Levels of Expertise

The Competency:	Basic:	Intermediate:	Advanced:
23. *Personnel/HR-Field Understanding . . .* Understanding issues and practices in other HR areas. (Organization Development, Organization Job Design, Human Resource Planning, Selection and Staffing, Personnel Research and Information Systems, Compensation and Benefits, Employee Assistance, Union/Labor Relations.)	• The T&D manager makes a presentation to a group of supervisors to *explain how the T&D mission relates to the other missions of other personnel functions* within the company. • The T&D manager lists the *human resource/personnel-related groups that meet frequently in his* area. He keeps track of and posts the issues they address in their meetings. • Etc.	• The T&D specialist writes a mission of the training and development department which *shows overlapping concerns with other personnel areas and yet presents the unique domain of training and development in the organiza-* tion. • *Knowing that new personnel information systems will allow much more sophisticated cataloging of* development actions, the T&D manager talks with the head of personnel information and asks to help develop the program for that application. • Having stayed up-to-date on *the state-of-the-art in performance appraisal and succession planning,* the T&D specialist is able to link several training programs with these practices and to	• After the T&D manager reviews the long-range personnel needs for the organization and gathers statistics about skills currently available in the organization, she *meets with the directors of compensation and staffing* to determine what each function can do to assure that the right skills are available when they are needed. • The T&D manager *chairs and coordinates the work of a task force of managers from the Compensation, Staffing, Labor Relations, and Personnel Research functions.* Their task is to develop a strategic plan for Human Resources that *presents an interpretation of the direction the HR departments will take.* • As part of an on-going HR planning group, the T&D manager *reviews professional development*
			the assessor reviews *what the executive did in each exercise*, makes a judgment about how appropriate her performance was in each situation, and *identifies patterns of behavior across the situation.* • Etc.

24. Presentation Skill . . .

Verbally presenting information such that the intended purpose is achieved.

---

trends affecting a broad range of HR practices, briefs the group on more important trends, and, with the group, *explores the potential impact of the trends* on human resource projects in the immediate future.

• Etc.

• When the T&D manager is asked to introduce the speakers in a one-day seminar on industry trends, *he presents personal tidbits which* will interest the participants and *reviews the skills* which they bring to the session.

• While giving a *standard lecture* reviewing several management theories in a course for new supervisors, the instructor *personalizes the material with a story from his own experience and still covers the material* in the allotted time.

• When asked to *present* the results of a well-designed training needs analysis to six branch managers who want to take action, the needs analyst *gets and keeps the group's attention by standing up, reviewing the major points she will cover and clearly presenting the data and its implications.* Her *eye contact* remains with the group throughout the presentation.

• Etc.

• When he feels nervous early in a presentation to 100 people, the T&D specialist uses *deep breathing, relaxation and visualization techniques to help reduce his tension.*

• When an instructor notices that several new employees with limited English-speaking skills are having a difficult time understanding *her standard presentation, she adjusts the lecture by defining and discussing the confusing words and by pausing and checking understanding* more frequently.

• When asked to make a presentation to manufacturing managers reviewing the Training and Development services and courses available to the company, the T&D specialist *works from a word outline, customizes the presentation to focus on the major needs of the group, and responds without defensiveness* to occasionally skeptical questions from the audience.

• Etc.

---

recommend how they can be more mutually supportive.

• Etc.

• An account executive representing a large T&D company has been invited to present his company's proposal for a major new training and evaluation program which will be used to develop employees across the country. He prepares a media assisted review of the proposal, *uses it to quickly review key points, then spends a good portion of the meeting listing, discussing, and responding to questions from the group. His responses are clear, address the issues, use language appropriate to the group, and convey confidence and professionalism.*

• When making a *presentation at an annual conference to a group of senior professionals,* the T&D specialist *mixes graphics, handouts, personal stories and well-organized presentations of key points.* The attendees rate the presentation as exceptional in both content and delivery.

• In a very tense meeting of top management to review the issues being raised in a key management development program, the T&D specialist *uses flip charts and*

Figure 4.6 (Continued)

The Competency Model for the T&D Field

Example Behaviors Illustrating Levels of Expertise

The Competency:	Basic:	Intermediate:	Advanced:
25. *Questioning Skill* . . . Gathering information from and stimulating insight in individuals and groups through the use of interviews, questionnaires and other probing methods.	• Working with an out-of-date operations manual and a knowledgeable terminal operator, the T&D specialist *interviews the operator and gathers enough information* to update the manual. • The T&D specialist *follows an interview outline to gather demographic data* about potential users of training and development services. • In order to determine their level of satisfaction from attending an orientation session, the T&D specialist *draws from a list of prepared questions to interview participants individually and as a group.* • Etc.	• A T&D specialist who is training supervisors in interviewing skills stresses the importance of *using reflective skills like empathizing and active listening, in order to help interviewees disclose information during the interviews.* • The T&D specialist develops a *set of self-analysis questionnaires* to help people in a career exploration program discover their own needs, goals, interests and capabilities. • Etc.	stories to illustrate key points. She *skillfully presents the issues and her recommendations* for executive action. The audience acknowledges that the issues should be addressed and agrees to meet in a problem-solving session. • Etc. • After the release of three well-liked foremen because of policy violations, the T&D specialist is asked to evaluate the training program which communicates company direction and philosophy. As part of the evaluation, she *designs a questionnaire which captures the true feelings of the workers* even though they are reluctant to express any opinions to management or the training department itself. • In preparation for designing a maintenance course for a new computer in the last stages of product development, the T&D specialist *questions reluctant design engineers, harried manufacturing production engineers, and taciturn quality control specialists to find out what the repair procedures will be* when the product is released three months hence. The T&D

26. Records-Management Skill . . . Storing data in easily retrievable form.

- A T&D specialist maintains attendance and continuing education unit records for participants in all company training programs and, following established procedures, prepares monthly reports for each operational unit.

- A T&D specialist establishes an AV/training materials resource center for training department staff. The services include cataloging, and indexing current and new acquisitions.

- Etc.

- When asked to design an inventory system for equipment scheduling and maintenance, the T&D specialist identifies information required and *designs a system for gathering and storing information.* She then trains the department administrative assistant to organize information for reporting and scheduling purposes.

- After participating in an external information management seminar, the T&D specialist *outlines the pros and cons of automated information storage and retrieval systems for his department* and briefs training peers at a monthly staff meeting.

- A T&D specialist works with the word processor to *establish methods for entering and retrieving a list of job tasks for a supervisory* training program.

- Etc.

specialist gets enough accurate information to help the technical writers prepare the operations manuals.

- During a key segment of a training program, the T&D specialist senses serious resentment in the audience. *Using carefully phrased, probing questions he draws from the group the underlying reasons for their attitude* and is able to defuse the situation.

- Etc.

- T&D specialist *develops recommendations to upgrade and automate the T&D department's record management system* so that periodic reports on cost effectiveness and attendance can be developed and used in planning and in reports to management.

- A T&D specialist, working with the data processing department develops a *framework for storing and retrieving data* from an extensive task analysis of the organization. The data is known to have far-reaching implications in identifying training needs, and *access to the information in readily usable forms is vital to the training* department.

- Etc.

Figure 4.6 (Continued)

The Competency Model for the T&D Field

Example Behaviors Illustrating Levels of Expertise

The Competency:	Basic:	Intermediate:	Advanced:
27. *Relationship Versatility* . . . Adjusting behavior in order to establish relationships across a broad range of people and groups.	• During the few minutes before a session where participants from several different organization units will discuss what needs to be done to support the use of important new skills on the job, the T&D specialist greets each person at the door and begins to make them comfortable about being there. • Realizing that a difference of opinion exists between two groups and that one group is more defensive about its position, the instructor *shifts to a listening mode and spends time letting the defensive group air its frustrations.* • Etc.	• *After working with a group of repair people* in a training class, where the course satisfaction ratings were high, the T&D specialist *meets with the company's Director of Finance* to begin to identify needs for a management development program. The director gets excited about the potential program and asks to shorten the time line for introducing it. • When working with a group of new trainees who are hesitant to take responsibility for their own learning and who prefer that the facilitator take a directive stance in leading class sessions, the T&D specialist *begins where they are by taking a directive position, then gradually moves to a non-directive style* as participants gain confidence and competence. • Etc.	• Management has decided to reorganize and has placed a previously line management controlled training program under the authority of the training department. The T&D specialist *involves the line manager in establishing quality control procedures and personally consults him throughout the transition.* The manager becomes a key supporter of the new structure. • During the development of an executive development plan where a large percentage of top management is antitraining, the T&D specialist implements a *strategy of meeting formally and informally with key executives to discuss their concerns and visions for company.* The executives ultimately provide a budget to fund a major new development initiative. • During a five-week executive development course in which three contenders for the presidency are present and initially unwilling to disclose their needs or ideas, the senior T&D specialist *builds a relationship with each individual and is even asked to help them develop consensus on a major com-*

pany problem that comes up for discussion during the program.

- Etc.

28. Research Skill . . .

Selecting, developing and using methodologies, statistical and data collection techniques for a formal inquiry.

- The T&D specialist develops a pre- and post-questionnaire to *assess knowledge change that has occurred* as a result of a series of seminars on the participative workplace.

- A non-exempt employee seeks advice from a T&D specialist on how to prepare for a supervisory position. The T&D specialist *selects standard interest and skill batteries to help the individual assess his development needs.*

- The T&D specialist develops a true-false multiple choice *test to assess knowledge levels* at the end of a computer-aided learning module on the basis of robot repair.

- Technical employees are frustrated by limited career options. The T&D specialist is asked to see if a job rotation system might make better use of and better develop their skills. As a first step she *selects generic inventories to help employees assess their skills.*

- Etc.

- When the researcher is asked to evaluate the reliability of a questionnaire, he *reviews the different approaches for measuring reliability and determines that a test-retest approach using people trained to code responses* will be most appropriate.

- The T&D manager prepares a *policy statement and guidelines for evaluation practices* to be used for all formal training and development events.

- The T&D specialist develops and validates a questionnaire for participants to send to their boss, peers and subordinates before a program. This questionnaire helps them identify *how their skill and style are perceived* by those they work with and to identify areas for development.

- Etc.

- When asked to show the effects of a training program on the productivity of a group of customer service reps, the evaluator recommends a nominal group technique for defining "productivity." She then *develops a pre- and post-measurement strategy* which managers feel will gather useful data and which her research colleagues agree will be valid.

- The T&D specialist is asked to evaluate the impact of a program whose objectives include attitude as well as skill and knowledge development. She develops an observation checklist for supervisors and a self-report format which *assesses post-course knowledge, attitudes and skill levels.*

- When asked to track the impact and identify the most successful ingredients of a multi-faceted program designed to help managers and employees develop a more open attitude toward change, the research specialist *develops an integrated research design which incorporates pre- and post-course questionnaires, analyzes project failures over time, and measures climate/attitude changes for all key groups.* The design wins honorable mention in a key research journal.

Figure 4.6 (Continued)

The Competency Model for the T&D Field

Example Behaviors Illustrating Levels of Expertise

The Competency:	Basic:	Intermediate:	Advanced:
29. *Training-and-Development-Field Understanding . . .* Knowing the technological, social, economic, professional, and regulatory issues in the field; understanding the role T&D plays in helping individuals learn for current and future jobs.	• The T&D specialist regularly reads and refers to articles in the *T&D Journal* and *Training Magazine.* • The T&D manager *notices an increase in the articles and talks dealing with* the application of Human Resource accounting practices to T&D and begins to learn about HRA before it becomes an issue in his organization. • Etc.	• The T&D specialist makes a presentation to her manager which shows how her train-the-trainer programs *incorporate advanced training techniques.* • Based on her attendance at *several annual T&D conferences and her broad reading about what is happening in the T&D field,* the T&D specialist notes and discusses the implementations of a trend toward learning designs where the learner takes more responsibility for the objectives and for application decisions. • Etc.	• The T&D specialist develops a plan for a three-year evaluation of the organization's training series for executives. He *develops an evaluation strategy* which tracks behavior change, participant reactions to programs and which compares program content with the organization's goals and strategic priorities and strategic weaknesses. • Etc. • The T&D manager is asked to justify why the T&D function shouldn't be eliminated due to declining financial resources and increasing numbers of qualified potential employees. The manager *describes the range of contributions that training and development can make to organizations* in difficult times and convinces the organization to retain the function. • The T&D specialist leads a conference session on *issues and trends in the T&D field.* The audience consists of training managers of Fortune 500 companies. • Etc.

30. *Training-and-Development-Techniques Understanding . . .*

Knowing the techniques and methods used in training; understanding their appropriate uses.

- In a presentation of a self-study supervisory development program, the T&D specialist *describes advantages and disadvantages of programmed instruction for this situation.*
- In a presentation for new trainers, the T&D specialist develops a list of *commonly used training and development techniques and the advantages and disadvantages of each.*
- Etc.

- As a result of hiring freeze, the T&D specialist *reviews the training techniques used throughout* all divisions and subsidiaries in the corporation. After studying course records and research findings, he develops a set of recommendations which indicate: (1) which courses must have a *live instructor using group interaction techniques;* (2) which courses could easily be converted to a *materials-based, self-instructional format;* (3) which should remain as they are.
- A lecture-based course has only been partially successful, although the content is accurate and complete for participant needs. The T&D specialist reviews the attitude and interest problems and proposes *six other ways the material could be more successfully presented.*
- Because an off-the-shelf training package includes case studies which do not quite fit the company's situation, the T&D specialist *recommends several alternatives to the case modules,* including role plays, demonstrations, participant development cases, guided imagery and other methods.
- Etc.

- A T&D specialist must develop a nine-module self-study program on drugs and effects for physicians. She sees her task as clearly presenting—in depth—a great deal of information, but also keeping the audience interested. She develops and uses a *format that incorporates graphics, space, summaries, case examples, diagrams, and short but clearly written essays.* Retention rates are 90 percent after the pilot.
- A T&D specialist who is preparing a guidebook for use as an aid in designing training and development programs, writes a *description of one hundred techniques used to help adults learn.*
- In producing a multi-course program to train nuclear power plant technicians, the T&D specialist designs a program which incorporates *assessment, computer-aided instruction, workshops, mentoring projects, simulations, interactive video, field trips, case studies and role plays.* Each technique is selected because of its leverage in helping achieve program objectives.
- Etc.

31. *Writing Skill . . .*

Preparing written material which follows generally accepted rules of

- When he is asked to *edit* a short manual written by a professional writer, the T&D specialist makes changes to assure the

- When given a topical outline, the T&D specialist creates a *coherent, precise and concise essay* for course background read-

- Given content outline, reference materials, and a helpful subject matter expert, the T&D specialist *writes branching programmed in-*

Figure 4.6 (Continued)

The Competency Model for the T&D Field

	Example Behaviors Illustrating Levels of Expertise		
The Competency:	*Basic:*	*Intermediate:*	*Advanced:*
style and form, is appropriate for the audience, creative, and accomplishes its intended purposes.	text conforms to generally accepted *rules* of grammar, punctuation and style. • Given a general content outline, a design, objectives, and rough draft, the T&D specialist *writes the script for a straight-forward ten-minute slide and tape* program about current issues in drug manufacturing. • A T&D specialist *rewrites the benefits section of a program brochure* to make it more relevant to the expected audience needs. • Etc.	ing. • A writer is given a design, objectives, content and audience description for a course and is asked to write the student guide. She *develops an approach* which the audience will find interesting, *uses words familiar to the audience*, and includes examples and stories to illustrate key points. The pilot test study shows interest and attention levels to be high. • Given a vague idea, the T&D specialist *writes the treatment, script, and storyboard* for an A-V presentation. • Etc.	struction materials that maintain reader interest and involvement. • A T&D specialist *writes a research report* which proposes several new practices for the T&D field. A leading applied research journal accepts it with minor revisions. • The T&D specialist *writes a proposal to develop an expensive instructional system* for an out-of-town client. The proposal is the only information that line and staff managers in the client organization review in making their decision. The proposal is accepted with the comment "You clearly communicated our needs, the purpose and advantages of your program, and why we should work with you." • Etc.

#8. Data-Reduction Skill

#9. Delegation Skill

#11. Feedback Skill

#12. Futuring Skill

#13. Group-Process Skill

#14. Industry Understanding

#15. Intellectual Versatility

#18. Negotiation Skill

#20. Organization-Behavior Understanding

#21. Organization Understanding

#23. Personnel/HR-Field Understanding

#24. Presentation Skill

#29. Training-and-Development-Field Understanding

#31. Writing Skill

For examples illustrating these competencies, see Figure 4.6.

The *strategist* role consists of "developing long-range plans for what the training and development structure, organization, direction, policies, programs, services, and practices will be in order to accomplish the training and development mission." It results in such outputs as:

1. "[The] Training and development [T & D] strategy included in the broad human resources strategy of the client organization."
2. "Identification (written/oral) of long-range T & D strengths, weaknesses, opportunities, threats."
3. "Descriptions of the T & D function and its outputs in the future."
4. "Identification of forces/trends (technical, social, economic, etc.) impacting T & D."
5. "Guidelines/plans for implementing long-range goals."
6. "Alternative directions for T & D."
7. "Cost/benefit analyses of the impact of T & D on the organization."

These outputs are listed in Figure 4.3 and are treated later in this book.

The strategist role requires these competencies:

#6. Cost/Benefit-Analysis Skill

#8. Data-Reduction Skill

#12. Futuring Skill

#14. Industry Understanding

#15. Intellectual Versatility

#17. Model-Building Skill

#20. Organization-Behavior Understanding

#21. Organization Understanding

#23. Personnel/HR-Field Understanding

#29. Training-and-Development-Field Understanding

For examples illustrating these competencies, see Figure 4.6.

Both roles in the leadership cluster are expected to maintain the same level of importance over the next five years. The role of training and development manager is positively correlated with the role of marketer and negatively correlated to such roles as evaluator, instructional writer, needs analyst, and theoretician. It requires the highest expertise in such competencies as Cost/Benefit-Analysis Skill and Organization Understanding. The role of strategist is positively correlated with that of training and development manager and negatively correlated with those of instructor and program administrator. It requires the highest expertise in Futuring Skill, Organization Understanding, and Training-and-Development-Field Understanding.

The Interface Cluster

The interface cluster includes four roles that are concerned more with the relationship between the training and development department and its environment than with internal operations of the department or its work processes. These roles include marketer, group facilitator, instructor, and transfer agent.

The *marketer* role consists of "selling training and development viewpoints, learning packages, programs and services to target audiences outside one's own work unit." It produces such work outputs as:

1. "Promotional materials for training and development programs and curricula."

2. "Sales presentations."

3. "Program overviews."

4. "Leads."

5. "Contracts with training and development clients (internal and external) negotiated."

6. "Marketing plan (developed and implemented)."

7. "Training and development programs and services [made] visible to target markets."

The marketer role requires these competencies:

#5. Computer Competency

#6. Cost/Benefit-Analysis Skill

#7. Counseling Skill

#11. Feedback Skill

#12. Futuring Skill

#13. Group-Process Skill

#14. Industry Understanding

#15. Intellectual Versatility

#18. Negotiation Skill

#19. Objectives-Preparation Skill

#20. Organization-Behavior Understanding

#21. Organization Understanding

#24. Presentation Skill

#25. Questioning Skill

#27. Relationship Versatility

#31. Writing Skill

For examples illustrating these competencies, see Figure 4.6.

The marketer role will maintain its present level of importance for the present, and is positively correlated with the roles of program administrator and theoretician.

The *group facilitator* role consists of "managing group discussions and group process so that individuals learn and group members feel the experience is positive." It results in such work outputs as:

1. "Group discussions in which issues and needs are constructively assessed."

2. "Group decisions where all individuals feel committed to actions."

3. "Cohesive teams."

4. "Enhanced awareness of group process, self, and others."

The group facilitator role requires these competencies:

  #1. Adult-Learning Understanding

#11. Feedback Skill

#13. Group-Process Skill

#15. Intellectual Versatility

#18. Negotiation Skill

#20. Organization-Behavior Understanding

#22. Performance-Observation Skill

#25. Questioning Skill

#27. Relationship Versatility

#30. Training-and-Development-Techniques Understanding

For examples illustrating these competencies, see Figure 4.6.

The group facilitator role will maintain its present level of importance for the immediate future. It is positively correlated with such other roles as instructor, marketer, and transfer agent—but negatively correlated with the roles of evaluator, media specialist, program administrator, and theoretician.

The *instructor* role consists of "presenting information and directing structured learning experiences so that individuals learn." It produces such work outputs as:

1. "Video tapes, films, audio tapes, computer-aided instruction, and other audio-visual materials facilitated."

2. "Case studies, role plays, games, tests, and other structured learning experiences facilitated."

3. "Lectures, presentations, stories delivered."

4. "Examinations administered and feedback given."

5. "Students' needs addressed."

6. "An individual with new knowledge, skills, attitudes, or behavior in his/her repertoire."

Although the instructor role will maintain its importance for the immediate future, the first output listed should become even more important over time.

The instructor role requires these competencies:

#1. Adult-Learning Understanding

#5. Computer Competence

#11. Feedback Skill

#13. Group-Process Skill

#15. Intellectual Versatility

#24. Presentation Skill

#25. Questioning Skill

#27. Relationship Versatility

#30. Training-and-Development-Techniques Understanding

For examples illustrating these competencies, see Figure 4.6.

The instructor role is positively correlated with group facilitator, marketer, and transfer agent roles. It is negatively correlated with the roles of evaluator, program administrator, and strategist.

The *transfer agent* role consists of "helping individuals apply learning after the learning process." It results in such work outputs as:

1. "Individual action plans for on-the-job/real world application."

2. "Plans (written/oral) for the support of transfer of learning in and around the application environment."

3. "Job aids to support performance and learning."

4. "On-the-job environment modified to support learning."

This role will maintain its present level of importance for the immediate future. It is positively correlated with such other roles as group facilitator, instructor, and marketer; it is negatively correlated with the media specialist, program administrator, and theoretician roles.

The transfer agent role requires these competencies:

#1. Adult-Learning Understanding

#11. Feedback Skill

#19. Objectives-Preparation Skill

#20. Organization-Behavior Understanding

#21. Organization Understanding

#27. Relationship Versatility

#30. Training-and-Development-Techniques Understanding

For examples illustrating these competencies, see Figure 4.6.

The Concept-Development Cluster

The concept-development cluster includes the three related roles—program designer, instructional writer, and theoretician—concerned most with planning HRD activities.

The *program designer* role consists "of preparing objectives, defining content, selecting and sequencing activities for a specific program." It produces such work outputs as:

1. "Lists of learning objectives."
2. "Written program plans/designs."
3. "Specifications and priorities of training content, activities, materials, and methods."
4. "Sequencing plans for training content, activities, materials and methods."
5. "Instructional contingency plans and implementation strategies."

This role is expected to maintain its present level of importance for the foreseeable future. It is positively correlated with other roles in this cluster and negatively correlated with that of program administrator.

The program designer role requires these competencies:

#1. Adult-Learning Understanding

#4. Competency-Identification Skill

#5. Computer Competence

#15. Intellectual Versatility

#17. Model-Building Skill

#19. Objectives-Preparation Skill

#20. Organization-Behavior Understanding

#30. Training-and-Development-Techniques Understanding

#31. Writing Skill

For examples illustrating these competencies, see Figure 4.6.

The *instructional writer* role consists of "preparing written learning and instructional materials." It results in such work outputs as:

1. "Exercises, workbooks, worksheets."
2. "Teaching guides."
3. "Scripts (for video, film, audio)."
4. "Manuals and job aids."
5. "Computer software."
6. "Tests and evaluation forms."
7. "Written role plays, simulations, games."
8. "Written case studies."

This role is expected to maintain its level of importance for the foreseeable future. However, one role output—computer software—is expected to grow in importance. This role is positively correlated with those of media specialist, program designer, task analyst, and theoretician—but negatively correlated with the training and development manager role.

The instructional writer role requires these competencies:

#1. Adult-Learning Understanding
#4. Competency-Identification Skill
#5. Computer Competence
#8. Data-Reduction Skill
#11. Feedback Skill
#14. Industry Understanding
#15. Intellectual Versatility
#16. Library Skills
#17. Model-Building Skill
#19. Objectives-Preparation Skill
#24. Presentation Skill
#25. Questioning Skill
#30. Training-and-Development-Techniques Understanding
#31. Writing Skill

For examples illustrating these competencies, see Figure 4.6.

The *theoretician* role consists of "developing and testing theories of learning, training, and development." It results in such work outputs as:

1. "New concepts and theories of learning and behavior change."
2. "Articles on training and development issues/theories for scientific journals and trade publications."
3. "Research designs."
4. "Research reports."
5. "Training models and applications of theory."
6. "Existing learning/training theories and concepts evaluated."

This role will maintain its present level of importance for the present. It is positively correlated with other roles in this cluster, but negatively correlated with the group facilitator, manager of training and development, marketer, program administrator, and transfer agent roles.

The theoretician role requires these competencies:

#1. Adult-Learning Understanding
#8. Data-Reduction Skill
#12. Futuring Skill
#15. Intellectual Versatility
#17. Model-Building Skill
#28. Research Skill
#31. Writing Skill

For examples illustrating these competencies, see Figure 4.6.

The Research Cluster

The research cluster includes three roles—evaluator, needs analyst, and task analyst—that focus on the need for formal, organized learning activities or the value of such activities in removing performance deficiencies.

The *evaluator* role consists of "identifying the extent of a program's, service's or product's impact." It produces such work outputs as:

1. "Instruments to assess individual change in knowledge, skill, attitude, behavior, and results."

2. "Instruments to assess program and instructional quality."

3. "Written and oral reports of program impact on individuals."

4. "Written and oral reports of program impact on an organization."

5. "Written and oral designs and plans for evaluation and validation."

6. "Written instruments to collect and interpret data."

This role is positively correlated with other roles in the research cluster; it is negatively correlated with the roles of group facilitator, instructor, manager of training and development, and program administrator.

The evaluator role requires these competencies:

#4. Competency-Identification Skill

#5. Computer Competence

#8. Data-Reduction Skill

#22. Performance-Observation Skill

#24. Presentation Skill

#25. Questioning Skill

#28. Research Skill

#31. Writing Skill

For examples illustrating these competencies, see Figure 4.6.

The *needs analyst* role consists of "defining gaps between ideal and actual performance and specifying the cause of the gaps." It results in such work outputs as:

1. "Performance problems and discrepancies identified and reported orally or in writing."

2. "Knowledge, skill, attitude problems, and discrepancies identified and reported orally or in writing."

3. "Tools to assess the knowledge, skill, attitude, and performance level of individuals and organizations."

4. "Needs analysis strategies."

5. "Causes of discrepancies inferred."

This role is positively correlated with others in this cluster and negatively correlated with training and development manager and program administrator.

The needs analyst role requires these competencies:

#4. Competency-Identification Skill

#5. Computer Competency

#8. Data-Reduction Skill

#11. Feedback Skill

#15. Intellectual Versatility

#20. Organization-Behavior Understanding

#21. Organization Understanding

#22. Performance-Observation Skill

#25. Questioning Skill

#28. Research Skill

For examples illustrating these competencies, see Figure 4.6.

The third and final role in the research cluster is that of *task analyst.* It consists of "identifying activities, tasks, subtasks, and human resource and support requirements necessary to accomplish specific results in a job or organization." It produces such work outputs as:

1. "List of key job/unit outputs."

2. "List of key job/unit tasks."

3. "Lists of knowledge/skill/attitude requirements of job/unit."

4. "Descriptions of the performance levels required in a job/unit."

5. "Job design, enlargement, enrichment implications/alternatives identified."

6. "Subtasks, tasks, and jobs clustered."

7. "Conditions described under which jobs/tasks are performed."

This role will retain its present level of importance for the immediate future. However, the fifth output above is expected to increase gradually in importance. The task analyst role is positively correlated with those of evaluator, instructional writer, and needs analyst and negatively correlated with that of training and development manager.

The task analyst role requires these competencies:

#4. Competency-Identification Skill

#8. Data-Reduction Skill

#11. Feedback Skill

#15. Intellectual Versatility

#19. Objectives-Preparation Skill

#22. Performance-Observation Skill

#25. Questioning Skill

#26. Records-Management Skill

#31. Writing Skill

For examples illustrating these competencies, see Figure 4.6.

The Unrelated Roles

Three HRD roles are not sufficiently correlated with any others to be placed in a role cluster. These are: the media specialist, the individual development counselor, and the program administrator.

The *media specialist* role consists of "producing software for and using audio, visual, computer, and other hardware-based technologies for training and development." It results in such work outputs as:

1. "T & D computer software."
2. "Written and oral lists of recommended instructional hardware."
3. "Graphics."
4. "Video-based material."
5. "Audio tapes."
6. "Computer hardware in working order."
7. "A/V equipment in working order."
8. "Media users advised/counseled."
9. "Production plans."
10. "Purchasing specifications/recommendations for instructional/training hardware."

Two work outputs of this role—training and development computer software and maintenance of computer hardware in working order—will increase in importance. This role is positively correlated with such others as instructional writer and program administrator; it is negatively correlated with the roles of group facilitator, individual development counselor, and transfer agent.

The media specialist role requires these competencies:

#1. Adult-Learning Understanding

#2. A/V Skill

#5. Computer Competence

#6. Cost/Benefit-Analysis Skill

#10. Facilities Skill

#11. Feedback Skill

#14. Industry Understanding

#15. Intellectual Versatility

#16. Library Skill

#19. Objectives-Preparation Skill

#24. Presentation Skill

#25. Questioning Skill

#30. Training-and-Development-Techniques Understanding

#31. Writing Skill

For examples illustrating these competencies, see Figure 4.6.

The *individual development counselor* role consists of "helping an individual assess personal competencies, values, and goals and identify and plan development and career actions." It results in such work outputs as:

1. "Individual career development plans."

2. "Enhanced skills on the part of an individual to identify and carry out his/her own development needs/goals."

3. "Referrals to professional counseling."

4. "Increased knowledge by the individual about where to get development support."

5. "Tools and resources needed in career development."

6. "Tools for managers to facilitate employees' career development."

7. "An individual who initiates feedback and monitors and manages career plans."

This role is expected to maintain its present level of importance for the foreseeable future. It is unrelated to any other role and is negatively correlated with the media specialist and program administrator roles.

The individual development counselor role requires these competencies:

#1. Adult-Learning Understanding

#3. Career-Development Knowledge

#4. Competency-Identification Skill

#7. Counseling Skill

#11. Feedback Skill

#15. Intellectual Versatility

#25. Questioning Skill

#27. Relationship Versatility

#28. Research Skill

For examples illustrating these competencies, see Figure 4.6.

The program administrator role consists of "ensuring that the facilities, equipment, materials, participants, and other components of a learning event are present and that program logistics run smoothly." It results in such work outputs as:

1. "Facilities and equipment selected and scheduled."

2. "Participant attendance secured, recorded."

3. "Hotel/conference center staff managed."

4. "Faculty scheduled."

5. "Course material distributed (on-site, pre-course, post-course)."

6. "Contingency plans for back-ups, emergencies."

7. "Physical environment maintained."

8. "Program follow-up accomplished."

This role is positively correlated with the media specialist and negatively correlated with the evaluator, group facilitator, individual development counselor, instructor, marketer, needs analyst, program designer, strategist, theorist, and transfer agent.

The program administrator role requires these competencies:

#2. A/V Skill

#10. Facilities Skill

#26. Records-Management Skill

For examples illustrating these competencies, see Figure 4.6.

Summing Up

HRD professionals must work within an organizational context. In small organizations they may need to adopt several, if not all, of the HRD roles described in this chapter. In larger organizations their roles may be more specific, as work in the HRD department is specialized. In most cases, however, no HRD professional will function in only one role capacity at all times.

References

1. Gibson, J., J. Ivancevich, and J. Donnelly, Jr. *Organizations: Behavior, Structure, Processes,* 5th ed. Plano, TX: Business Publications, 1985.

2. *Competency Analysis for Trainers: A Personal Planning Guide.* Toronto: Society for Training and Development, 1979.

3. *The EDS Curriculum Plan: An Outline of Learning Experiences for the Employee Development Specialist.* Washington, D.C.: Bureau of Training, 1976.

4. Pinto, P., and J. Walker. *A Study of Professional Training and Development Roles and Competencies.* Baltimore, MD: American Society for Training and Development, 1978.

5. "A Self-Development Process for Training and Development Professionals." *Training and Development Journal* 33 (1979) 5: pp. 6–13.

6. Varney, G. "Developing OD Competencies." *Training and Development Journal* (April, 1980): pp. 30–33.

7. Neilsen, E. *Becoming an OD Practitioner.* Englewood Cliffs, NJ: Prentice-Hall, 1984.

8. *Instructional Design Competencies: The Standards.* Iowa City, Iowa: International Board of Standards for Training, Performance and Instruction, 1986.

CHAPTER 5

Planning a career in HRD.

HRD practitioners are responsible for helping others recognize and develop their potential. Thus, it is reasonable to expect that practitioners themselves will be able to assess the opportunities in their own field and their own strengths and weaknesses. To help others, you must first be able to help yourself.

This chapter briefly describes the scope of HRD activities in the U.S., growth opportunities in the field, the importance of personal preferences in career planning, considerations in finding your first HRD job, resources for building role competencies, and potential career paths for practitioners beyond the first job. ■

Opportunities in HRD

Individual career planning involves a gradual narrowing of choices based on information about various occupations and personal strengths, weaknesses, and preferences relevant to those occupations. Experienced HRD practitioners are likely to utilize reading and contacts with professional colleagues to learn what opportunities are available. Prospective or inexperienced practitioners will probably be less aware of such opportunities.

It is worthwhile, then, to begin with a description of the scope of HRD activities in the U.S. and point out likely growth areas.

Scope of HRD Activities in the U.S.

Until recently there has been only spotty information about the scope of HRD activities in the U.S.—mainly because government policy has focused primarily on formal education and on issues associated with external, not internal, labor markets. In addition, there are unique problems in researching employer-sponsored training, education, and development—not the least of which is a definition of what they are. After all, work experience itself can be considered a developmental activity, and individually-initiated job assignments with a developmental component are sometimes hard to distinguish from required job tasks. An enlightening history could be written on the continuing evolution of research on HRD.

Interest in HRD has increased as a result of the perceived failure of mainstream economic theory since 1964.[1] Recent research indicates where job opportunities in HRD are likely to be, based on the amount of employer-sponsored training, what kind of people are trained, and how they are trained.

To summarize some of this information:

- Approximately 15 million people receive formal training each year by their employers.[2]
- Employers spend approximately $30 billion per year on organized training and educational events.[3]
- Employers spend approximately $180 billion per year for informal (on-the-job) instruction.[4]
- In the banking industry, internal training departments offer about 45 percent of planned instruction, operating departments about 25 percent, and outside educational institutions only about 5 percent.[5]
- Production employees receive the most formal instruction of any single group, followed by professional employees. However, executives receive the most education per person, followed by professionals.[6] See Figure 5.1, from *Training* Magazine's Industry Report, 1985.

Figure 5.1   Hours of training delivered

	Hours of Training Delivered			
Job Category	1 % Providing Training [1]	2 Mean Number of Individuals Trained [2]	3 Mean Number of Hours Delivered	Projected Total Number of Hours Delivered
Executives	67.1	6.7	41.4	40.5 million
Professionals	48.6	53.5	38.3	216.9 million
Sales Representatives	37.1	43.1	37.7	131.3 million
First-line Supervisors/Foremen	64.4	36.0	36.4	183.8 million
Middle Managers	69.9	22.4	36.3	124.8 million
Senior Managers	60.0	14.3	35.7	66.7 million
Customer Service	45.7	58.8	33.9	198.4 million
Production Workers	32.4	118.7	33.4	279.7 million
Administrative	48.7	28.2	19.2	57.4 million
Office/Clerical	53.0	35.9	18.8	77.9 million
Grand total number of hours delivered				1,377.4 million

[1] Percent of all U.S. organizations with 50 or more employees providing training.
[2] Average number of individuals based on only those organizations providing training in each job category.
[3] Average number of hours of training delivered per employee based on all organizations providing training in each category.

Source: "Where the Dollars Go," by D. Feuer. Reprinted with permission from the October, 1985, issue of *Training, The Magazine of Human Resources Development.* Copyright © 1985, Lakewood Publications Inc., Minneapolis, MN (612) 333-0471. All rights reserved.

- The highest percentage of organizations provide training on management and supervisory skills. The second highest percentage provide training on technical skills to keep professionals up to date in their fields.[7] See Figure 5.2, from *Training* Magazine's Industry Report, 1985.

- Training departments spend the greatest percentage of time on providing instruction about work methods or procedures. Technical skills account for the second greatest percentage of time; customer relations is third.[8]

- Organizations are most likely to use external consultants to furnish instruction for executives; next most likely to use them for training managers; and third most likely to do so for clericals.[9] See Figure 5.3, from *Training* Magazine's Industry Report, 1982.

- Formal training is most often delivered by lecture, less often by one-on-one instruction, and least often by computer-assisted in-

Figure 5.2 General types of training

Types of Training	General Types of Training			
	% of Total Providing [1]	% In-House Only [2]	% Outside Only [3]	% Both In-House and Outside [4]
Management Skills and Development	74.3	10.3	18.7	45.3
Supervisory Skills	73.7	14.9	12.7	46.2
Technical Skills/ Knowledge Updating	72.7	24.9	8.3	39.5
Communication Skills	66.8	19.6	10.8	36.4
Customer Relations/ Services	63.6	22.6	10.8	30.3
Executive Development	56.5	6.6	20.4	29.5
New Methods/ Procedures	56.5	28.0	2.3	26.2
Sales Skills	54.1	15.1	8.1	30.9
Clerical/Secretarial Skills	52.9	16.8	14.2	22.0
Personal Growth	51.9	10.8	11.2	30.0
Computer Literacy/ Basic Computer Skills	48.2	13.4	9.8	24.9
Employee/Labor Relations	44.9	16.3	7.7	21.0
Disease Prevention/ Health Promotion	38.9	13.5	7.5	17.9
Customer Education	35.7	17.7	1.7	16.2
Remedial Basic Education	18.0	5.0	6.9	6.0

[1] % of sample who offer this type of formal training.
[2] Among all organizations, % who offer only training designed, developed and delivered by in-house staff.
[3] Among all organizations, % who offer only training designed, developed and delivered by outside consultants or vendors.
[4] Among all organizations, % who offer training designed, developed and delivered by both.

Source: "Where the Dollars Go," by D. Feuer. *Training* Magazine, October, 1985. Reprinted by permission.

Figure 5.3   Average number of trainers by industry

Average Number of Trainers
by Standard Industrial Classification [1]

Industry Classification	Average No. of Full-Time, Head-Office Trainers per Company	Average No. of Full-Time Field Based Trainers per Company
1. Construction	11.0	17.7
2. Retail trade	10.6	17.0
3. Transportation, communication, public utilities	9.3	17.8
4. Membership organizations, societies, associations, churches, and religious groups	6.7	13.0
5. Banking, finance, insurance and real estate	6.4	10.7
6. Manufacturing	5.9	13.2
7. Hotels, lodging and food services	5.6	9.3
8. Health services	5.6	25.4
9. Educational services	5.5	12.3
10. Business services	5.3	14.4
11. Mining, oil drilling	5.0	6.0
12. Wholesale trade	4.5	16.0

[1] Calculated by dividing reported number of trainers by number of organizations reporting 1 or more trainers.

Source: "Trainer Tally Varies." *Training* Magazine, October, 1982, p. 24. Reprinted by permission.

struction, interactive video, and videodiscs.[11] See Figure 5.4, from *Training* Magazine's Industry Report, 1983.

By considering these facts and examining the figures, prospective practitioners can develop useful insights about potential job opportunities in HRD.

Likely Growth Areas in HRD

In what industries are HRD efforts expected to grow over the next decade? What professional roles will be most promising? In what geographical areas is demand likely to be greatest? These questions cannot be answered with certainty, but there is enough information to make some realistic predictions.

Figure 5.4 Preferences in delivery

| Instructional Format | % of Respondents | | Desirability Ranking (1982) * |
	Currently Using	Not Currently Using, but will be Using in 12 Months	
Lectures	89.4%	3.2%	N/A
Overhead transparencies	83.7%	3.7%	2
Videocassettes	78.3%	6.7%	4.5
Role playing	77.0%	4.8%	4.5
Slides	74.7%	3.9%	6
Case studies	71.3%	5.4%	7
16mm films	70.6%	3.5%	8
One-to-one instruction	68.3%	4.1%	10
Audiocassettes	61.4%	3.2%	11
Self-tests	56.8%	5.4%	3
Games and simulations	54.2%	5.6%	9
Programmed instruction	39.5%	7.4%	N/A
Sound filmstrips	38.4%	2.0%	13
Computer-assisted instruction	19.1%	12.2%	12
Interactive video	9.1%	7.4%	N/A
Videodiscs	4.6%	2.0%	N/A

*Numbers in this column reflect the rank order of desirability ratings of instructional formats as reported by respondents to TRAINING Magazine's 1982 census. The No. 1 ranked format, "participant exercises," was inadvertantly excluded from the 1983 usage question.

Source: "Development and Delivery of Training." *Training* Magazine, October, 1983, p. 50. Reprinted by permission.

The industries offering the most potential for growth in HRD, in rank order starting with the best, are:

1. Communications, including telephone and computer companies.
2. Education, particularly at the community college level.
3. Health services, including hospitals and nursing home chains.
4. Manufacturing.
5. Banks and financial institutions.[12]

In all of these fields except education, deregulation has served as an HRD catalyst. Employees in these fields must learn how to think and act more competitively. In health services, employees must work harder to contain costs while preserving quality service and coping with rapid technological change. In manufacturing, they must work more productively, to spread the higher cost of U.S. labor over more goods and services than are produced by foreign competitors. In education, the discovery of HRD as a tool for economic development is likely to prompt growing support, particularly at the State government level, for using community colleges to supply educational services to business and industry.

HRD professionals skilled in the following roles will probably be most in demand:

1. Instructional writers, particularly those who design, develop, and implement computer-based and computer-assisted instruction.
2. Group facilitators, particularly those in organization, management, and supervisory development.
3. Individual development counselors, particularly those serving as career specialists.
4. Instructors, particularly those skilled in classroom delivery.
5. Evaluators.[13]

Computerized instruction will be a growth field for some time to come. It can deliver instruction geared to the time schedules and specialized needs of individuals in a way that classroom instruction cannot. At the same time, there is an equally great need to improve the interaction within groups and between groups in organizations. That accounts for the demand for group facilitators. Growing career awareness among employees calls for those who can advise individuals on their careers. The roles of instructor and evaluator are traditionally important in HRD: the first because much training is still offered by lecture; the second because organizations are requiring more qualitative and quantitative proof that instruction has, in fact, solved a performance problem or seized an opportunity to avert future problems.

Geographically, U.S. demand for HRD practitioners will probably be greatest in the South, Southwest, and West; least in the Midwest and Northeast. Industries and people are moving south and west, making those areas fruitful for growth. At the same time, population and industrial conditions are stagnant or even declining in midwestern and most northeastern states. Where industries and people are, the opportunities in HRD will be greatest.

Self-Assessment

Before establishing career goals and action plans, the prospective HRD practitioner should consider his or her personal strengths, weaknesses, preferences, and other factors. Several complete guides on this self-assessment process are available:

- *Career Planning for HRD Professionals: A Leader's Guide and Materials.* American Society for Training and Development, Washington, D.C. (1983)
- *Careers in Training and Development.* American Society for Training and Development, Washington, D.C. (1983)
- *Up the HRD Ladder: A Guide for Professional Growth,* by N. Chalofsky and C. Lincoln. Addison-Wesley, Reading, Mass. (1983)
- *Finding the Right Job in Training: A Leader's Guide.* American Society for Training and Development, Washington, D.C. (1983)
- *Your Career in HRD: A Guide to Information and Decision Making.* American Society for Training and Development, Alexandria, Va. (1985)

Prospective practitioners should find these detailed guides useful, but here we will raise only a few of the many self-assessment issues.

What Are Your Preferences?

A good place to begin career planning is with your personal values and preferences. Consider the following questions:

1. Who do you want to work for? In other words, what kind of a boss do you want? Describe the type of person you would most prefer. Then describe the type of person you would not prefer at all.

2. In what type of organization do you want to work? What type of organization would you avoid? Think about:
   a. *Organizational purpose.* Would you feel most comfortable pursuing profits (business/industry) or serving other people (government/not-for-profit)? Why?
   b. *Culture.* Would you prefer a strict hierarchy of authority (military), somewhat strict (business/government), or not at all strict

(self-employed consultant)? To what extent do you want a say in decisions affecting you?

   c. *Size.* How large or small an organization would you prefer to work in? For what reasons?

Describe the kind of organization in which you would most prefer to work and the kind in which you would not want to work at all.

3. Where do you want to work? Where do you not want to work? Think about:

   a. *Region of the world.* Do you want to remain in the U.S.?

   b. *Region of the country.* Do you have preferences for certain states or regions?

   c. *Population density.* Would you prefer to work in a large city, a medium-sized one, a suburb, or in a small town?

Describe the kind of location where you would most prefer to work and the kind where you would not want to work at all.

4. In what type of HRD department do you want to work? What type would you want to avoid? Think about:

   a. *Size.* How much would you like to run a one-person show? Be one of two people in HRD? Be part of a team of three or more?

   b. *Up-to-dateness.* How much would you like to begin with an HRD department that is somewhat behind the times, one that is state-of-the-art, or one ahead of the times? Why?

   c. *Relationships.* Some HRD departments struggle for recognition. Would you prefer to work in one where relations with other parts of the organization are very good, one where relations are stable, or one where relations are presently rather poor? Why?

   d. *Trainees.* Do you have preferences about the kind of people you want to train? Would you prefer employees of an organization, customers, franchise owners, or some special group? Do you have preferences about groups you might want to avoid?

Describe the kind of HRD department in which you would most prefer to work and any kind which you would most prefer to avoid.

5. In what type of job do you want to work at present? What types of jobs would you want to avoid? Think about:

   a. *Job specifications.* Do you have special preferences about education and experience requirements associated with a particular job?

b. *Task responsibilities.* Do you have preferences about the kind of work you want to do? Would you prefer to fill most of the roles outlined in *Models for Excellence* or only some of them? Which ones interest you most? Least? What accounts for your interests?

c. *Salary.* Do you have an absolute minimum salary requirement? To what extent would you be willing to accept a less-than-average salary now for the chance of a much better job in the future? To what extent would you be willing to accept a higher-than-average salary now with little chance for a better job in the future?

d. *Growth potential.* To what extent would you prefer a job that allows you to grow in skill? How important is this to you?

e. *Flexibility.* To what extent would you prefer a job that allows you freedom to mold it according to your creativity? To what extent could you tolerate one that would not allow for much change?

Describe the kind of job in HRD that you would most prefer at this time. Then describe the kind of HRD job which you would most prefer to avoid.

Assessing Your Strengths and Weaknesses

A strength contributes to realization of a career goal or preference; a weakness impedes that realization.

Look carefully at your answers to the preceding questions. Focus particularly on those concerning the kind of job you want. Then consider: What are your strengths and weaknesses relative to that job? How well-prepared are you at this time to be hired for the job you want?

To help assess your strengths and weaknesses, complete the exercise in Figure 5.5. Then score yourself, using the table in Figure 5.6, and list your strengths and weaknesses.

Resources for Building HRD Competencies

Once you know what you want to do and how well-prepared for it you are, you may want to establish a self-development plan to build your competencies for your first HRD job. There are several ways to do this:

Directions: Complete the questionnaire which follows. Use it to assess your HRD strengths and weaknesses and as a guide for preparing for a job in the field. Compare your answers to the competencies associated with different roles in Figure 5-6.

ASTD COMPETENCY STUDY

A. From the list of 15 possible Training and Development Roles below, select the three roles that are *most important to you* by "X"ing the box to the left of those roles. The roles may be important for your present job or for a future job. They will be the roles that you want to emphasize in your self-development planning.

☐ 1. EVALUATOR. . .The role of identifying the extent of a program, service or product's impact. Key outputs: *reports* (written and oral) of program impact on organization and individuals, *evaluation designs* and plans, *instruments* to assess program and instructional quality, and individual change.

☐ 2. GROUP FACILITATOR. . .The role of managing group discussions and group process so that individuals learn and group members feel the experience is positive. Key outputs: *group decisions* where individuals all feel committed to action; enhanced *awareness* of group *process,* self and others; *discussions* in which issues and needs are constructively assessed; *cohesive* teams.

☐ 3. INDIVIDUAL DEVELOPMENT COUNSELOR. . .The role of helping an individual assess personal competencies, values and goals, and identify and plan development and career actions. Key outputs: enhanced *skills of individuals* in identifying and carrying out development needs/goals, *tools* and resources for career development, individual career development *plans, knowledge of* where to get development support.

☐ 4. INSTRUCTIONAL WRITER. . .The role of preparing written learning and instructional materials. Key outputs: teaching guides, manuals and job aids, exercises, workbooks, worksheets, role plays, simulations, games, case studies, tests, evaluation forms, scripts.

☐ 5. INSTRUCTOR. . .The role of presenting information and directing structured learning experiences so that individuals learn. Key outputs: students' *needs* addressed; individuals with *new knowledge, skill, attitudes or behavior* in their repertoires; lectures, *presentations,* stories delivered; structured learning events directed.

☐ 6. MANAGER OF TRAINING AND DEVELOPMENT. . .The role of planning, organizing staffing, controlling training and development operations or training and development projects, and of linking training and development operations with other organization units. Key outputs: department or project *objectives; budgets; staff* selected, developed and evaluated: T&D actions *congruent* with other HR and organization actions; positive work *climate; information* exchanged; problem *solutions;* T&D *standards, policies and procedures.*

☐ 7. MARKETER. . .The role of selling Training and Development viewpoints, learning packages, programs and services to target audiences outside one's own work unit. Key outputs: *marketing plans* developed and implemented, sales *presentations, leads, promotional* materials, *contracts.*

☐ 8. MEDIA SPECIALIST. . .The role of producing software for and using audio, visual, computer and other hardware–based technologies for training and development. Key outputs: *advice* and counsel to media users, video-based *material, graphics, lists* of recommended instructional hardware, AV *equipment* in working order, production *plans,* software and hardware *recommendations.*

☐ 9. NEEDS ANALYST. . .The role of defining gaps between ideal and actual performance and specifying the cause of the gaps. Key outputs: written and oral *reports* on performance problems, and on knowledge, skill and attitude discrepancies; inferences of *causes* of discrepancies; needs analysis *strategies and tools.*

☐ 10. PROGRAM ADMINISTRATOR. . .The role of ensuring that the facilities, equipment, materials, participants and other components of a learning event are present and that program logistics run smoothly. Key outputs: *contingency* plans for emergencies; select on and scheduling of *facilities, equipment and faculty; course material* distributed; participant *attendance* secured and recorded.

☐ 11. PROGRAM DESIGNER. . .The role of preparing objectives, defining content, selecting and sequencing activities for a specific program. Key outputs: *specifications, sequencing* plans and *priorities* for training content, activities, materials and methods; lists of learning *objectives;* written program *plans* and designs; contingency plans and *implementation* strategies.

Figure 5.5 Self-assessment questionnaire (*Source: American Society for Training and Development.*)

☐ 12. STRATEGIST. . .The role of developing long-range plans for what the training and development structure, organization, direction, policies, programs, services and practices will be in order to accomplish the training and development mission. Key outputs: identification of *long-range* T&D strengths, weaknesses, opportunities, threats; long-range *plans* included in the broad human resource strategy of the organization; identification of *forces and trends* affecting T&D; *alternative directions* for T&D.

☐ 13. TASK ANALYST. . .Identifying activities, tasks, sub-tasks, human resources and support requirements necessary to accomplish specific results in a job or organization. Key outputs: *lists* of key job/unit *tasks and outputs;* lists of knowledge/skill/attitude *requirements* of job/units; *descriptions* of performance levels, sub-tasks, tasks and job clusters; descriptions of *conditions* for job performance.

☐ 14. THEORETICIAN. . .The role of developing and testing theories of learning, training and development. Key outputs: new *concepts and theories* of learning and behavior change; training *models* and applications of theory; *articles* on T&D issues; research *designs* and reports.

☐ 15. TRANSFER AGENT. . .The role of helping individuals apply learning after the learning experience. Key outputs: plans for support of transfer of learning; individual action plans for on-the-job/real world application.

B. Evaluate your present level of competency on each of the 31 competencies listed below using the following scale:

1. *Low or beginning* level of competency: Probably not familiar with some of the key principles; not especially confident about demonstrating this competency in relatively simple situations.

2. *Intermediate* level of competency: Having a deep understanding and skills; able to function in a broad range of moderately difficult situations.

3. *Advanced* level of competency: Having a broad and deep understanding and skills; able to function in complex, varied situations and be a model of subject matter mastery and skills.

	ADVANCED		
		INTERMEDIATE	
			BEGINNING

1. *Adult-Learning Understanding*. . .Knowing how adults acquire and use knowledge, skills, attitudes. Understanding individual differences in learning . . . . ( ) ( ) ( )

2. *A/V Skill*. . .Selecting and using audio/visual hardware and software . . . . ( ) ( ) ( )

3. *Career-Development Knowledge*. . .Understanding the personal and organizational issues and practices relevant to individual careers . . . . ( ) ( ) ( )

4. *Competency-Identification Skill*. . .Identifying the knowledge and skill requirements of jobs, tasks, roles . . . . ( ) ( ) ( )

5. *Computer Competence*. . .Understanding and being able to use computers . . . . . ( ) ( ) ( )

6. *Cost/Benefit-Analysis Skill*. . .Assessing alternatives in terms of their financial, psychological, and strategic advantages or disadvantages . . . . ( ) ( ) ( )

7. *Counseling Skill*. . .Helping individuals recognize and understand personal needs, values, problems, alternatives and goals . . . . ( ) ( ) ( )

8. *Data-Reduction Skill*. . .Scanning, synthesizing, and drawing conclusions from data. . . . . ( ) ( ) ( )

9. *Delegation Skill*. .Assigning task responsibility and authority to others . . . . ( ) ( ) ( )
10. *Facilities Skill*. . .Planning and coordinating logistics in an efficient and cost-effective manner. . . . . ( ) ( ) ( )

11. *Feedback Skill*. . .Communicating opinions, observations and conclusions so that they are understood . . . . ( ) ( ) ( )

Figure 5.5 (Continued)

124

12. *Futuring Skill*. . .Projecting trends and visualizing possible and probable futures and their implications .... ( ) ( ) ( )

13. *Group-Process Skill*. . .Influencing groups to both accomplish tasks and fulfill the needs of their members .... ( ) ( ) ( )

14. *Industry Understanding*. . .Knowing the key concepts and variables that define an industry or sector (i.e., critical issues, economic vulnerabilities, measurements, distribution channels, inputs, outputs, information sources) .... ( ) ( ) ( )

15. *Intellectual Versatility*. . .Recognizing, exploring and using a broad range of ideas and practices. Thinking logically and creatively without undue influence from personal biases .... ( ) ( ) ( )

16. *Library Skill*. . .Gathering information from printed and other recorded sources. Identifying and using information specialists and reference services and aids ... ( ) ( ) ( )

17. *Model-Building Skill* . . .Developing theoretical and practical frameworks which describe complex ideas in understandable, usable ways .... ( ) ( ) ( )

18. *Negotiation Skill*. . .Securing win-win agreements while successfully representing a special interest in a decision situation .... ( ) ( ) ( )

19. *Objectives-Preparation Skill*. . .Preparing clear statements which describe desired outputs .... ( ) ( ) ( )

20. *Organization-Behavior Understanding*. . .Seeing organizations as dynamic, political, economic, and social systems which have multiple goals; using this larger perspective as a framework for understanding and influencing events and change .... ( ) ( ) ( )

21. *Organization Understanding*. . .Knowing the strategy, structure, power networks, financial position, systems of a SPECIFIC organization .... ( ) ( ) ( )

22. *Performance-Observation Skill*. . .Tracking and describing behaviors and their effects .... ( ) ( ) ( )

23. *Personal/HR-Field Understanding*. . .Understanding issues and practices in other HR areas (Organization Development, Organization Job Design, Human Resource Planning, Selection and Staffing, Personnel Research and Information Systems, Compensation and Benefits, Employee Assistance, Union/Labor Relations) .... ( ) ( ) ( )

24. *Presentation Skill*. . .Verbally presenting information so that the intended purpose is achieved .... ( ) ( ) ( )

25. *Questioning Skill*. . .Gathering information from and stimulating insight in individuals and groups through the use of interviews, questionnaires and other probing methods .... ( ) ( ) ( )

26. *Records-Management Skill*. . .Storing data in easily retrievable form .... ( ) ( ) ( )

27. *Relationship Versatility*. . .Adjusting behavior in order to establish relationships across a broad range of people and groups .... ( ) ( ) ( )

28. *Research Skill*. . .Selecting, developing and using methodologies, statistical and data collection techniques for a formal inquiry .... ( ) ( ) ( )

29. *Training-and-Development-Field Understanding*. . .Knowing the technological, social, economic, professional, and regulatory issues in the field; understanding the role T&D plays in helping individuals learn for current and future jobs ...... ( ) ( ) ( )

30. *Training-and-Development-Techniques Understanding*. . .Knowing the techniques and methods used in training; understanding their appropriate uses . ( ) ( ) ( )

31. *Writing Skill*. . .Preparing written material which follows generally accepted rules of style and form, is appropriate for the audience, creative, and accomplishes its intended purposes .... ( ) ( ) ( )

Figure 5.5 (Continued)

DIRECTIONS: Compare your answers on the questionnaire in Figure 5-5 to the competencies listed in this figure. Use a blank sheet of paper to list differences between actual and desirable skill levels for the roles in which you wish to be proficient.

THE ROLES/COMPETENCIES MATRIX

This chart illustrates the level of expertise required in each competency area. Competencies and roles are both listed from most to least frequently occurring.

- ● = Advanced requirement.
- ○ = Intermediate requirement.

Requirements are only listed for competencies which sixty percent (60%) or more role respondents said are critical now and/or in five years for the role.

	Manager	Marketer	Instructional Writer	Media Specialist	Needs Analyst	Group Facilitator	Strategist	Evaluator
15. Intellectual Vers.	●	○	●	●	●	●	●	
11. Feedback Skill	●	○	●	●	●	●*		
1. Adult Lrng. Und.	○		●	●		●		
25. Questioning Skill		●	●	○	●	●		●*
5. Computer Comp.	○	○	○	●*	○			○
8. Data reduction Skill	●		●		●		●	●*
20. Org. Behavior Und.	●*	○			●	●		
31. Writing Skills		●	●*					○
4. Competency ID.			○		●			○
19. Object. Prep.		●	●	○				
24. Presentation Skill	●	●*	●	●				○
27. Relationship Vers.	●	●				●*		
30. T&D Techniques Und.			●	○		○		
14. Industry Und.	●	●*	●	○			●	
21. Organization Und.	●	●			○		●*	
6. Cost/Benefit Analysis	●*	○		○			●	
12. Futuring Skill	●	●					●*	
13. Group Process Skill	●	●				●*		
17. Model Building Skill			●				●	
22. Perf. Observ. Skill					●	●		●
18. Negotiation Skill	●	●*				○		
28. Research Skills					○			●*
2. AV Skill				●*				
3. Career Dvlp. Know.	○							
7. Counseling Skill		○						
10. Facilities Skill				○				
15. Library Skills			●*	○				
23. Pers./HR Field Und.	○						●*	
26. Records Mgnt. Skill								
29. T&D Field Und.	●						●*	
9. Delegation Skill	●*							
TOTALS	18	16	14	14	10	10	10	8

* Indicates the highest expertise level for the competency.

Figure 5.6 Scoring the questionnaire (*Source:* Models for Excellence.)

1. Gain relevant experience.
2. Enroll in formal or informal educational programs.
3. Enroll in training programs.
4. Do independent reading on the subject.
5. Locate people proficient in the skill and observe them doing it or ask them to describe how it is done.

Depending on the skill you wish to acquire, some of these approaches may work better than others. For example, it is relatively easy and often effective to observe and then try to imitate a good classroom instructor; it is not too useful to watch an instructional writer.

Let's examine these five approaches in more detail:

1. Gain relevant experience. If you are enrolled in a college HRD program, you may have the opportunity to gain relevant experience through an internship. If you are not a student but would like to make a career move into HRD, then:

- Try to gear your job to assignments that will develop skills you need. Volunteer to do training, write instructional materials, prepare visual aids, or other such tasks. Above all, build support from your supervisor.
- Join voluntary associations—charities, community groups, even political campaigns—and ask for jobs that will develop the HRD-related skills you need.
- Volunteer to teach a class at a local community or senior college. Many colleges want part-time faculty with skills in specific areas. You will acquire teaching experience this way.
- Volunteer to lead self-help groups, like those found in many churches or synagogues. You can acquire group facilitation skills in such settings.
- Tailor your hobbies around HRD-related matters.
- Write (for publication if possible) on HRD-related topics.

There are undoubtedly other ways to build your skills. Be imaginative.

2. Enroll in educational programs. The ASTD has published a *Directory of Academic Programs* (1982), presently available on computer database. This lists over 200 colleges and universities that offer degrees or certificates in the field. Your local library also may have directories of accredited and nonaccredited colleges that will award graduate or undergraduate credit for life experiences in many fields—including HRD. Consult the library as well for directories of correspondence courses that enable you to learn at home on your own time.

For more information on educational programs, see:

- *How to Get the Degree You Want: Bear's Guide to Non-Traditional College Degrees,* 8th ed., by J. Bear. Ten Speed Press, Berkeley, CA (1982).
- *Directory of External Degrees from Accredited Colleges and Universities,* edited by W. Haponski and S. Haponski. ETC Associates, Clayville, NY (1985).
- *The Correspondence Educational Directory,* 3rd ed., by J. Jones. Racz Publications, Oxnard, CA (1984).
- *Guide to 5000 Home Study Diploma-Certificate Programs,* by J. Smart. Smartco, Rocheport, MO (1984).
- *Guide to External Degree Programs in the U.S.,* edited by E. Sullivan. ACE, Washington, D.C. (1983).
- *Learning Independently: A Directory of Self-Instruction Resources,* 2nd ed., by P. Wasserman et al. Gale Research, Detroit, MI. (1982).

3. Enroll in training programs. Many colleges, universities, professional societies, and HRD vendors offer Train-the-Trainer seminars. Lasting from one day to two weeks, they are often concentrated and highly useful for learning about a specific HRD role. Some typical titles are: Effective Delivery Skills for Instructors, Preparing Instructional Materials, and Performing Needs Analysis.

Both the ASTD and the publishers of *Training* issue annual guides to consultants, some of whom offer public seminars (*ASTD Buyer's Guide; Marketplace Directory.*) If you join a professional society in HRD (an advisable move), your name will be placed on mailing lists that will bring you many brochures about specialized training.

4. Do independent reading. Many good books and articles are available on any specific HRD skill. Look through the reference sections of this book as a starting point.

5. Observe others. You can only observe or talk to others if you create the opportunity. Attend local chapter meetings of ASTD or other HRD-related organizations. Find out the names of people who are especially proficient in one or more skills of interest to you. Then arrange to talk with these people. In many cases they can tell you what they do, show you examples, and recommend learning projects to build your skills.

Getting Your First Job in HRD

If you have never had HRD experience, the choice of a first job is important. In many ways it will establish behaviors that can last throughout your career and can affect your values, skills, and even future employability. For these reasons, you should choose your first job with great care.

There are many excellent general guides available on handling the job search, preparing a resumé, and interviewing. Rather than repeat this information, our discussion will focus on concerns unique to HRD.

Your Resumé

The purpose of a resumé is to get an interview—to open the door. A few suggestions are:

1. Always state a general career objective but tailor it, if possible, to one organization. For example: "A job as instructor at the XYZ Corporation."

2. Provide general information about yourself first—but make it brief. Be sure to include your address or addresses, phone number(s), hobbies, health condition, and whether you will relocate. Birthdate, height, weight, and marital status are optional.

3. If you have no work experience directly relevant to HRD, list education first. Be sure to give the name and address of your school, gradepoint (if high), academic major and minor, dates attended, and dates of graduation. List any courses pertinent to the job (e.g., speech, technical writing, management, computer science).

4. List work experience next. Be sure to provide the name of the employer, your job title, dates of employment, and salary. Sometimes it helps to furnish a one-sentence description of what you did on the job.

5. List any professional affiliations—particularly if you are a member of such organizations as the ASTD, the American Society for Personnel Administration (ASPA), the National Society for Perfor-

mance and Instruction (NSPI), the Society for Applied Learning Technology, the American Management Association, or the Society for Technical Communication.

6. List references last.

Once you gain experience, you should structure your resumé differently.

Finding Out About Openings

For a newcomer, it might seem difficult to find information about job openings. Here are some suggestions:

1. Inquire about placement with the national headquarters of ASTD (1630 Duke Street, Box 1443, Alexandria, VA 22313) and NSPI (1126 Sixteenth St. NW, Suite 214, Washington, D.C. 20036).

2. Obtain from ASTD national headquarters a list of Placement Chairpersons in all chapters throughout the U.S. Send resumés to them and ask about opportunities in their areas.

3. If you are in school, enroll in its placement service. Meet recruiters and ask them for the names of the HRD managers in their organizations to whom you can send your resumé.

4. Read advertisements in your local newspaper as well as those in monthly issues of *Training and Development Journal, Performance and Instruction, Personnel Administrator, Personnel Journal, Training,* and *Training News.*

5. Attend national conventions of ASTD, NSPI, and ASPA. Look for the placement service. Have plenty of resumés with you.

6. Speak with relatives, friends, and teachers. Find out if any faculty members at your school are members of ASTD, meet them, and explain what kind of job you are looking for. This is one of the best sources of information for a student.

7. Inquire at your local Job Service and employment agencies. Explain your aims carefully, because many agencies unfamiliar with HRD may have trouble distinguishing it from personnel management.

8. Attend local ASTD chapter meetings. To find out where your chapter is, contact National ASTD headquarters. Get to know peo-

ple who can help you. They may be aware of job openings—or already have them.

9. Contact large employers in your area. Most organizations with more than 300 employees will have a training department. If nothing else, talk to the personnel manager about employers in the area known for their training efforts.

The Job Search

Contact organizations in which you want to work. It is helpful to:

1. Prepare a list of people you want to contact.
2. Establish a goal to reach at least one or two people a day during an intensive job hunt. Keep a log of who you reached and what they said.
3. Make contacts by letter, phone, and personal visit.

Many entry-level HRD jobs are never listed anywhere. Sometimes organizations promote or transfer from within; sometimes advertising is only through specialized employment agencies or national journals. Bear this in mind but also remember that employers will be impressed by determined people with appropriate skills and a definite career goal. You may get a shot at an HRD job when you show the desire for one, provided the company has an opening or can create one and does hire from the outside.

The Interview

A good job search should produce some interviews. Keep these suggestions in mind:

- Dress appropriately.
- Try to relax.
- Prepare yourself by researching the company. Know about its business and, if possible, its HRD program.
- Be ready to show how you can fit in. Sell yourself by relating your knowledge and skills to the job opening. If possible, show some examples of your work.

- If you do not know what the job opening is, ask about it first. Get the information you need to relate your abilities to the job.

- Be prepared to answer tough questions about what you want, how you want it, when you want it, and how the job fits into your long-term career goals.

- Speak honestly about your strengths and weaknesses.

- Ask your own questions about the company, the HRD effort, and the job. Remember that the aim is to satisfy yourself as well as get a job offer.

- If asked about salary requirements, talk about ranges—high teens, low twenties or thirties. Another way to deal with the question is to say you want the "going rate."

- After the interview, always send a thank-you note to the interviewer.

Practicing the interview process can help you prepare for it. Ask a friend to play the interviewer and spend an hour or two fielding questions. Think about how you would answer such typical questions as:

1. What do you want to do with your life?
2. Why should we hire you?
3. What do you know about HRD? This organization?
4. What are your strengths and weaknesses?

By knowing what you want and why you want it, you will be prepared to interview effectively for a job—provided you also have the skills.

Choosing Your Career Path

After you have gained some experience in HRD you will want to consider future career paths. There are numerous alternatives. You can:

1. Increase the scope of your present job.
2. Decrease the scope of your present job.
3. Seek promotion from one HRD role (e.g., instructional writer, instructor, evaluator) to another (manager).
4. Move to a larger organization.
5. Move to a smaller organization.

6. Move from a regional office to corporate headquarters.

7. Move from corporate headquarters to a regional office.

8. Move from an HRD department in a line division (e.g., marketing) to a central HRD department.

9. Move from a central HRD department to one in a line division.

10. Move out of a specialized HRD job to one with only some HRD components.

11. Move out of HRD and into a different career or occupation.

12. Move out of HRD and into higher-level management jobs.

Some of these career moves have been described at length elsewhere.[14] Recent information suggests that one-fourth of practitioners aspire to the role of HRD manager, about 15 percent to that of chief executive, about 15 percent to related but higher-level jobs in human resources management, about 14 percent to external consulting, about 12 percent to jobs in their organizations outside HRD, about 6 percent to academia, about 5 percent to their own businesses other than consulting, and about 5 percent to other choices.[12]

Let's examine our list of 12 career paths in more detail:

Increase the Scope of Your Present Job

One potential career move is to expand the range of competencies you use on the job. For example, you may adopt another HRD role or add competencies to what you already do. This choice is useful if you are feeling stale on the job and want to revitalize what you do. Of course, you may need to seek additional education and training to acquire needed competencies. In most cases, your superior will consent to, if not actually encourage, such development.

Decrease the Scope of Your Present Job

Another potential career move is to reduce the scope but increase the depth of your present duties. For example, you may give up one or more roles but improve your facility with those you keep. This career choice is appropriate if the department is expanding (more people often means greater specialization) or if you are intensely interested in just one or two roles and their corresponding competencies.

Seek Promotion in HRD

A traditional career aspiration is to move up the chain of command. Many trainers begin as instructors or instructional writers. In a large HRD department, the next step up is to supervisor of instructors in areas like professional, technical, or managerial training or as a unit chief responsible for media, instructional design, or evaluation. The final move is to manager of a training department. Variations in these career paths may depend on the nature of the industry or size of the organization.

Shift to a Larger Organization

Many HRD practitioners begin in relatively small organizations—including banks, hospitals, government agencies, or manufacturing plants. As their competence increases, they may begin to feel that they are stagnating. One career move is to remain in the same industry but shift to a larger organization.

Shift to a Smaller Organization

Movement up the traditional chain of command is not always easy. People at the top tend to remain in their jobs longer than those at the middle or bottom—thus restricting the upward mobility of qualified people as they gain competence. This problem is expected to worsen in the U.S. over the next decade, because the number of people in age groups customarily associated with middle and upper management jobs will increase as never before.[15] Unfortunately, a corresponding increase in middle and upper-level jobs is not likely. In fact, just the reverse is true—organizations are reducing such jobs to improve communication and save money.[16]

One alternative to traditional upward career movement is to shift from a large to a smaller organization. The individual is usually "promoted" in the sense that the change often means a more impressive job title. For example, a technical trainer-instructor with 15 years' experience might be able to move to a smaller organization and be called Director of Training. In many cases it means changing to the role of generalist, who enacts several roles, rather than being a specialist, who concentrates on only one.

Shift from a Regional Office to Headquarters

In some organizations, trainers start out in field offices, where they run their own show and do everything in that location. Corporate-level trainers, in contrast, may produce training materials and deliver specialized instruction—such as executive training. A career move from a regional to corporate headquarters is thus a possibility if you want increased specialization.

Shift from Corporate Headquarters to Regional Office

This is the reverse of the previous career move: a shift from corporate headquarters to a regional office. This change is desirable when you want greater autonomy and wish to become more of a generalist than specialist. It may also be a good idea from the organization's standpoint, because it will create a bridge for communication between corporate and regional offices.

Shift from a Line to Staff HRD Department

Large organizations sometimes maintain specialized HRD operations in line (operating) departments distinct from a more general but larger staff HRD department. For example, some firms split off training for computer operators and programmers from training that serves the remainder of the organization. One possible career move is thus from one of these specialized HRD units, where technical skill is usually highly prized, to a central HRD department where instructional skill is often more important.

Shift from a Staff to a Line HRD Department

Some HRD practitioners begin in a large, central HRD staff department. There they learn how to design, deliver, and evaluate instruction. When they long for career movement and have specialized skills in some area other than HRD (e.g., computer programming, marketing, production), they may want to consider moving into an operating department to head up specialized HRD units.

Move Out of an HRD Specialization to a Job with HRD Components

Many jobs require instructional skills. For example, a field sales manager may devote substantial time to training new sales representatives. For those who see more promise in a career related to (but outside of) HRD, such a career move might be worth considering.

Move Out of HRD Completely

Not everyone wants to make a lifelong career of HRD. In the past, few people even thought of HRD as a profession distinct from others. This view is changing among practitioners but is still not necessarily accepted by all managers or in all organizations.

Some people might want to try other occupations where they think they can do better. Many ex-trainers have become HRD consultants, though the allure of this career change has dimmed for all but a few. Some trainers think of moving into academia, but teaching opportunities in traditional higher education settings require a great deal of writing and publication in addition to teaching.

The skills of HRD are certainly transferable to other fields. Instructors can become speakers and salespersons. Instructional writers can become technical writers, editors, or even reporters. Media specialists can use their talents in radio, television, or libraries. These are just a few examples. Of course, career moves of these kinds may require experience, education, and talents different from the typical skills picked up in HRD work. Additional education might be needed.

Move into Higher Management

In the past it was rare for personnel or HRD practitioners to move up the ladder to higher management. Now, however, more of them are aspiring to such jobs.

A job in HRD tends to have high visibility—especially for classroom instructors and those involved in management training. Indeed, many firms rotate their highest potential talent through a tour of duty in the department for just this reason. Although there is a potential for HRD professionals to move up the management ladder, those who want to do so should supplement their present credentials and experience with those appropriate to new goals. Making friends with people who can help may also be important.

References

1. Carnevale, A. "Human Capital: Notes for the Future. In *The Workforce of the 80s,* H. Sredl and W. Rothwell, eds. Washington, D.C.: American Society for Training and Development, 1983.

2. Carnevale, A. "The Learning Enterprise." *Training and Development Journal* 40 (1986) 1: pp. 18–26.

3. Ibid.

4. Ibid.

5. Calvert, R. Jr. "Training America: The Numbers Add Up." *Training and Development Journal* 39 (1985) 11: pp. 35–37.

6. Feuer, D. "Where the Dollars Go." *Training* 22 (1985) 10: pp. 45–53.

7. Ibid.

8. Ibid.

9. Ibid.

10. Swanson, R., and N. Mosier. "Adult Education in America." *Training* 20 (1983) 10: pp. 54–55; 58–60; 64; 66; 68.

11. "Development and Delivery of Training: Media, Methods, and Means." *Training* 20 (1983) 10: pp. 47; 50–53.

12. Lee, C. "Trainers' Careers." *Training* 22 (1985) 10: pp. 75–80.

13. Ibid.

14. Chalofsky, N., and C. Lincoln. *Up the HRD Ladder: A Guide for Professional Growth.* Reading, MA: Addison-Wesley, 1983.

15. Carnevale, A. *Jobs for the Nation: Challenges for a Society Based on Work.* Washington, D.C.: American Society for Training and Development, 1984.

16. Debats, K. "Cut the Fat." *Personnel Journal* 61 (1982) 11: p. 811.

For More Information

Archer, E. "Human Resource Professionalism: An Unexpected Source of Conflict." *Personnel Administrator* 31 (1986) 7: pp. 97–98, 100, 102–104.

Bear, J. *How to Get the Degree You Want: Bear's Guide to Non-Traditional College Degrees* 8th ed. Berkeley, CA: Ten Speed Press, 1982.

Brinkerhoff, D., and A. Smith. "Write a Resumé, Not an Obituary." *Training* 23 (1986) 7: pp. 37–39.

Carnevale, A., and H. Goldstein. *Employee Training: Its Changing Role and an Analysis of New Data.* Washington, D.C.: American Society for Training and Development, 1983.

Directory of Executive Recruiters. Fitzwilliam, NH: Consultants News, 1986.

Hansen, G. "Professional Education for Careers in Human Resource Administration." *Personnel Administrator* 29 (1984) 1: pp. 69–70, 72–73, 75–76, 78–80, 95.

Haponski, W., and S. Haponski, eds. *Directory of External Degrees from Accredited Colleges and Universities.* Clayville, NY: ETC Associates, 1985.

International Directory of Executive Recruiters. Fitzwilliam, NH: Consultants News, 1984.

Jones, J. *The Correspondence Educational Directory,* 3rd ed. Oxnard, CA: Racz Publications, 1984.

"Recruitment Services Directory." *Personnel Journal* 65 (1986) 8: pp. 80–104.

Schuman, N., and W. Lewis. *Revising Your Resume.* New York: Wiley, 1986.

Smart, J. *Guide to 5000 Home Study Diploma-Certificate Programs.* Rocheport, MO: Smartco, 1984.

Sullivan, E., ed. *Guide to External Degree Programs in the U.S.* Washington, D.C.: ACE, 1983.

Wasserman, P., et al. *Learning Independently: A Directory of Self-Instruction Resources,* 2nd ed. Detroit: Gale Research, 1982.

3

Coordinating HRD with organizational strategy.

The HRD department is strongly influenced by the environment that surrounds it. In particular, the overall strategic plans of the organization and the specific plans for human resources can imply much about possible HRD initiatives. But what is strategic, long-range organizational planning? How can it affect HRD? What is human resources planning and how can it affect HRD? Part Three addresses these questions, focusing on the relationship between the organization's long-term objectives and the role of HRD in helping bring them about.

CHAPTER 6

Organizational strategic planning.

This chapter describes organizational strategic planning and the role of HRD in helping to realize long-range organizational plans. ■

The Need for Strategic Planning

HRD is not an end in itself. Rather it is a means of helping an organization achieve its goals while helping individuals realize their career aspirations. Most organizations have a purpose, a distinct reason for existing. On a simplistic level, business firms exist to make a profit; government agencies exist to provide a service to the public at the lowest possible cost; nonprofit enterprises exist to provide a service and charge users only enough to recoup expenses incurred in the process. Beyond such obvious purposes, each organization has its own unique reason for existing that provides a sense of direction to its activities. It also has objectives by which to measure periodically how well that purpose is being achieved. The purpose of the organization and its objectives influence its HRD plans—that is, the number of people and the types of skills needed. At the same time, the number of people and their skills influence the relative ease or difficulty of changing the organization's purpose and objectives.

Organizations do not exist in a static environment. Changes in technology, economic conditions, governmental policies, and other areas may affect an organization's prospects for successfully achieving its purpose. As such environmental changes affect organizations, managers must often reconsider their organization's purpose and the number and type of people they need to achieve that purpose.

The railroads serve as a classic example of what can happen to companies that fail to reconsider their purpose as times change.[1] During the 19th century, trains were the fastest mode of transportation. But as automobiles, trucks, and aircraft became more prevalent, railroads lost most of their customers. Rather than take advantage of this trend—the railroads could have purchased auto or plane manufacturers and could thus have altered their purpose—they are now financially bankrupt and must depend on governmental subsidies for their survival.

The plight of the railroads dramatizes the need for managers to take a long-term view of their organization's purpose and to plan accordingly. This activity is called *strategic planning*. It is the focus of this chapter, because it significantly influences—and is, in turn, influenced by—HRD.

The Strategic Planning Process

Simply defined, strategic planning (SP) is the process by which an organization determines how it will achieve its purpose over the long term, given expected opportunities and problems presented by the outside environment and the strengths and weaknesses of the organization itself. In business and industry, SP is synonymous with how the firm will compete; in government and nonprofit enterprises, SP is synonymous with how the organization or agency will continue to meet the needs of its constituency or service users in light of changing conditions, laws, rules, and regulations.

SP theorists do not totally agree on steps in the process and even on the definition of their field. However, most would agree with Glueck and Jauch [2] that SP requires members of an organization to:

Formulate: 1. Organizational goals and objectives (and reformulate those already existing).

Analyze: 2. The environment in which the organization operates—or plans to operate—in order to detect potential threats or possibilities for action.

3. The organization's strengths and weaknesses relative to the environment.

Choose:

4. Among the range of possible strategies for the organization.

5. A promising grand strategy to command the highest priority and integrate all organizational activities over time— but plan for contingencies in the event of unexpected environmental change.

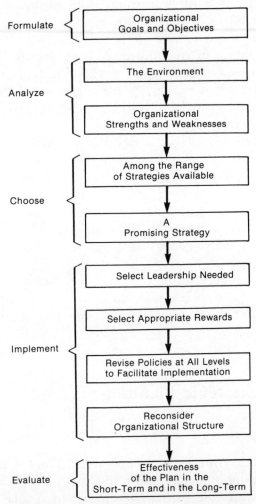

Formulate { Organizational Goals and Objectives

Analyze { The Environment → Organizational Strengths and Weaknesses

Choose { Among the Range of Strategies Available → A Promising Strategy

Implement { Select Leadership Needed → Select Appropriate Rewards → Revise Policies at All Levels to Facilitate Implementation → Reconsider Organizational Structure

Evaluate { Effectiveness of the Plan in the Short-Term and in the Long-Term

Figure 6.1 The strategic planning process

Implement:	6. The proposed strategy by selecting appropriate leaders and rewarding them for behavior and results consistent with strategy.
	7. Policies at all levels and across all function areas that are consistent with strategy.
	8. An organizational structure consistent with the plan.
Evaluate:	9. The effectiveness of the plan in the short-term and long-term.

Strategic plans can be classified into two types: (1) comprehensive plans, which attempt to integrate all functional activities and corporate subdivisions to achieve organizational objectives, and (2) market-specific plans, which identify only markets that the organization should enter or develop in the future. A 1982 survey conducted by the American Management Association revealed that, while 90 percent of 156 responding firms had strategic plans, 70 percent of them were market specific.[3] However, management theorists more commonly mean comprehensive plans when they refer to SP.

Methods of conducting the SP process also differ. In general, three approaches are used: the top-down, the bottom-up, and the negotiated. In the first approach, corporate grand strategy is formulated at the highest level of management and then communicated to lower levels. In the second, grand strategy is consolidated from independent plans in otherwise autonomous enterprises comprising the corporation. In the third, grand strategy is proposed either at top or bottom and then negotiated.[4]

Strategic planning deals only with how the organization can achieve its purpose in the long run. It is preceded by two steps: a prophetic vision of the organization's future and an articulation of organizational purpose.

Key Steps in Strategic Planning

Visualizing the Future

To most Americans, imagination is not a trait closely associated with managing an organization. Although the pioneering spirit runs deep in American culture, it is tempered by a love of the practical, concrete, and useful. Knowledge and creativity are not prized for their own sake but rather for their potential applications. Americans are generally pragmatic and often even anti-intellectual.

The problem is that, without imagination, managers cannot recognize potentially profitable opportunities or predict long-term consequences of their actions. Short-sightedness and complacence are often called the biggest failings of managers in the U.S. since World War II. Organizations reward managers based on short-term goal achievement, not on long-term consequences. To make matters worse, the average tenure of top managers in U.S. corporations is just five years, much too short to judge the long-term results of their actions.

Imagination is actually the essence of entrepreneurial skill. An entrepreneur is one who recognizes an opportunity before others do and takes full advantage of it. No business would exist today except for the initiative of some entrepreneur who recognized the potential for making money and took considerable financial and personal risks to back an unproven venture.

Joseph Schumpeter,[5] an early critic of capitalism, predicted its ultimate decay as a result of what he believed would be a decline in entrepreneurial skill. As capitalism triumphed and alleviated material needs, Schumpeter argued, fewer people would be willing to take risks. At the same time, big corporations would increasingly be led by professional managers—not the founding entrepreneurs. Such professionals would be loathe to risk their jobs or future employment prospects by leading their firms into risky but highly profitable activities. The result: economic decline.

Contemporary observers of American business believe that Schumpeter was at least partially correct in his predictions. Approximately 90 percent of all wealth is concentrated in the hands of 200 large corporations; the remainder is distributed among remaining businesses in the U.S. Most managers in the largest corporations are indeed professionals, and many are products of business schools that emphasize the accountant's love of prudence, conservatism, and short-term results.[6] However, Schumpeter was wrong about a decline in the number of entrepreneurs: more new, small businesses have been formed in the past ten years than ever before, and they employ more people than their giant counterparts combined.

It is thus in the largest U.S. corporations, and government bodies—not in small business—where there is what might be called a *crisis of vision* or at least a crisis in implementing a vision of the future.

What is vision? It is a clear, concrete picture in the mind of leaders who know what they want to achieve. In the case of a manager it is a sense of what the organization should look like and how it should function in its environment. A vision is also:

1. Founded on an in-depth knowledge of the industry and of the organization's potential in it.

2. Directed toward gradual strengthening of the organization so that, in time, the vision is realized through a series of gradual (or perhaps revolutionary) changes in outlook and point of view.

3. Characterized by flexibility and by creativity. The aim is to achieve what is desirable, not just what is possible or what observers believe to be practical.[7]

The power of vision is that it is sustained and relatively enduring.

What has contributed to a crisis in vision? There seem to be two main causes: (1) a simple lack of imagination, and (2) a lack of sufficient charisma and political power to excite others to act.

Imagination, essential for visualizing the future, is not taught in business schools; rather, it is more closely associated with the study of the arts and humanities. It is the ability to reperceive reality and reinterpret it creatively. In an organizational context, it is the ability to look beyond past traditions and conceive a new future and the organization's place in it. Techniques for creative thinking can be used to stimulate imagination (see box).

Imagination is essential for senior managers whose main function is setting the direction of their organization. However, imagination is not enough by itself. An additional skill is needed: the ability to inspire, enthuse, and even infect others with the same vision. All great leaders of the past not only possessed a vision but were successful in getting others to accept it and to work on making it a reality. Some of the best examples of combining vision, inspiration, and enthusiasm have been demonstrated by religious leaders and statesmen. Napoleon was able to inspire his countrymen with a vision of a unified Europe; Mohammed inspired his followers with a vision of a world unified in religion. The same skill, though of lesser scope, can be seen in the corporate world: Lee Iacocca inspired Chrysler's employees to work harder and temporarily sacrifice their self-interest for the future survival of the company.

Before undertaking strategic planning, it is essential for top corporate managers to have some sense of what they think the organization should be like in the future. Only then can they proceed to the next step.

Three Techniques for Creative Thinking

Three approaches have been shown to be especially helpful to small groups in facilitating creative thought: brainstorming, Nominal Group Technique (NGT) and the Delphi procedure.

Brainstorming consists of what the 19th-century writer Matthew Arnold called "the free play of the mind around an idea." To apply it, simply ask a small group (five to six people) to write down everything that comes into their minds about a topic provided to them. They should be given a time limit and should make no attempt to criticize the quality of the ideas. When the time limit is up, the ideas should be counted.

NGT is a variation of brainstorming. Persons in a small group spend several minutes thinking silently about an open-ended topic or question. They then write their ideas down on index cards and pass them to someone who records ideas. All ideas are summarized on a flip chart in full view of all participants. They then vote on the ideas, ranking them in order of usefulness.

The Delphi technique requires a panel of experts, selected by a group seeking to generate ideas. The experts never meet as a group—instead, each receives a questionnaire that simply inquires about a given problem. The experts' responses are pooled by the group conducting Delphi. A report summarizing all responses and another questionnaire are sent back to the experts. Each one examines the report and votes on the relative value of the ideas. This process is continued until a consensus of experts is reached.

For more on techniques for creative thinking, see:

- *Group Techniques for Program Planning,* by A. Delbecq, A. Van de Ven, and D. Gustafson. Scott, Foresman, & Co., Glenview, IL (1975).

- *Games Trainers Play,* by J. Newstrom and E. Scannell. McGraw-Hill, NY (1980).

Articulating Organizational Purpose

The articulation of organizational purpose stems from a vision of the future and, to some extent, a sense of present and past. An organization's purpose is sometimes called its mission, its reason for existing. A mission is never fully achieved, unless the organization is temporary. It unifies an organization and provides a sense of direction and a rationale for that direction.

As early as 1924, Mary Parker Follett, in her classic book *Creative Experience,*[8] proposed her famous Law of the Situation and thus reinforced the importance of articulating purpose:

> When you have made your employees feel that they are in some sense partners in the business, they do not improve the quality of their work, save waste in time and material, because of the Golden Rule, but because their interests are the same as yours.

In order to create this "feel," it is essential to know first precisely *what* business the organization is in and *how* it will conduct business.

Superficially, the question of purpose or mission appears to be a moot point. A hardware store exists to make a profit by selling hardware; an automobile manufacturer exists to make a profit by selling cars. But there is far more to it than that. Consider: why should a hardware store exist? If it is simply a matter of profit, more can be made in other businesses or investments. Why hardware? What does that business include or exclude? Discount stores sell hardware and make more money by buying and selling it in volume. Can it be that the old-fashioned hardware store, in which a customer can drop in and pose questions to knowledgeable clerks, is really in the business of providing a service that most discount stores do not?

The more that owners of the hardware store understand the unique purpose of their business, the greater their advantage against competitors. The same principle applies to all other businesses. With a sense of a clearly defined purpose, an organization is in a position to establish a business philosophy that is consistent with it. In this way, managers and employees alike have defined their organization's market—the specific group of consumers they wish to serve. In the case of the hardware store, the market may consist largely of people who feel they need help in making a purchase or, ultimately, in using the merchandise. The owners will be in a good position if (1) they hire those knowledgeable enough to give good advice, and (2) they think of even more ways to help their customers and thus capitalize on their chief market strength.

As organizations grow and age, they sometimes lose sight of their purpose. Think again of the railroads. Over a hundred years ago, their purpose was transportation. They provided the fastest mode of travel and freight delivery. Then times changed, but railroad managers never looked beyond trains to redefine company purpose. They missed marvelous opportunities to purchase new and eventually more profitable automobile and aircraft manufacturers.

Before strategic planning is possible, managers and employees alike must have some sense of the organization's purpose. The process of articulating that purpose will be worthwhile in itself, since it will reveal what managers believe their business is.

Determining Organizational Goals and Objectives

An organizational goal is a desired end state or condition which an organization attempts to realize. A goal is somewhat more general than an objective, which is measurable. Goals and objectives stem from a sense of purpose and from a vision of the future shared by those in the organization. Determining goals and objectives is the first step in strategic planning.

Different observers have asserted contrasting theories about the nature of goals. Talcott Parsons [9] believes that organizational goals are derived from what society needs. Petro Georgiou,[10] on the other hand, believes that goals are essentially distilled from the common wishes of those who are employed by—or have a stake in—the organization.

Hall explains the nature of goals succinctly:

> Organizational goals by definition are creations of individuals, singly or collectively. . . . The collectively determined, commonly based goal seldom remains constant over time. New considerations imposed from without or within deflect the organization from its original goal . . . changing the activities of the organization. . . . The important point is that the goal of any organization is an abstraction distilled from the desires of members and pressures from the environment and internal system.[11]

Although organizations may have only one purpose (i.e., reason for existence), they have several goals (i.e., what is to be achieved). Each

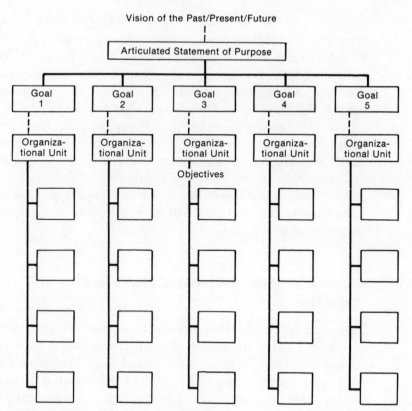

Figure 6.2   The hierarchy of objectives

part of the organization has a goal that contributes to the continuing achievement of the overall mission; each work group and each job has a goal that also contributes to the mission. This concept is illustrated in Figure 6.2.

From goals, objectives are derived for measuring to what extent the goals were or are to be achieved during a specified time period. They range from broad objectives for the entire organization to more specific objectives for parts of the organization, work groups, and even individuals in their respective jobs. All organizations have objectives, though they are not always clearly articulated or understood. When they are articulated, the result is a well-defined hierarchy of objectives that makes priorities explicit.

How are organizational goals and objectives established and implemented? Management theorists are not in total agreement on the answer.

In explaining their disagreement, it is useful to make several distinctions about the nature of organizations and decision-making. On the one hand, classical management theorists such as Frederick Taylor and Henri Fayol assumed that organizations should be structured logically, that tasks should be specialized, and that managers should make decisions solely on the basis of what works the best. They assumed, then, that organizations should be treated rationally—that is, the best solution for any problem should be selected solely for its usefulness. They completely ignored the idea that worker feelings or power struggles between managers or work groups could, in fact, influence the relative ease or difficulty of making or implementing decisions. Human Relations theory, however, pointed out that organizations could be treated politically—that is, the best solution for any problem should be selected solely for the power and personal advantage it would yield to individuals or work groups. Subsequent theorists hypothesized that every organization has two sides: *the formal*, consisting of the allocation of work responsibilities and authority conferred by virtue of position, and the *informal*, consisting in part of worker feelings and expectations about those responsibilities and that authority.

In the context of goal and objective setting, exponents of the formal organization maintain that goals and objectives are purely rational and are intended to maximize profits or to ensure timely, efficient, and effective service delivery. Exponents of the informal organization assume that goals and objectives are largely political and are intended to maximize the power of those who control the organization.[12] Still others point to both formal and informal organizations, arguing that the process of developing goals and objectives is political but the goals and objectives ultimately selected will be rationally related to maximizing profits or ensuring efficient and effective operations. Most observers would probably agree with this last position.

Only after determining organizational goals and objectives is it possible to proceed to the next step in strategic planning.

Analyzing the Environment

The term *environment* usually refers to the world outside an organization. The organizational environment is that which provides inputs (e.g., land, labor, capital, raw materials, and technology) and to which outputs are directed (i.e., markets). Every organization is dependent on the environment for its very existence—in fact, all organizations are growing even more dependent as a result of: (1) the increasing rate of technological change, (2) the proliferation of government regulations, and (3) the rise of foreign competition.

As a step in the strategic planning process, environmental analysis identifies characteristics of the environment most critical to the organization and predicts how those characteristics are likely to change in the future. Through environmental analysis, the organization can prepare itself for changes that are often outside its control to influence but are within its control to deal with. Research has shown that the more information managers have about the future, the more likely the organization will be successful in coping with it.

Not all organizations exist in the same environment. Indeed, the most critical characteristics of environment vary by industry and by the size of the organization. For example, what affects General Motors does not necessarily affect IBM. They rely on different supplies of raw materials and use different labor skills. A cyclical downturn in the national economy is more likely to affect GM, which sells most of its cars to private individuals in the U.S., than IBM, which sells its computers and office equipment both to individuals and businesses worldwide. On the other hand, the effect of an economic downturn will probably have less influence on the biggest company in the auto industry, GM, than on smaller competitors like Ford or Chrysler. By virtue of size, GM has market power over its smaller competitors.

In general, there are four types of environments—the placid randomized, the placid clustered, the disturbed reactive, and the turbulent field.[12] In the first type, there is no competition and resources are available but require some effort to locate. Governmental agencies usually exist in this environment. Success depends on just doing as well as possible under the circumstances. In the second type, there is no direct competition but resources are heavily concentrated in certain areas. Charitable organizations and some retailers operate in this environment. Success depends on positioning the organization as closely as possible to resources or consumers. In the third type, several competing organizations jockey for favorable positions. Many businesses in the U.S. face this kind of environment, competing for consumer dollars against counterparts in their own industry. Success depends not only on positioning the organization and its products or services so as to attract the most attention but also on preventing competitors from attaining a more favorable market position. In the fourth type, competing organizations jockey for positions while the environment itself changes. Firms dealing with high technol-

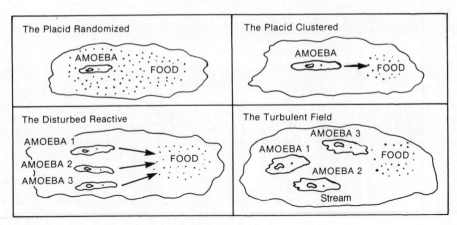

Figure 6.3   Four types of environments

ogy—computers, electronics, and aerospace—face these conditions. Success depends on simultaneously keeping track of changes in the environment, positioning the organization to take advantage (or minimize disadvantages) of environmental change, and preventing competitors from attaining favorable positions. Figure 6.3 depicts these environmental states in a simplified form.

Depending on the type of environment in which they operate, organizations will differ in the importance they attach to such factors as technology, economics, suppliers, distributors, and social trends. Figure 6.4 provides a list of environmental factors that could affect organizational success or failure. By analyzing the present and future importance and status of these factors, managers can gain a sense of how their organization will and should fare in the future.

Environmental analysis typically relies on a variety of forecasting techniques, used to predict changes in relevant aspects of the external environment:

1. Economic conditions can be forecast by using leading indicators, consumer sentiments, futures markets, per capita income, and other information.

2. Technological change can be predicted by expert opinion or by hypothetical scenarios of future events.

3. Governmental/legal changes, like technological change, can be forecast by expert opinion through such methods as the Delphi and Nominal Group Technique.

Figure 6.4 Environmental factors

Characteristics	Description	How Important is this Characteristic to the Organization?	Why?	How will this Characteristic Change in 5 Years? 10 Years?	Why?
Economic	Includes all factors affecting the state of the business cycle	How much is the organization affected by changes in general business conditions?	Provide the reasons	What will be the likely state of the economy over the long term?	Provide the reasons
Governmental	Includes all factors affecting laws, regulations, policies	How much is the organization affected by regulations?		What factors might influence changes in laws or regulations?	
Market	Includes all factors affecting who can or will purchase or use the organization's products/services	How much is the organization dependent on one kind of market?		What factors might affect the kind of market the organization will serve?	
Technological	Includes all factors affecting the supply of resources needed by the organization and machinery or knowledge affecting work processes	How much is the organization dependent on a few key supplies or on certain types of knowledge or technology?		What factors might affect the future supply of resources and/or the means of making the product or providing the service?	
Social	Includes public attitudes about the organization and its products or services	How much is the organization dependent on current lifestyles or attitudes?		What factors might alter public attitudes?	
Geographic	Includes all factors affecting the location of key suppliers, distributors, competitors, or consumers	How much is the organization dependent on certain suppliers, etc. in a certain location?		What factors might alter the physical location of suppliers, distributors, consumers, or competitors?	

154

4. Market changes can be forecast through changes in population growth, social changes, and analysis of competitors.

5. Geographic changes can be forecast by examining census figures, population growth, and movements of important suppliers, manufacturers, and distributors.

6. Social changes can be forecast through issue analysis and expert opinions on the sociopolitical environment.[13]

Depending on what is to be analyzed, techniques vary in their relative effectiveness. Environmental analysis is far from an exact science, and it is usually easier to forecast that environmental change will take place than to forecast the nature or degree of change.

Analyzing Organizational Strengths and Weaknesses

To establish the long-term direction of an organization, managers need more than information about future changes in the environment. They also need good information about the status of the organization: its present standing relative to what managers desire for it or relative to competitors in the same industry. Any organization has internal strengths and weaknesses. A strength is what contributes to goal achievement; a weakness is that which impedes goal achievement. Both are characteristic of the world inside the organization, its inner workings or *internal environment.* The choice of strategy (i.e., how to achieve goals and objectives) is dependent on a comparison of external and internal environments.

The analysis of organizational strengths and weaknesses—sometimes called *internal appraisal*—assesses how well the organization is achieving its purpose at present. Of all steps in strategic planning, internal appraisal is the most difficult.

There are three major problems associated with internal appraisal: objectivity, methods, and criteria. Objectivity requires management to judge the performance of all parts of the organization in a critical way. The problem is that top managers are responsible for their organizations. Indeed, they are the principal stakeholders in (and often apologists for) the status quo. They can hardly be objective in their assessments. Research has shown that managers become so committed to a course of action that even when it appears to fail they will persist in the same course.[14] Nor can they rely entirely on information provided to them by subordinates: research has shown that people filter their communication to their superiors and will emphasize the positive so as to preserve their chances of being rewarded. Even superiors will conceal their mistakes or perceived shortcomings from those reporting to them.

A second problem concerns methods of conducting internal appraisal. How can strengths and weaknesses be identified? In the U.S., most organizations rely on financial reports. They are published annually by corporations which have stockholders. Managers within the organization receive financial information even more frequently and can use this information along with figures on production and sales to detect some potential problems.

Unfortunately, numbers provide information primarily about results of operating problems. They seldom help to pinpoint cause. They may show, for example, that sales are sluggish but not whether the cause is a general economic downturn, an incompetent sales force, or something else. For this reason, managers often have more trouble identifying the cause of problems than recognizing their symptoms.

A third problem in conducting internal appraisal has to do with the selection and application of criteria—that is, yardsticks for measuring strengths and weaknesses. There is, after all, no such thing as a strength or weakness viewed in isolation. A strength exists only when compared to some criterion, some standard or value indicator of what should be. The same is true of a weakness.

Sources of criteria may vary from the subjective opinions of managers or employees to academic research findings, industry practices, professional (i.e., expert) opinion, workflow analysis, or governmental regulations or laws. Some theorists have listed organizational attributes that should be considered in an internal appraisal. Others have surveyed managers to determine what they believe should be considered. Figure 6.5 depicts some of these attributes.

Several methods are useful for top managers who want to examine organizational strengths and weaknesses. They include: portfolio analysis, performance audits, attitude surveys, quality circles, and behavioral science approaches to organizational diagnosis.

Portfolio analysis is a relatively old appraisal method. For business firms, two major approaches to portfolio analysis are prominent: the General Electric (GE) Model and the Boston Consulting Group (BCG) Model.

The GE Model was created to assist decision-makers in that company,

Figure 6.5 Attributes to consider in internal appraisal

Function	Description	What Criteria can be used for Appraisal?	How can those Criteria be used?
Finance/ Accounting	Raises or invests funds and keeps track of them	• Cost of capital • Good tax conditions • Good systems for budgeting and profit planning	• Compare with industry " "
Marketing	Determines what products or services to offer, what to charge for them, where and how to sell them	• Market share • A good mix of products or services • Good market research • Good pricing policies • Good distribution • Good promotion strategies	• Compare with competitors " " " " "
Operations/ Production	Produces goods or delivers the services	• Low cost production • Good procedures for designing, scheduling, assessing quality • Use of facilities • Ability to meet the demand	• Compare with competitors " " "
Personnel	Sets policies for recruitment of people and maintaining a workforce capable of doing the work	• Good mix of skills and experience of top management • Good integrated policies on recruitment, staffing, training, compensation, etc. • Participative climate and high morale	• Compare with industry " • Compare across many organizations

which consists of over 40 different businesses. Each business is placed on a grid based on its comparative strengths and industry attractiveness. If placement on the grid is positive, GE invests more and expands the business; if placement results are mixed, GE exercises restraint and caution; if placement results are negative, GE reduces investments and may try to sell the business.

The BCG Model is similar. Companies that comprise the corporation are placed on a grid based on market share and market growth. The results reveal whether each business can be classified as a star showing great promise, a problem child showing potentials unrealized, a cash cow showing continued promise, or a dog showing little hope of success.

In the performance audit, an independent analyst (or team of analysts) conducts an examination of an entire organization or its parts. The results are reported to top management for purposes of assessing how well results match intentions or how well resources are used in obtaining results. A performance audit—sometimes called a management audit—can address any issue. It need not focus only on financial matters, but is useful for identifying and correcting other deficiencies.

Attitude surveys are useful for detecting employee morale problems, assessing training needs, thwarting unionization efforts, and identifying perceived strengths or weaknesses in daily operations. Conducting a survey is not difficult, and standardized questionnaires are available, making it possible to compare results in one organization to results in many others.

Quality circles have gained much attention in recent years. Supervisors are trained as group leaders and use work time to help their employees consider ways to improve operations. Higher management evaluates the suggestions and either accepts or rejects them. If suggestions are rejected, reasons must be fed back to the circle.

Other approaches to diagnosing organizational strengths and weaknesses have been developed by industrial psychologists. Levinson [15] suggests that an organization can be examined by having an outside consultant develop a case history, much like that used in psychoanalysis, which relies on consultant feelings, documents, information from other organizations, and facts about how the organization is structured. Hornstein and Tichy [16] recommend that managers of an organization work together in a structured setting to develop their own diagnostic model. Nadler and Tushman [17] suggest a three-step process: (1) Identify what is to be studied, (2) determine what characteristics are most important, and (3) decide how well parts of the organization work together or interact with the environment. Weisbord [18] has developed a model useful in assessing how well six aspects of an organization work together: its purposes, rewards, structure, leadership, methods of coordinating technology, and methods of resolving conflict.

When the internal appraisal is completed, top managers are able to consider a range of possible strategies.

Considering Strategic Options

In any planning activity, there is always a range of possible strategies. The question is: what are they? Answering that question is a step in the strategic planning process that identifies how many ways an organization can potentially achieve its purpose and objectives successfully over time. It typically requires a comparison of external trends and internal strengths and weaknesses in order to generate a list of possible directions. How are such comparisons made? Who makes them? What are some of the possibilities that decision-makers can choose?

To compare external trends with internal strengths and weaknesses, all that is necessary is a *means* and a *method*. The *means* is simple enough: set external trends and internal strengths/weaknesses up in a way that allows comparison (see Figure 6.6). Selecting a *method* is more difficult. Some common ones include: planning committees, reports generated by strategic planning units or consultants, or judgments of managers at all levels of the organization.

Top managers—the chief executive and reporting subordinates— bear primary responsibility for generating strategic alternatives. This view is consistent with the notion of *timespan of discretion:* top-level managers are responsible for creating strategy and their performance can only be judged as a function of how well that strategy works.[19] In contrast, middle managers are responsible for working within the long-term strategy established by superiors and for creating medium- and short-range plans consistent with that strategy. Field supervisors are responsible for overseeing the work of employees and for daily, weekly, or monthly tactics necessary for implementing medium- and short-range plans. Figure 6.7 depicts the relationship between management level and plans.

Organizations generally select their grand strategy from six basic possibilities. They are: (1) growth, (2) retrenchment, (3) turnabout, (4) integration, (5) diversification, and (6) combination.[20]

A growth strategy simply means that the organization will try to do more of what it is already doing. Resources will be directed to increasing market share, expanding the size of the market served, and perhaps increasing the workforce.

Retrenchment is the opposite of growth: external conditions do not favor the organization, so it will pare down its workforce or its scale of operations to cut possible losses and conserve scarce resources.

A turnabout strategy tries to reverse the decline of a faltering enterprise.

Figure 6.6 Comparing external trends with organizational strengths and weaknesses

	Environment		Internal Attribute	Organization	
External Aspect	How Important is this Aspect to the Organization?	How will this Aspect Change in 5–10 Years?		What Criteria can be used for Appraisal?	How can those Criteria be used?
Economic			Finance/ Accounting		
Governmental			Legal/ Governmental Relations		
Market			Market		
Technological			Production/ Operations		
Social			Personnel		
Geographic			Location of Facilities		
Others?			Others?		

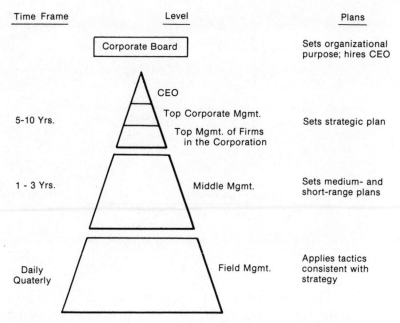

Figure 6.7 How planning relates to management level

An integration strategy calls for acquiring or merging with key suppliers (i.e., those firms that provide raw materials or other resources essential to corporate operations), competitors, or distributors (i.e., those firms that transport or sell the corporation's finished products or offer its services).

Diversification strategy involves entering into a new business that appears to offer more promise for the future.

A combination strategy involves implementing two or more of the above strategies in different parts of the organization at the same time.

Selecting the Strategy

Before the best strategy can be identified, top managers must consider several important factors. Their selection will be, in part, a function of (1) what they value, (2) the (perceived) purpose of the organization, (3) the alternative strategies they recognize and consider, (4) pressures exerted by groups inside or outside the organization, and (5) the size of the organization relative to its industry.

Values are, of course, what managers perceive as desirable or undesir-

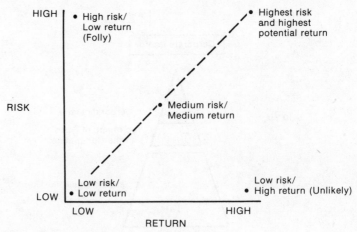

Figure 6.8   The risk/return trade-off

able. They pervade all aspects of strategic planning and guide decision-making among alternatives. Selecting a strategy frequently involves a trade-off between risk and return. The greater the risk, the greater the potential payoff; the less the risk, the less the potential payoff (see Figure 6.8). The question is: to what extent are top managers willing to accept risk (possible loss of company assets) for return (high profits)? In most cases, managers tend to be *risk averse;* they accept the prospect of lower returns as long as risk is low. There are exceptions: venture capitalists, who back fledgling and unproven ventures, sometimes accept high risk for the prospects of high returns. Entrepreneurs are less risk averse than most professional managers. To select a strategy, managers must assess what they hope to achieve.

To select a strategy, top managers should also consider—or even reconsider—the purpose of the organization. Are they content to remain in the same business, even if future prospects look bleak? If not, how will a changed sense of purpose affect the organization? Suppose a new business is acquired through diversification. Will the present management team possess the necessary expertise to run that business?

In selecting a strategy, top managers should also be receptive to their options. As William Haney [21] has pointed out, managers are often prone to "blinderedness"—a painful inability to see beyond the present way of doing things. Radical alternatives rarely occur to them. They must therefore make a deliberate effort to generate alternatives and try out those that appear promising, even the ones that at first seem outlandish.

To select strategy, top managers must also sense that important groups inside and outside the organization will favor—or at least not disfavor—their selection. Strategy is not chosen solely by top managers and then imposed on others. Internal and external coalitions play an important part in strategic choice. The process of selecting strategy is more revealing about power and decision-making in the organization than the choice ultimately made.[22]

Finally, the size of the organization relative to its industry is an important determinant of appropriate strategy. The reason: industry leaders frequently have great market power as a result of their size and dominance. If General Motors drops the price of cars, it is national news and may force similar drops by competitors. If a smaller competitor drops prices, GM may be able to survive quite well without following suit.

Implementing the Strategy

Implementation puts the strategic plan into action by adapting the organization to meet expected changes in external conditions. Frequently criticized as the least effectively handled step in strategic planning, it requires changes in four key areas: the organization's leadership, rewards, policies, and structure.

Changes in strategy frequently call for changes in leadership. Each part of the organization must be led by a person with the right mix of education, experience, motivation, and attitudes for implementation. Leaders attuned to one strategy are not always the best ones to engineer dramatic change. Leadership changes are particularly important at the highest management levels because strategic direction is guided, if not also formulated, by those at the top. But despite the key importance of leadership in implementing strategic plans, it is quite difficult to identify—let alone find—the right person for the right job at the right time. This is a major problem confronting all U.S. corporations.[23,24,25] The matter is complicated, because short-term needs frequently conflict with long-term needs.

Adopting a new strategy frequently requires the organization to reconsider the way it rewards management and employee performance. Most agree that people will do what they are rewarded for doing, though theories of motivation and rewards may differ. Nevertheless, it is easy enough to think of instances when desired behavior is not rewarded properly.

In addition to change in leadership and rewards, a new strategy often requires a change in (or review of) policies. A policy is a predetermined and articulated stand on issues relevant to the organization and is intended to serve as a guide to action. Policies flow from a sense of the organization's purpose and from a philosophy of what the organization is doing. Some examples should illustrate the point. Suppose top managers decide that marketing and advertising specialists will do a more effective job in promoting the organization's products or services than field representatives. The result: a policy prohibiting field representatives from any independent, local advertising of company products or services. Another example: suppose top managers decide that employee education in electronics will improve the organization's general performance. The result could easily be a policy of reimbursing employee tuition and fees for any college courses in electronics—but not for any other subject.

When a company's grand strategy changes, all existing policies should be reviewed to ensure they are consistent with the change. Consider the examples above. If a firm decides to adopt a combination strategy—growth in the existing business and diversification into a new business—it may be necessary to rethink policies on advertising by field representatives and on employee tuition reimbursement. After all, local advertising may stimulate growth, and tuition reimbursement for courses other than electronics may help equip employees with skills they need to work effectively in a new business.

As an aid in rethinking policy, managers may draw on techniques from a specialized field of study called *policy analysis*.[26] It uses a variety of methods to examine the likely future impact on organizational performance of changes in policy. Policy analysis is closely related to another specialized field, called *evaluation research,* which examines results of policy changes on organizational performance.

A new strategy often calls for a corresponding change in the allocation of work duties and responsibilities—that is, the structure of the organization. Rhenman [27] found that the root of most problems in implementation was a structure inappropriate to support it. Chandler,[28] the first strategic planning theorist, hypothesized that structure is always an outgrowth of strategy. Research has revealed, however, that the structure existing when a new strategy is contemplated can influence what strategy is chosen.[29] One reason is that structure often determines who the strategists are. There are five general types of organizational structure: entrepreneurial, functional, divisional, project, and matrix. They form a con-

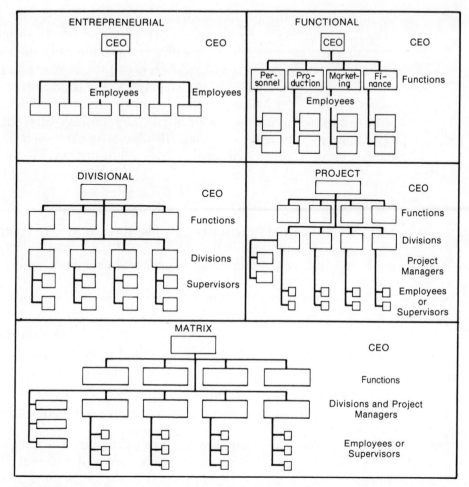

Figure 6.9 Types of organizational structure

tinuum in which the entrepreneurial is the least complex and matrix is the most (see Figure 6.9).

In an entrepreneurial structure, all employees answer to one manager. In the functional structure, managers are inserted between the top manager and employees. These managers oversee such traditional functions as personnel, finance, marketing, and operations. In the divisional structure managers, are added below functions to concentrate on some unique division of the work—for example, product or service types, geographical regions, or (in a multiservice or multiproduct corporation) the industry. In the project structure, a layer of management is added below divisions to oversee every work project from beginning to end. In matrix management, the structure is the same as in the project type, though there is one important difference: project managers are equal, not subordinate, to divisional managers.[30] There is no universally correct structure; however, some are more appropriate than others for dealing with different environments or for implementing different strategies. Dynamic environments call for a flexible structure such as project or matrix; more stable environments call for more traditional structures.

Evaluating the Strategy

Evaluation, the final step in strategic planning, is used to compare strategic results or outcomes with organizational goals and objectives. There are four basic requirements for a successful evaluation effort:

1. Managers must be motivated to evaluate. They must want to do it.
2. Some method must be devised to collect information about results.
3. The information collected must lend itself to comparison with organizational goals and objectives. The outcomes of means (strategy) have to be examined relative to ends (goals and objectives).
4. Managers must be willing to act on the results of evaluation.[2]

Much research has been devoted to evaluation of strategic planning. Several writers have shown that a dizzying array of different performance measures can be used to gauge success in the evaluation process.

How HRD Fits Into Strategic Planning

When surveyed, top managers have indicated they want proactive human resource (HR) departments capable of participating in the formulation and implementation of strategic plans.[31] There is good cause for this position: productivity leaders across industries share a tendency to handle their human resources strategically.[32] There is equally good cause for HR practitioners to pay heed: their career success may depend increasingly on their ability to think strategically, to adopt the long-term perspective of top managers. Of all HR activities, HRD efforts have the greatest potential to facilitate realization of organizational plans—but are also least likely to be used for this purpose at present. Strategic human resources development does not yet exist.

Obstacles to Linking Strategic Planning With HRD Initiatives

In recent years, much attention has been devoted to long-range and strategic planning for training departments. However, the unfortunate side effect is that such exclusive attention on planning for the HRD department implies that management of organizational learning is the prerogative of that department. Yet every HRD professional knows that this is utterly untrue: the learning process so permeates what happens in organizations that managing it is a key—if not the single key—to strategic success. Everyone shares some responsibility for the learning process, including line managers, prospective learners, and, of course, HRD professionals. HRD department plans can only grow out of learning plans for the entire organization over time and can be successful only when integrated with such other activities as recruitment, compensation, and individual career planning.

While there has been a wealth of abstract theorizing on the relationship between organizational strategic planning and planning for human resources or for training departments, there has been precious little solid research on these subjects. In fact, just a few references can encompass much of the major research.[33,34,35,36] Less theorizing and no research has been done on the more complicated issue of organizational learning.[37,38,39]

Based on the research that *has* been done, what are the major impediments to linking organizational strategic plans and long-term instructional/learning initiatives? To summarize them briefly, they include: simple ignorance of the potential strategic value of HRD efforts; the experiential nature of planning; the short-term focus of most training departments; the past-centered orientation of traditional methods of instructional planning; the possibility that instructional efforts could have a longer-term impact than organizational strategy; and, the low status of HRD professionals in the management hierarchy.[36]

Clearly, no attempt will be made to link organizational and instructional plans if decision-makers are ignorant or unconvinced of the potential benefits. Nor is such awareness likely to come from formal management education, which too often emphasizes the value of short-term results. The typical graduate business school curriculum, crucial for its role in anticipatory socialization to professional management practice, does well to offer one or two class periods on HRD in a course on human resources management. Such scant coverage of tools for organizational learning is unlikely to induce sensitivity to the issue.

Despite the wide coverage given to linkages between organizational and instructional plans in professional HR literature, many outside the HR field have never heard of the idea. As one corporate planner explained to a researcher,

> It seems the first requirement [for linking HRD and strategic plans]. . . . is a motivation to do so. I'm not sure there is a solution to lack of leadership from the top. But once your strategic goals are identified, it seems to me that it would be a simple matter to base training on them. Nobody here has thought about it.[36]

When decision-makers lack knowledge of the issue or motivation to deal with it, progress is unlikely.

Organizational strategic planning is not entirely different from learning and instruction—they are both inherently experiential and learning-oriented. Strategy-making does begin with organizational goals and objectives. But they remain tentative, not fixed in concrete, and are subject to revision as a result of unexpected external change or increased experience gained through implementation. Indeed, the process of implementation is much like that of experiential learning, because the act of grappling with problems prompts discoveries unforeseen at the time of strategy formulation.

Corporate planners are aware of this problem, even if HR practitioners are not. One told a researcher that "you can't walk through a door when you don't know where it is."[36] The point is obvious: a need is only a need when recognized. A second planner made the same point in a different way, remarking that "you can't nail Jell-o to a tree." In other words, a plan is so indefinite when initially conceptualized that there is a danger in taking it literally as given. A third planner voiced the same opinion more directly:

> Training has to be designed some time after the implementation of strategy, not in anticipation of it or concurrent with it. There is simply too much changed as a plan is being implemented. If we tried to use training as a tool for implementation, it would be a big waste of time and money.[36]

Of course, employee development and education are more long-term than training, but they too may suffer from the same problems.

HRD departments are notorious for their myopia. They tend to be driven too often by fads or products. It is not surprising that some managers persist in thinking of HRD as suitable only for quick fixes of performance problems without regard to long-term consequences.

Traditional methods for planning instruction only make matters worse. They are inherently past-oriented and centered on individuals only; rarely are they future-oriented and centered on long-term organizational change. Much of the problem can be traced to modern educational thinking, which still does not differ markedly from John Dewey's assertion in 1938 that traditional educators believe "the subject-matter of education consists of bodies of information and skills that have been worked out in the past; therefore, the chief business of the school is to transmit them to the new generation."

Commentators inside and outside the HRD field consistently criticize it for a similar stance. The real issue amounts to this: should HRD be an adaptive function or a maintenance function?[40] Maintenance activities coordinate and routinize tasks that take place inside an organization; adaptive activities help an organization adjust to conditions and changes that take place outside. When the focus of organized instruction is on socializing newcomers "to the ways things are done here" and on short-term change efforts like training, it is a maintenance function that does little more than serve as a rite of passage.[41] But when the focus is on evoking new insights and on long-term change efforts like development, it becomes an adaptive function that can prepare an entire institution to deal with demands of the future. The choice is not absolute, since both functions are appropriate at times. The problem is that HRD practitioners have rarely exercised the adaptive side of their function.

Organizational learning plans may actually have longer life spans than strategic plans. In the truest sense, of course, organizations do not learn in the same way as individuals or progress through the same developmental stages as work groups, but they are collections of people and therefore exhibit some of the same qualities that typify human existence.[38] Organizational learning really consists of two components: the aggregate knowledge, skills and abilities of people in the organization plus an institutional memory of past practices and experiences. The more that changes in strategic direction call for new knowledge, skills and abilities or for practices different from those used in the past, the more the likelihood of resistance to change. What has been learned is difficult to change in a short period of time—or even over several years.

Finally, HRD professionals rarely enjoy the high status associated with the top management team that is primarily responsible for organizational strategy formulation. More often, HRD practitioners report to Vice Presidents of Personnel or their equivalents. One result is to interpose an information filter—the personnel executive—between key strategists and HRD. At best, this information filter buffers contradictory signals about desirable instructional initiatives for the training department; at worst, it reduces or even distorts information about long-term organizational goals and plans. As a result, those best able to provide consultation to others about the issue of learning are excluded from participation in strategy formulation. This means that the elements of human potential, ability, and motivation are utterly left out of corporate plans. Perhaps even worse, strategists have not tapped the skills of their in-house experts on group facilitation, whose talents could work wonders.[42]

There are thus formidable impediments to linking organizational and instructional initiatives. The challenge facing present and future HRD practitioners is clear: to overcome these impediments and others.

Overcoming the Obstacles

It is most unlikely that future decision-makers will enjoy more stable external environments. Indeed, just the opposite is true. As the basis of the economy moves away from manufacturing and toward information processing, a central problem will be how to increase the speed and effectiveness with which technological and informational advances can be translated into the workplace. Overcoming traditional resistance to change is likely to emerge as a key problem of this decade. A possible solution lies in future-oriented instruction, planned over the long term and intended to deal simultaneously with needs and their implications for job transfer. Along the way, HRD practitioners *and* line managers will have to rethink what they are doing.

First, HRD people will have to take the lead in educating and informing others of potential roles in strategic planning that can be played by training, employee education, and development. They can do so by circulating professional literature to raise consciousness, by gaining visibility through seminars on strategic planning and on HRD, by successfully facilitating the start-up of strategic planning in organizations that have not formally practiced it, and by setting an example so that others can see the differences between short-term, medium-term, and long-term employee improvement efforts.

It is true that HRD practitioners cannot do everything themselves. But they can do what they presumably do best: serve as change agents, performance engineers, and learning facilitators. To overcome simple ignorance of the value of HRD as a strategic tool, they need to raise the issue and provide information; to overcome lack of motivation, they need to use the best available evaluative data to point out benefits of adopting a long-range view of human development and organizational learning.

Second, the experiential nature of strategic planning is less an impediment than an opportunity to link it to HRD. Assume that adult identity stems from experience and that organizations change what they do based on experience. Further assume that John Dewey was right when he said:

> We always live at the time we live and not at some other time, and only by extracting at each present time the full meaning of each present experience are we prepared for doing the same thing in the future.[43]

Is it not possible to simulate in the present likely future external conditions that will be encountered by the organization, work groups, individuals, and job incumbents? If experience, which is inherently past-oriented, is one key to learning, then why not simulate likely conditions of the future to produce artificial experience?

The benefits of this approach should be apparent. If people define their learning needs based on experience, then won't they do a better job of it when they have experienced future possibilities first-hand? Experiential exercises can be developed for this purpose. They may, of course, include simulations, games, case studies, critical incidents, and roleplays. While there is always danger that forecasts of the future will be mistaken, there is an equal and perhaps greater danger in encouraging the unspoken assumption that the future will be the same as the more certain present or past.

Third, the notorious myopia of training departments is not an uncorrectable condition. HRD practitioners are short-sighted because they are rewarded for it by those who have never thought of an alternative. As experts on human performance, HRD practitioners should take the lead in pointing out the implications of reward systems within which they function and suggesting alternatives more likely to produce favorable long-term outcomes.[44]

Fourth, the past-centered orientation of instructional planning is an impediment that can be overcome by placing traditional needs assessment information in a larger context. Popular approaches, such as performance and competency analysis (described in Chapter 13), can serve to identify present organizational strengths and weaknesses. The traditional results of instructional needs assessment information should be paired with what is expected in the future so that activities become adaptive-oriented and thus capable of facilitating organizational learning. Quite apart from identifying learning needs, such analysis is a basis for examining how well the strategic planning process itself is being implemented. In this sense, HRD practitioners are able to function as strategy analysts and engineers.

Fifth, it is probably true that organizational learning has a life span longer than that of strategic plans—even 20-year plans. After all, individuals can work in organizations for 30 years or more without significantly altering what they have learned through cultural immersion during those years. Yet there is a common link between organizational learning and planning: both are influenced by life cycle. Just as learning interests for individuals are influenced by their central life concerns and crises in each developmental stage, so learning interests for organizations are influenced by their stage of development. What we need is more information about what kinds of long-term learning strategies work best in different organizational stages.

Finally, it is also probably true that HRD professionals rarely enjoy direct participation in formulating organizational strategy. As a result, the element of human potential is often missing in long-term plans. While participation might be a goal for which practitioners can strive, it is not essential for linking organizational and instructional initiatives. In fact, HRD planning can be conducted apart from strategic planning. HRD people need only show that strategic plans imply the need for knowledge, skills, and abilities that must be acquired over time. When decision-makers understand that, they will begin to see the advantage of establishing long-term learning plans.

No longer can HRD professionals remain complacent, assuming that methods used in the past will serve them in the future. No longer can they assume—or buy into the expectations of others—that their efforts are only quick fixes for removing immediate skill or knowledge deficiencies. They must, instead, master strategic thinking and begin to focus on facilitating organizational as much as individual learning. As they do so, the value of their efforts will become increasingly obvious.

References

1. Naisbitt, J. *Megatrends.* New York: Ballantine, 1983.

2. Glueck, W., and L. Jauch. *Business Policy and Strategic Management,* 4th ed. New York: McGraw-Hill, 1984.

3. "Members Want to Know." *Management Review* 71 (1982) 8: p. 36.

4. Naylor, T. "Effective Use of Strategic Planning, Forecasting and Modeling in the Executive Suite." *Managerial Planning* 30 (1982) 4: pp. 4–11.

5. Schumpeter, J. *Capitalism, Socialism and Democracy.* London: Allen and Unwin, 1943.

6. Mandt, E. "The Failure of Business Education—and What to Do About It." *Management Review* 71 (1982) 8: pp. 47–52.

7. Gluck, F. "Vision and Leadership in Corporate Strategy." In *Strategic Planning: Concepts and Implementation,* J. Ryans, Jr. and W. Shanklin, eds. New York: Random House, 1985.

8. Follett, M. *Creative Experience.* London: Longman, Green & Co., 1924.

9. Parsons, T. *Structure and Process in Modern Societies.* New York: The Free Press, 1960.

10. Georgiou, P. "The Goal Paradigm and Notes Toward a Counter Paradigm." *Administrative Science Quarterly* 18 (1973) 3: pp. 291–310.

11. Hall, R. *Organizations: Structure and Process,* 2nd ed. Englewood Cliffs, NJ: Prentice-Hall, 1977.

12. Emery, F., and E. Trist. "The Causal Texture of Organizational Environments." *Human Relations* 18 (1965): pp. 21–32.

13. Starling, G. *The Changing Environment of Business: A Managerial Approach,* 2nd ed. Boston: Kent Publishing, 1984.

14. Staw, B. "Knee-Deep in the Big Muddy." *Organizational Behavior and Human Performance* 16 (1976) 1: pp. 27–44.

15. Levinson, H. *Organizational Diagnosis.* Cambridge, MA: Harvard University Press, 1972.

16. Hornstein, H., and N. Tichy. *Organization Diagnosis and Improvement Strategies.* New York: Behavioral Science Associates, 1973.

17. Nadler, D., and M. Tushman. "A Diagnostic Model for Organizational Behavior." In *Perspectives on Behavior in Organizations,* J. R. Hackman, E. E. Lawler and L. W. Porter, eds. New York: McGraw-Hill, 1977.

18. Weisbord, M. "Organizational Diagnosis: Six Places to Look for Trouble With or Without a Theory. *Group and Organization Studies* 1 (1976): pp. 430–447.

19. Jaques, E. *Timespan Handbook*. London: Heinemann, 1964.

20. Glueck, W., and L. Jauch. *Business Policy and Strategic Management*, 4th ed. New York: McGraw-Hill, 1984.

21. Haney, W. *Communication and Organizational Behavior*. Homewood, IL: Richard Irwin, 1973.

22. March, J., and H. Simon. *Organizations*. New York: Wiley, 1958.

23. Gerstein, M., and H. Reisman. "Strategic Selection: Matching Executives to Business Conditions." *Sloan Management Review* 24 (1983) 2: pp. 33–49.

24. "Wanted: A Manager to Fit Each Strategy." *Business Week* (Feb. 25, 1980): pp. 166–173.

25. "What's Wrong With Management?" *Dun's Business Month* 119 (1982) 4: pp. 48–52.

26. Stokey, E., and R. Zeckhauser. *A Primer for Policy Analysis*. New York: W. W. Norton, 1978.

27. Rhenman, E. *Organization Theory for Long Range Planning*. New York: Wiley-Interscience, 1973.

28. Chandler, A. *Strategy and Structure: Chapters in the History of American Industrial Enterprise*. Cambridge, MA: Massachusetts Institute of Technology, 1962.

29. Galbraith, J., and D. Nathanson. "The Role of Organizational Structure and Process in Strategy Implementation." In *Strategic Management*, D. Schendel and C. Hofer, eds. Boston: Little, Brown & Co., 1979.

30. Davis, S., and P. Lawrence. *Matrix*. Reading, MA: Addison-Wesley, 1977.

31. Foltz, R., K. Rosenberg, and J. Foehrenbach. "Senior Management Views the Human Resource Function." *Personnel Administrator* 27 (1982) 9: pp. 37–51.

32. Misa, K., and T. Stein. "Strategic HRM and the Bottom Line." *Personnel Administrator 28 (1983) 10: pp. 27–30.*

33. Devanna, M., C. Fombrun, N. Tichy, and E. Warren. *Study of Human Resource Management Issues in Strategy Formulation and Strategy Implementation*. Unpublished manuscript, 1981.

34. Fombrun, C., N. Tichy, and M. Devanna, eds. *Strategic Human Resource Management*. New York, Wiley, 1984.

35. Nininger, J. *Managing Human Resources: A Strategic Perspective*. Ottowa: The Conference Board of Canada, 1982.

36. Rothwell, W. *Management Training in Support of Organizational Strategic Planning in Twelve Illinois Organizations*. Unpublished doctoral dissertation, University of Illinois, Urbana-Champaign, 1985.

37. Argyris, C., and D. Schön. *Organizational Learning: A Theory of Action Perspective*. Reading, MA: Addison-Wesley, 1978.

38. Bedeian, A. *Organizations: Theory and Analysis,* 2nd ed. Chicago: Dryden, 1984.

39. March, J., and J. Olsen. "The Uncertainty of the Past: Organizational Learning Under Ambiguity." *European Journal of Political Research* 3 (1975) 160ff.

40. Katz, D., and R. Kahn. *The Social Psychology of Organizations,* 2nd ed. New York: Wiley, 1978.

41. Belasco, J., and H. Trice. *The Assessment of Change in Training and Therapy.* New York: McGraw-Hill, 1969.

42. Hulett, D., and J. Renjilian. "Strategic Planning Demystified." In *Organization Development: Present Practice and Future Needs,* S. Sherwood, ed. Washington: American Society for Training and Development, 1983.

43. Dewey, J. *Experience and Education.* New York: Collier Books, 1971, p. 49. (Reprint of 1938 edition.)

44. Lawler, E. "The Strategic Design of Reward Systems." In *Strategic Human Resource Management,* C. Fombrun, N. Tichy and M. Devanna, eds. New York: Wiley, 1984.

For More Information

Abell, D. *Defining the Business: The Starting Point of Strategic Planning.* Englewood Cliffs, NJ: Prentice-Hall, 1980.

Ackoff, R. *Creating the Corporate Future: Plan or Be Planned For.* New York: Wiley, 1981.

Bell, D. *The Coming of Post-Industrial Society.* New York: Basic Books, 1973.

Buchele, R. (1962). "How to Evaluate a Firm." *California Management Review* (1962): pp. 5–17.

Burke, W. *Organization Development: Principles and Practices.* Boston: Little Brown, 1982.

Cathcart, J. "How to Conduct a Strategic Planning Retreat." *Training and Development Journal* 40 (1985) 5: pp. 63–67.

Chatov, R. "The Role of Ideology in the American Corporation." In *The Corporate Dilemma,* D. Votaw and S. Sethi, eds. Englewood Cliffs, NJ: Prentice-Hall, 1973.

Hill, R., and J. Hlavacek. "Learning from Failure." *California Management Review,* 19 (1977) 4: pp. 5–16.

Latham, G. "The Appraisal System as a Strategic Control." In *Strategic Human Resource Management,* C. Fomsrun, N. Tichy, and M. Devanna, eds. New York: Wiley, 1984.

Mason, R., and E. Mitroff. *Challenging Strategic Planning Assumptions.* New York: Wiley, 1981.

Mintzberg, H. "Organizational Power and Goals: A Skeletal Theory." In *Strategic Management: A New View of Business Policy and Planning,* C. Hofer and D. Schendel, eds. Boston: Little Brown, 1979.

Nolan, J. *Management Audit.* Radnor, PA: Chilton Book Co., 1984.

O'Connor, R. *Company Planning Meetings.* New York: The Conference Board, 1980.

Pastin, M. "The Fallacy of Long Range Thinking." *Training,* 23 (1986) 5: pp. 47–53.

Rowe, A., R. Mason, and K. Dickel. *Strategic Management: A Methodological Approach.* Reading, MA: Addison-Wesley, 1986.

Ryans, J., Jr., and W. Shanklin. *Strategic Planning: Concepts and Implementation.* New York: Random House, 1985.

Sashkin, M. "True Vision in Leadership." *Training and Development Journal* 40 (1986) 5: pp. 58–62.

Shallcross, D. "Creativity: Everybody's Business." *Personnel and Guidance Journal* 51 (1973): pp. 623–626.

Steiner, G., H. Kunin, and E. Kunin. "Formal Strategic Planning in the United States Today." *Long Range Planning* 16 (1983) 3: pp. 12–17.

Suchman, E. *Evaluative Research.* New York: Russell Sage Foundation, 1965.

Thierauf, R. *Management Auditing: A Questionnaire Approach.* New York: Amacom, 1980.

Toffler, A. *The Third Wave.* New York: William Morrow, 1980.

Utterback, J. "Environmental Analysis and Forecasting." In *Strategic Management,* D. Schendel and C. Hofer, eds. Boston: Little, Brown & Co, 1979.

Zemke, R. "Stalking the Elusive Corporate Credo." *Training* (June 1985): pp. 44–51.

CHAPTER 7

Human resources planning.

This chapter describes human resources planning as it relates to strategic planning and HRD. A strategic plan serves as a guide for the long-term direction of an organization. Implementing this plan requires the organization to marshal and deploy its resources, both human and financial. Human resources planning (HRP) is intended to ensure that the right people with the right skills are on hand at the right time to facilitate implementation of strategy.

HRP integrates all HR activities with overall strategic plans and coordinates such different activities as hiring, promotion, and training. Much has been written about it. However, there is not much evidence from the real world that human resources are actually being planned for in any systematic and comprehensive way by a majority of the largest corporations, much less the small ones.[1] ■

What Is Human Resources Planning?

Recent years have seen an explosion of interest in human resources planning. Numerous academic and professional articles and several books have dealt with the subject. What accounts for such intense attention to HRP? There are several possible answers to this question, including:

1. *The crucial importance of HRP.* An organization's long-term success depends largely on its collective human skills, talents, and performance. Leadership is particularly important.

2. *The difficulty of HRP.* Planning for the long-term use and development of people is not as easy as planning for production, finance, or marketing. Individuals affect plans made about them and, indeed, must participate in the planning process if they are to be committed to realizing the goals and objectives of the plan.

3. *The pervasiveness of HRP.* Unlike plans for other business functions, HRP pervades an entire organization. It is not the sole responsibility of the personnel or human resources department. Instead, everyone has a part in establishing future goals and in helping implement them.

U.S. organizations lag far behind the Japanese and West Germans in systematic planning for human resources.

Despite obvious interest in the subject and the existence of a professional society and journals devoted exclusively to HRP, there is no agreement on a single definition of HRP. One study of this issue uncovered more than 20 definitions and 25 models of HRP.[2] At this writing, the number of definitions and models has more than doubled. In this respect, HRP is like HRD: both have been treated in so many ways that simple definitions have become elusive.

Generally speaking, HRP consists of translating organizational plans at various levels into HR plans that guide long-term acquisition, use, and development of employees. Some believe that this has emerged as one of the most important current challenges facing organizations.

HRP is needed in order to:

• *Integrate HR initiatives and organizational plans.* Implementing a strategic plan requires the right kinds of people. Unless organizational and HR plans are integrated, personnel initiatives may retard or even block those of the organization.

• *Integrate HR initiatives horizontally.* There is strong interdependency among such typical HR activities as recruitment, selection, orientation, training, development, education, compensation, benefits, labor relations, and employee appraisal. Without integration of these initiatives, one HR activity can retard, impede, or completely block others.[3]

A Model of HRP

While there are many models of HRP, most require:

1. The integration of HRP and strategic planning.
2. Analysis of future HR demands.
3. Analysis of HR supplies.
4. Analysis of environmental trends and conditions likely to affect the availability of HR supplies.
5. Comparisons of HR demands and anticipated supplies.
6. Action to match HR demands and supplies.
7. Evaluation of plans and results.

This process is depicted in Figure 7.1.

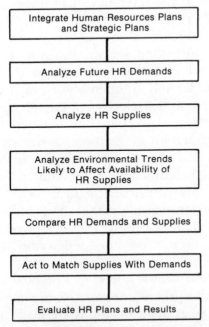

Figure 7.1 A model of human resources planning

There are other ways to conceptualize HRP. Alpander,[4] for example, distinguishes between long-term and short-term HR plans. A long-term (or strategic) HRP focuses on relating the organization's environment to personnel policies. A short-term (or operational) HRP focuses instead on such daily concerns as what individual will be promoted into what job or will be transferred geographically. An alternative is to distinguish between technical and management plans. A technical plan compares HR supplies and demands; a management plan identifies ways to coordinate organizational activities to close the gap between supplies and demands.

HR planning methods differ in much the same ways as strategic planning methods. A top-down approach ignores individuals and work groups, concentrating instead on the collective HR needs of an entire organization over time. A bottom-up approach analyzes individual and work group needs to derive HR objectives for the organization. A negotiated approach synthesizes specific needs of individuals and work groups with the collective HR needs of the organization.[5]

Key Steps in Human Resources Planning

Integrating HRP and Strategic Planning

The first step in HRP is to integrate it with strategic planning. Despite its importance, this step may be the most neglected in actual practice. For example, research by English[6] revealed that fewer than 10 percent of large companies establish HR plans before or at the same time as business plans. Walker[7] lamented the attitude of managers who think that integration is unnecessary because talented people are always available externally. He also criticized the tendency of business planners to devote all their attention to finance and marketing while leaving their personnel counterparts to remain ignorant of long-range corporate objectives. Lorange and Murphy[8] identified specific integration problems: insufficient information on which to base promotion decisions; frustration among managers about incentive and compensation practices; limited participation of HR professionals in the selection of the top management team; and little interaction between corporate and personnel planners.

Much of what has been written on integration consists of exhorting HR professionals to make the attempt. It is considered one way to upgrade the status of the personnel function. Some contend that a key difference between successful and unsuccessful firms is the ability to deal with human resource issues strategically rather than focus exclusively on short-term issues of individual selection, training, promotion, appraisal, and job design.[9] Numerous case studies describe attempts by various firms to integrate HRP and strategic planning.[10,11,12,13]

Unfortunately, however, there is little agreement on how to go about such integration. A method that works in one organization may not work in another, largely because most strategic decisions are made and implemented informally.[14] Differences in organizational cultures and management values require tailor-made approaches in each setting.

Despite these complications, it is possible to suggest ways to approach integration effectively:

1. Examine the purpose of the organization.[15] In what ways can the personnel or HR function contribute to this purpose? Is HR mentioned in any formal purpose statement of the organization?

2. Include HR issues in the strategic planning process.[13] During organizational planning, have guidelines been established for recruitment, training, performance appraisal, and other HR functions?

3. Consider strategic plans in personnel initiatives. Before taking action, do personnel professionals at least check what they propose to do against strategic objectives?

4. Build communication links between organizational and HR planning functions. Do corporate and personnel planners talk to each other? How can the amount and quality of their interaction be improved?

Walker [7] provides a checklist of other issues to consider in improving the integration of strategic and HR planning.

Predicting Future Human Resource Demands

The second step in HRP is to forecast the numbers and kinds of people who will probably be needed by the organization in the future. This issue has attracted more attention than any other in HRP. Indeed, some have suggested that forecasting is the key component of HRP.

There are two major problems associated with this step: first, identifying a predictor of HR demands; second, conducting the forecasting process itself.

To analyze future HR demands, planners need some way to correlate numbers of employees and amounts of work load or work outputs. Several variables have been used or suggested:

1. *Historic variables.* Planners know how many employees the organization has and what production levels they have achieved. If production must be increased by 50 percent, for example, then staffing should be increased by that amount.

2. *Intuitive variables.* Planners survey managers, who estimate intuitively how many people they will need to produce at a given level.

3. *Productivity variables.* Using historical data, planners forecast future productivity per worker and then divide output by a productivity index.[16]

4. *Time-series variables.* Historical staffing levels are adjusted to take seasonal and cyclical trends into account.[17]

Unfortunately, not one of these methods is totally satisfactory. Historic variables do not consider the potential of existing staff to improve their productivity. Intuitive variables are just guesses prone to overestimation or underestimation. Productivity variables do not necessarily include limits on growth. Time-series variables are prone to miscalculation. Even worse, all these variables concentrate attention on numbers of people rather than on their skills, and on past history rather than on work outputs under uncertain future conditions.

Methods of conducting the forecasting process are quite advanced in theory but not in practice. They include:

1. *Regression analysis.* Planners use statistical techniques to correlate numbers of employees and quantities of work.

2. *Linear programming.* Planners use specialized mathematical techniques to determine the optimal solution to a complex problem. The focus is on personnel changes that must be made to achieve certain objectives, given identified constraints. It is a powerful approach though not commonly used. Its focus also tends to be more short-term than long-term.

3. *Judgmental approaches.* Planners can use delphi analysis, curve fitting, and other social science approaches to supplement statistical methods with expert opinions.

Rarely is an attempt made to identify skills or knowledge needed by people to deal with future conditions that might be quite different from current conditions.

Analyzing Human Resource Supplies

The third step in HRP is to analyze the current work force of the organization. At this point, planners should consider how well future demands can be met with people already in the organization. There are two approaches: static models and flow models.

A static model is comparable to an accountant's balance sheet. It represents current human resources at one point in time. There are two types:

1. *Succession charts,* which depict the readiness of employees for promotion. Such charts are most commonly used for the highest management levels, but they can be developed for all but entry-level jobs in an organization.
2. *Skill inventories,* which list the known abilities of every employee. Hundreds of items can be cross-referenced, including prior work experience, education, training, knowledge of foreign languages, publications, hobbies or interests, and career aspirations.

Though static models were once quite popular, they have not been successful. Succession charts have limited use because they tend to be largely subjective; skill inventories, despite widespread interest in the 1960s, have proven to be unwieldy and are not utilized as much as they could be.[7]

A flow model is much like an accountant's income statement. It represents expected changes or human resource movements over time. There are, after all, only six possible changes that an individual can make: in, out, up, down, across, or grow in an existing job by improved performance, behavior, knowledge, or skills. Markov or semi-Markov analysis is used in flow modeling.[18] The basic idea of Markov analysis is to estimate probabilities that employees will remain in their present positions or will move to new positions. Historical data can provide some guidance in estimating these probabilities, but accuracy can be improved by using expert opinion to supplement the historical data.

Substantial progress has been made in analyzing expected future HR supplies. Sophisticated computer simulations can even be used to assess the potential impact of changes in personnel policies. Such simulations are costly, however, and still out of reach for all but large organizations. Microcomputers and HRP software may in time make such simulations affordable for even small firms.

Analyzing Environmental Trends

The fourth step in HRP is to analyze external environmental trends likely to affect the future availability of HR supplies. At this point, planners should consider how well future HR demands can be met by the external labor market. This step has particular importance when there is a significant discrepancy between supplies available internally and expected future demands. For example: when AT&T was forced to divest, an entirely new breed of profit-oriented management talent was needed. It was not available internally because the firm had been so heavily regulated.[19]

Few firms have the resources needed to keep track effectively of variables affecting the entire external U.S. labor market. The Bureau of Labor Statistics (BLS) publishes an *Occupational Outlook Quarterly* and other publications that some consider useful. Unfortunately, BLS assumptions may not bear up for the needs of one firm in one area and would not, in any case, help multinationals dealing across national boundaries.

The external supply of labor depends on such variables as:

- *Fluctuations in the business cycle.* As the nation enters a recession, unemployment increases. The external supply of labor, viewed in the aggregate, is relatively plentiful. As the nation enters a recovery, unemployment decreases, and the external supply of labor grows more scarce. The problem is that increases in unemployment are not uniform: for example, white-collar workers are less prone to layoff than skilled or unskilled production labor. Even in the depths of a recession, some labor shortages in special occupations remain acute.

- *Social trends and attitudes.* Depending on the mood of the nation, people can be more or less inclined to work in certain occupations or for certain companies. During the Vietnam war many talented college students avoided academic majors in business because many leading corporations were so closely associated with the "atrocities" of the military-industrial complex. During the 1980s college students are favoring preparation in relatively high-paid occupations like business, accounting, engineering, or computer science over low-paid but socially desirable occupations like teaching.

- *Demographic trends.* The availability of labor is obviously influenced by birthrates. Between 1946 and 1964, one-third of the present U.S. population was born.[20] It was the largest generation in history, and its age cohorts are already in the labor market. Employers have grown to expect a relatively plentiful supply of college-educated labor. However, birthrates declined after 1964 and the participation rate of young people in college has slipped as well. The number of young people entering college is expected to plummet by as much as 25 percent between 1985 and 1992.

Other variables influence availability of labor—including geographical movements of business, technological innovations, and employee satisfaction levels that affect turnover.

Comparing HR Demands and Supplies

The fifth step in HRP is to compare HR demands and supplies. At this point, planners determine how well present HR inventories match up to what will be needed in the future. From this comparison they can then begin to weigh alternative methods—that is, initiatives of the personnel department and other departments—to meet HR demands.

Despite the obvious importance of this step, little guidance is available from published sources about how to make the comparison. What evidence exists suggests that few, if any, organizations use a comprehensive approach to establish separate yet coordinated objectives for different HR activities. As a result, the horizontal integration of such different functions as recruitment, selection, training, and appraisal does not exist.

Acting to Match HR Supplies with Demands

The sixth step in HRP is to take action to match HR supplies and demands. It is to HRP what implementation is to strategic planning. Yet it is obvious that, without being preceded by a systematic and comprehensive comparison of HR supplies and demands, this step—crucial as it is—is unlikely to be successful.

The range of possible HR actions is staggering to contemplate. (Look at Figure 7.2, which represents areas included in the HR function.) Consider:

- Changes in organizational or work group structure or job design can alter HR supplies and demand by reallocating work duties, thus meeting some old HR demands while creating new ones.
- Changes in HRP itself can alter how the organization assesses its HR supplies and demands. The result: new definitions and thus new ways of looking at old issues.
- Changes in selection practices can affect how the organization meets

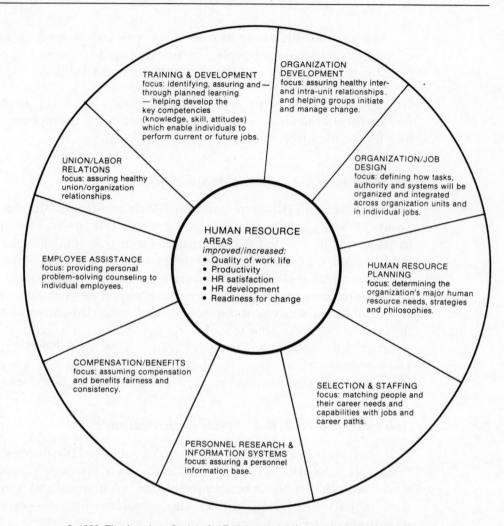

Figure 7.2 The human resource wheel   (*Source: Models for Excellence.*)

its HR needs by changing the basis on which people are hired, promoted, demoted, or transferred.

- Changes in personnel research and information systems can affect amounts and kinds of data that managers can use to identify and cope with problems of HR supplies and demands.

- Changes in compensation and benefits can affect employee turnover, retention, and behavior, thus affecting HR supplies and demands.

- Changes in employee assistance programs can affect individual, and through it organizational, performance. The result can be changes in HR supplies and demands through changes in individual productivity.
- Changes in union/labor relations practices can affect how well the organization functions. Labor contracts can influence HR supplies and demands by limiting management prerogatives on employee selection, retention, promotion, transfer—and, of course, compensation.
- Changes in training, education, and development can affect individual productivity on a present job or in preparation for a future one. The result: possible change in HR supplies and demand.
- The introduction of organization development programs can affect how people in the organization adapt to pressures inside and outside and how well work groups interact. The result: possible changes in HR supplies and demand.

Any of these areas can furnish tools for altering existing HR supplies or for meeting HR demands. However, none of these actions taken individually can solve all supply and demand problems. For example, changing compensation and reward practices will work only if employees value the rewards, have the skills to perform well enough to achieve them, and believe that there is some reasonable chance they can actually attain what they want.

Matters are complicated further in two respects: changes in any area of the HR wheel will affect all other areas to some extent; and, the scope and time frames of change efforts can vary.

The activities of the HR wheel are interdependent. Suppose that the structure of an entire organization is changed. The effect will be much like tugging on one strand of a spider web—the entire web will vibrate. For instance:

1. A reorganization will change reporting relationships, tasks, roles, work groups, and even individual jobs. There will be a major shift in how the work is allocated, with a corresponding change in the distribution of human resources. New work demands will be created while old ones are given up.

2. A reorganization will change HR planning methods. Historical data on staffing levels will become useless under new conditions without precedent.

3. A reorganization will affect selection and staffing because the nature of jobs, work groups, reporting relationships, and other matters will change. New managers, created by the reallocation of duties, may not have the same values and expectations as their predecessors.

As these changes are felt, they will create others. The initial effects of a reorganization will produce many side effects. These can include a fundamental shift in perceptions about quality of work life, levels of productivity and employee satisfaction, appropriate employee development activities, and degrees of readiness for change. The result: a dramatic alteration in HR supplies and demands under radically new conditions.

The scope and time frame of change efforts also can differ, which will in turn influence the extent of changes in HR supplies and demands. Look at Figure 7.3, which depicts the hierarchy of plans. Consider:

• Changes in organizational strategic plans will affect long-term, intermediate-term, and short-term HR initiatives. When a new strategy is adopted, new HR demands are created and the value of existing supplies is changed.

Figure 7.3 The hierarchy of plans

- Changes in coordinative plans will affect HRP at all levels. When a middle manager adopts a new approach in interactions with others, the effects are subtle but still affect the entire organization.

- Changes in operational plans will affect HRP at all levels but primarily at the operational level. How a field supervisor approaches tasks and deals with employees will have an effect, but it will be very subtle and its impact primarily short-term.

The range of potential HR actions that can be taken to match supplies and demands is thus quite broad. Because one change can affect conditions in all HR areas, coordination of efforts is vital. However, there is little evidence that such coordination is either achieved or even attempted in most organizations.

Evaluating HR Plans and Results

The seventh and final step in HRP is to evaluate HR plans and results. At this point, planners take stock of how well plans are being implemented or have been implemented. As might be expected, evaluation can scarcely be successful if nobody has considered alternatives, established objectives for each area of the HR wheel, or taken action to coordinate and integrate HR activities.

There are two approaches to evaluating HRP: first, by dollar value; second, by managerial judgment.

The dollar-value approach places a so-called "bottom-line figure" on HR initiatives—that is, compares the cost of taking action to solve a problem (i.e., an HR initiative) with the cost of not taking action. If the difference results in a net savings, the HR action is or was justified; if the difference results in a net loss, the HR action is or was unjustified. This method can be used to weigh alternative change efforts before action or convince hard-nosed managers that past actions were not just expensive boondoggles. Various methods for utilizing the dollar-value approach have been suggested.[21,22,23]

The managerial approach compares results with intentions. Of course, it can only be used when:

1. The desired outcomes have been specified in advance.
2. There is some way to assess outcomes.
3. Managers will value results.

4. Results are linked to what managers value—strategic plans or individual intentions, for example.

Relatively little has been written about the managerial approach to evaluating HRP—probably because HR professionals are more worried about demonstrating the bottom-line value of their efforts than they are about whether the results matched up to intentions.

How HRP Relates to HRD

Human resources planning is best understood as a process in which an organization's present HR supplies are compared with its expected future needs and actions are taken over time to narrow any gaps. HRP is thus quite broad, encompassing any and all activities on the HR wheel (Figure 7.2). In contrast, human resources development (HRD) refers to organized learning experiences sponsored by an employer and designed and/ or conducted in the work setting for the purpose of improving work performance while emphasizing the betterment of the human condition through integration of organizational goals and individual needs. It is narrower than HRP and consists of:

- *Training,* focused on job tasks in the present.
- *Education,* focused on individual preparation for advancement.
- *Development,* focused on the individual as a vehicle for organizational learning.

These HRD activities can change existing HR supply and demand relationships by furnishing individuals with new skills, knowledge, behaviors, and insights that they can use to improve work performance and thus work output.

Any HRP action can affect HRD efforts; any HRD action can affect HR supplies and demands and, through them, HRP. To elaborate:

1. A change in organizational, work group, or job design will create learning needs. When the allocation of job duties changes, individuals must acquire a new repertoire of skills to do the work and interact with other people in new social groupings. Training may be needed.

2. A change in selection and staffing practices will also create learning needs. The skills, knowledge, and abilities of people entering or advancing in the organization will affect what they need in their present training and future education and development.

3. A change in personnel research and information systems will probably produce new learning needs as well. The quality and quantity of data collected about human performance and satisfaction will affect identification of areas in which new skills, knowledge, or behaviors are needed.

4. A change in compensation and benefit practices will influence employee motivation and, through it, learning needs. Such a change will affect the motivation of people to perform and learn how to improve their performance.

5. A change in employee assistance programs will influence learning needs by changing individual perceptions of self and others. As a result, individuals will need to approach job task and interpersonal relations in new ways. This may require training.

6. Changes in union/labor relations practices will influence the work setting and, through it, change conditions in which learning occurs and the job tasks and interpersonal relations of individual employees. The result can be new learning needs.

7. Changes in training, education, and development practices will alter individual knowledge, skills, attitudes, and (potentially) job performance. The result: new learning needs for supervisors and even co-workers who deal with individuals who have developed a new awareness of self, others, and job tasks. New HR supplies and demands for the organization may also be a result.

8. Changes in organization development practices will create the need for new interpersonal skills in dealing with self, members of an individual's work group, and members of other work groups. Training, education, and development are tools for furnishing such skills and reinforcing large- and small-scale OD interventions.

While this is a rather simplistic summary, it demonstrates that HRD efforts can play an important role in reinforcing HRP initiatives. At the same time, planned learning experiences will change an organization's supply and demand relationships in the present and future.

References

1. Nkomo, S. "The Theory and Practice of HR Planning: The Gap Still Remains." *Personnel Administrator* 31 (1986) 8: pp. 71–73,75–76,78–80,83–84.

2. Milkovich, G., L. Dyer, and T. Mahoney. "HRM Planning." In *Human Resource Management in the 1980s,* S. Carroll and R. Schuler, eds. Washington, D.C.: Bureau of National Affairs, 1983.

3. Alpander, G. *Human Resource Management Planning.* New York: Amacom, 1982.

4. Ibid.

5. Milkovich, G., and T. Mahoney. "Human Resources Planning and Personnel Administration and Industrial Relations Policy." In *ASPA Handbook of Personnel and Industrial Relations,* D. Yoder and H. Heneman, Jr., eds. Washington, D.C.: Bureau of National Affairs, 1979.

6. English, J. "Human Resource Planning: The Ideal Versus the Real." *Human Resource Planning* 7 (1984) 2: pp. 67–72.

7. Walker, J. *Human Resource Planning.* New York: McGraw-Hill, 1980.

8. Lorange, P., and D. Murphy. "Strategy and Human Resources: Concepts and Practice." *Human Resource Management* 22 (Spring-Summer, 1983): pp. 111–135.

9. Misa, K., and T. Stein. "Strategic HRM and the Bottom Line." *Personnel Administrator* 28 (1983) 10: pp. 27–30.

10. Baytos, L. "A 'No Frills' Approach to Human Resource Planning." *Human Resource Planning* 7 (1984): pp. 39–46.

11. Bright, W. "How One Company Manages Its Human Resources." In *The Challenge of Human Resource Planning: Selected Readings,* J. Walker and K. Price, eds. New York: The Human Resource Planning Society, 1982.

12. Cashel, W. "Human Resources Planning in the Bell System." In *The Challenge of Human Resource Planning: Selected Readings,* J. Walker and K. Price, eds. New York: The Human Resource Planning Society, 1982.

13. Dyer, L. "Studying Human Resource Strategy: An Approach and an Agenda." *Industrial Relations* 23 (Spring, 1984): pp. 156–169.

14. Dyer, L. "Bringing Human Resources into the Strategy Formulation Process." *Human Resource Management* 22 (Fall, 1983): pp. 257–271.

15. Gould, R. "Gaining Competitive Edge Through Human Resource Strategies." *Human Resource Planning* 6 (1984) 2: pp. 83–94.

16. Wikstrom, W. *Manpower Planning: Evolving Systems.* New York: The Conference Board, 1971.

17. Burack, E., and N. Mathys. *Human Resource Planning: A Pragmatic Approach to Staffing and Development.* Lake Forest, IL: Brace-Park Press, 1980.

18. Stewman, S. "Markov and Renewal Models for Total Manpower System." *Omega* 6 (1978): pp. 341–351.

19. Tichy, N., C. Fombrun, and M. Devanna. "Strategic Human Resource Management." *Sloan Management Review* (Winter, 1982): pp. 47–61.

20. Jones, L. *Great Expectations: America and the Baby Boom Generation.* New York: Ballantine, 1980.

21. Cascio, W. *Costing Human Resources: The Financial Impact of Behavior in Organizations.* Boston: Kent Publishing, 1982.

22. Flamholtz, E., and R. Kaumeyer. "Human Resource Replacement Cost Information and Personnel Decisions." *Human Resource Planning* 3 (1980) 2: pp. 111–138.

23. Lapointe, J. "Human Resource Performance Indexes." *Personnel Journal* 62 (July, 1983): pp. 545–553.

For More Information

Bennison, M., and J. Casson. *The Manpower Planning Handbook.* London: McGraw-Hill, 1984.

Craft, I. "A Critical Perspective on Human Resource Planning." *Human Resource Planning* 3 (1980) 2: pp. 39–52.

Director, S. *Strategic Planning for Human Resources.* New York: Pergamon Press, 1985.

Edwards, I., C. Leek, R. Loveridge, R. Lumley, J. Mangan, and M. Silver, eds. *Manpower Planning: Strategy and Techniques in an Organizational Context.* Chichester, UK: John Wiley, 1983.

Frantzreb, R. *Microcomputers in Human Resource Management.* Roseville, CA: Advanced Personnel Systems, 1986.

Frazee, I., and R. Nichols. "Mainframe HR Software: Current Issues and Market Trends." *Personnel Administrator* 31 (1986) 7: pp. 83–96.

Schwartz, R. "Practitioners' Perceptions of Factors Associated with Human Resource Planning Success." *Human Resource Planning* 8 (1985): pp. 55–66.

Stix, D. "Reward Management: The Integrating Process of Human Resources Strategy." In *Handbook of Wage and Salary Administration*, 2nd ed., M. Rock, ed. New York: McGraw-Hill, 1984.

4

HRD and the individual.

HRD efforts are intended to provide new knowledge, skills, and attitudes for individuals. Hence, HRD is fundamentally focused on individual change. Obviously, individuals differ in the roles they play, the positions they hold, and the ability and motivation they bring to the job or role. Further, they have plans and aspirations of their own, distinct from organizational plans. But what variables influence individuals? How do those variables affect how well they enact their roles and perform their jobs? What is individual career planning, and how can organizations contribute to such planning? Part Four addresses these questions, focusing on the relationship between the individual and HRD.

CHAPTER 8

The individual: socialization and performance.

This chapter focuses on the individual. It discusses issues important to organizational socialization and individual performance.

HRD aims at individual learning for improved work performance. However, individuals vary in knowledge, skills, and abilities. To be effective, HRD efforts must take into account these individual differences.

Each organization has a unique culture with its own norms, values, and status hierarchy. The selection of individuals is not finished when they are hired; rather it is a gradual process of socialization involving how to perform a role, how to interact with other people, and how to behave in the organizational culture.

Individual performance is influenced by physiological, environmental, psychological, and motivational variables. ∎

Socialization

When people are hired into an organization they must make a transition from a broad environment to a unique culture. The term for learning how to enact a role in a unique setting or work culture is *socialization*. It involves not only mastering technical skill (the *what* of a job) but also interpersonal skill (the *how* of dealing with others) and cultural skill (the *how* of dealing with unspoken values, beliefs, and norms).

Perhaps a simple example will illustrate the crucial importance of each of these skills. John Martin was hired as Corporate Director of HRD in a company employing 500 people. With John's 20 years' experience in HRD in the industry, few could question his knowledge of the field and products manufactured by the firm. During his first week, he was treated cordially by everyone. The next week, John arranged meetings with each of the company's top managers to discuss plans for the HRD department.

John had already met the top managers during his lengthy interview process for the job. At that time he was heartened by the glowing reports he received about the department and about the company's strong commitment to developing human resources.

In these meetings, however, John began to hear quite a different story. Company executives complained bitterly about the high-handed practices of the company president. They said he wanted to make all the decisions himself. As a result, they frequently faced embarrassment when decisions made without their advice went hopelessly awry. John also heard several times that his predecessor was fired for poor performance. In reality, he was given only lip service and never any real resources. No fewer than two Vice Presidents and three Division Managers separately advised John to brace himself for similar treatment.

It is apparent from this simple example that John already possesses the necessary technical skill—he knows about HRD in the industry. Further, we can infer that he is also highly proficient in interpersonal skills: he was able to extract very sensitive information from others despite being a newcomer. It is clear that, to succeed, John will have to learn quickly about the organization's culture so he can find a way to avoid the fate of his predecessor.

Key Stages in Socialization

John made swift progress in socialization, which consists of several stages:

1. Role anticipation
2. Role development.
3. Role stabilization.[1]

Whenever a person enters a new role, he or she will experience these stages—whether the move is from outside the organization or from one position to another with the same employer. The experience will be most intense when the transition is from outside, because the individual faces orientation not only in a new role (the job) but also in a new culture (work group and organization).

In the first stage—role anticipation—individuals prepare for and enter a new role.[2,3,4,5] Education serves as one form of role preparation. Some occupations—medicine, law, and advanced graduate work in any field—entail lengthy indoctrination that immerses the student in the values and skills associated with professional practice. If properly handled, education helps ease the transition from school to work; if improperly handled, it builds expectations that sharply vary from reality. The result is *reality shock*—utter disorientation.

Recruitment serves as another form of role preparation. What recruiters say about the job and the organization raises expectations. If realistic, what they say can ease the school-to-work or environmental-organizational transition; if unrealistic in that only positive features are highlighted, the outcome is again likely to be reality shock—and greater likelihood of quick turnover or employee dissatisfaction.[6]

In the second stage—role development—individuals acquire a concrete, realistic sense of role. Four basic conflicts must be resolved if the role development stage is to be completed successfully:

1. *A conflict between effective and ineffective interpersonal relationships.* Can the individual acquire necessary social skills for getting along with supervisors and co-workers?
2. *A conflict between effective and ineffective task proficiency.* Can the individual apply the necessary work skills to perform the job?
3. *A conflict between effective and ineffective cultural proficiency.* Can the individual learn "the way things are done here," the unspoken assumptions and values of the organization and work group?
4. *A conflict between personal and organizational goals.* Can the individual make reasonable progress toward life and career goals in the organization and job role? [1]

Individuals vary in how much importance they attach to each of these conflicts and how much they are affected by the conflicts.

If the resolution process is successful, the individual progresses to the next stage of socialization. If conflicts are not satisfactorily resolved, the result is voluntary or involuntary turnover.

In the third and final stage of socialization—role stabilization—individuals have been accepted as competent by other people. However, they face two major conflicts:

- *That between role demands and life off the job.* Can the individual strike a balance between what is required by the organization and what is required to have a satisfying personal life away from it?

- *That between the individual's work group and other groups.* Can the person strike a balance between the norms and values of his or her co-workers and those of others with whom interaction is necessary? [1]

These conflicts continue as long as the individual remains in the same role and organization. As in the second stage, individuals must learn to cope with these conflicts. If they cannot do so, turnover or dissatisfaction is likely.

HRD and Socialization

Individuals do not bear sole responsibility for their own socialization; rather, they share that responsibility with organizations. HRD is one tool—and a most useful one—for facilitating entry into a role or organization. Formal, planned learning experiences can be geared to the needs and interests of people undergoing the socialization process.

During the role anticipation stage individuals are highly motivated to learn about opportunities available to them, prospective employers, practice in their future occupations, and subsequent career paths. HRD practitioners can facilitate preparation for employment by:

- Working more closely with educators to ensure that prospective recruits still in school form realistic expectations of future work roles.

- Providing opportunities for cooperative education. Through internships, apprenticeships, part-time, and summer jobs students can gain insight about prospective future roles and employers.

- Opening company training programs to high school or college students. Often the problems raised or issues addressed in these programs can start some thinking about the kinds of real-life demands that face people working in particular roles.

Of course, realistic recruitment and selection is also important. Instead of focusing solely on job tasks, the recruiter should also describe policies and practices related to pay, promotion, transfers, and the likely expectations of co-workers and supervisors.[6]

When entering a new organization, people are highly motivated to learn everything they can about their jobs, work group, department, organization and the role expectations of others. Much can be learned through observation, questioning, and reflection. In many cases, newcomers are bombarded with too much too fast and with too little structure. HRD practitioners can facilitate effective organizational entry by:

- Preparing realistic orientation programs to introduce newcomers to other people in the organization and to their work duties. Approaches to orientation can vary.[7,8,9] It is important, however, to give employees *structured* orientation so they are not confused by a maze of new information and people.
- Offering structured on-the-job and off-the-job training geared to key tasks and responsibilities associated with new roles.

Perhaps most important, HRD people should open dialogues with newcomers so they will not hesitate to ask questions either about the job or the organization. In some cases, it may be desirable to rotate new recruits briefly through different parts of the organization so that they can see first-hand how their departments and jobs fit into a larger pattern.

During the role development stage, newcomers confront the key issues of establishing effective interpersonal relationships, acquiring job competence, becoming aware of cultural norms, and resolving goal conflicts. Remembering that the importance of each of these issues varies by individual, HRD professionals can facilitate role development by:

1. Providing continued opportunities for training to improve job competence.
2. Providing—when needed or desirable—instruction on interpersonal skills and (for supervisors) team-building and counseling. This will at least partially deal with the issue of interpersonal relationships.

3. Structuring some learning events with the participation of experienced employees who understand the organizational culture. Through realistic job simulations, case studies, and discussion groups these employees can help newer employees become aware of cultural norms.

4. Sponsoring education so that individuals can pursue personal goals by preparing themselves for advancement.

Other approaches can also be useful. Formal or informal mentoring programs, in which experienced employees are given partial responsibility for development of newcomers, can do much to reduce the time usually necessary for integration into the work group and for awareness of cultural norms. In addition, mentors—often selected informally by the person in need of help—can contribute greatly to future advancement.[10]

The first supervisor of any newcomer is crucial to subsequent success, through the guidance, opportunities for challenging work, and feedback on performance that he or she provides. While HRD people rarely control choice of mentor or first supervisor, they can train supervisors on providing guidance, challenging individuals, and giving feedback through various means.[11]

During the role stabilization stage individuals must learn to strike a balance between personal and work life and between their work group and other groups. HRD practitioners can facilitate success in this stage by:

1. Counseling people on work-related problems.

2. Training supervisors on counseling techniques and on the importance of empathy.

3. Making referrals to professional counselors for personal problems when appropriate.

4. Providing opportunities for planned learning about processes and conflicts within and between work groups.

Perhaps most important, HRD practitioners can help people in the role stabilization stage to plan for future career moves and develop new or deeper interests in their present roles.

Performance

Improving individual performance is what HRD is all about. The question is: what is performance? Some people define it simply as behavior or outcomes of behavior. Unfortunately, there is no single theory of performance with which everyone agrees. No single discipline has a monopoly on performance; rather, many disciplines focus on some specific facet.

Figure 8.1 provides an overview of important variables in performance. The discussion that follows is organized around parts of this model.

Physiological Variables

Physiological variables include mental and physical abilities. Briefly defined, *ability* is the present capacity to engage in certain behavior. An *aptitude* in an undeveloped or underdeveloped capacity to engage in certain behavior.

Ability, of course, significantly influences performance. People vary in the nature and extent of their talents. They are gifted in different

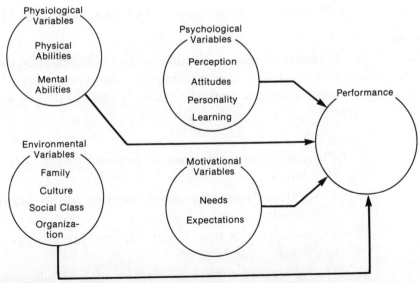

Figure 8.1 Variables influencing individual performance

ways: some possess such physical abilities as stamina and resistance to heat or cold; some possess great facility with numbers, words, or reasoning.

Organizations have long recognized the importance of abilities. It is not uncommon to find selection tests that screen people on the basis of their mental abilities and aptitudes. Nor is it unusual for prospective employees to undergo physical tests prior to selection.

However, organizations are rarely, if ever, concerned with an individual's *complete* range of present abilities and aptitudes. More important to an organization is *skill,* defined as a task-specific ability. (In fact, under equal opportunity laws, all selection tests must be job related.)

Physiological variables set the boundaries of individual development: people cannot exceed their own physical and mental limitations. At the same time, few jobs require individuals to perform at their limits. Indeed, many jobs do not even call for development of individual aptitudes that might improve job performance.

When dealing with a problem of individual performance, the HRD professional can begin with several questions about ability. To what extent is the person

- Physically able to perform the job or specific tasks involved in it?
- Mentally able to perform the job or specific tasks involved in it?

If the answer to either question is "only to a small extent," then HRD activities like job-specific training will not improve performance.

Other questions might be asked. To what extent does the individual possess

- Physical aptitudes that would improve present job performance if developed?
- Physical aptitudes that *might* improve future job performance if developed?
- Mental aptitudes that would improve present job performance if developed?
- Mental aptitudes that *might* improve future job performance if developed?

If the answers to these questions are "to some extent" or "a great extent," then it might be worthwhile to invest in training, education, or developmental efforts to transform an aptitude into an ability.

Environmental Variables

Environmental variables include background (family, culture, social class) and present work context.

An individual's childhood environment is important because family values, social class, and culture influence development and available opportunities. In the U.S., we admire the individual who can rise from an impoverished childhood to a successful position. Yet paradoxically, great admiration is also shown for those who have family and social class advantages and use them productively.

Organizations have long used upbringing as a selection criterion. Preferences are still shown for people who resemble job interviewers in terms of values, attitudes, dress, and background—even though this can violate equal opportunity laws. And to some extent, selections into organizations are self-initiated. People tend to seek jobs in organizations that are consistent with their self-concept. Since self-concept is in part a result of upbringing, its effects are subtle yet pervasive.[5]

Culture can be understood as the unspoken pattern of values that guide behavior in work groups and organizations. Socialization, described in the first part of this chapter, is a process of learning about the culture. It is important because culture regulates behavior and thereby influences individual performance.

When approaching a performance problem, the HRD professional can ask several questions about environment. To what extent is the person

- Likely to be aware of particular organizational expectations as a result of his or her upbringing, culture, and social class?
- Familiar with the organizational culture?

If answers to these questions are "only to a small extent," then training alone probably will not eliminate performance or behavior problems. An individual who fails to show up for work and does not call in is either unaware that a call may be expected or willfully refuses to make the call. Either behavior may result from upbringing or cultural background and will require more than training to remedy.

Psychological Variables

Psychological variables include individual perception, attitudes, personality, and learning. Perception is the way an individual interprets events, situations, and people. Attitudes are predispositions to action, acquired through experience. Personality refers to relatively fixed attributes of an individual, resulting from experience with the environment, that make him or her unique. Learning is a change in perception, attitude, or behavior.

Perception. Individuals perceive—that is, interpret—the world in different ways. Their perceptions depend partially on role, group affiliations, individual attitudes, and values. Consider some examples:

- An instructor watches a trainee tapping his pencil on the top of his book and staring off into space in the middle of a training lecture. The instructor is annoyed because he interprets these behaviors as signs of boredom. In reality, the trainee is at the peak of concentration.

- An instructor is annoyed because a trainee constantly asks what he considers trivial questions about an unpopular company policy. The instructor calls a coffee break and warns the trainee about his "disruptive" behavior. The trainee is shocked: he was merely curious and wanted to explore every point of the policy so that it was clear to him.

- A manager ignores the work of her best performer. The employee starts looking for another job, because he interprets the lack of feedback as a sign that his boss does not care about his future. In reality, his boss has been so pleased with his work that she is only biding her time until she can engineer a promotion for him.

These situations illustrate how easy it is for the same event or behavior to be perceived in different ways.

Perceptions are influenced by such factors as:

1. *Characteristics of perceivers.* People tend to judge another person by their own standards.

2. *Needs and goals.* People tend to judge events by how they think they are affected by them.

3. *Emotional state.* Depending on moods, people can interpret the same event in different ways.

4. *Surroundings.* People associate the meaning of an event with their attitudes about the surroundings.

5. *Past events.* People can associate the meaning of something that happens in the present with similar events experienced in the past.

When approaching a problem of individual performance, the HRD professional can ask several questions about perception. To what extent

- Does the person perceive the opportunity to perform? (Is it clear what behavior is called for under particular circumstances?)
- Has the person successfully perceived opportunities to perform in the past? (Has he or she demonstrated appropriate performance at any time?)

If the answer to either one of the primary questions is "to a great extent," then the problem is not caused by faulty perception. The source of the problem rests elsewhere, and it will take further analysis to determine what corrective action to take. Training, education, or development may not be appropriate because they are expensive and assume that the problem stems from lack of knowledge or skill.

Attitudes. Individuals learn attitudes from those around them. Consider the following situations:

1. An employee tells a co-worker: "The managers here just don't know what they're doing. A year ago we had a reorganization. Today we had another one. Our reporting relationships change faster than in a banana republic."

2. Before interviewing a job candidate, a manager explains to another that "the guy probably won't fit in here."

3. After asking a group of trainees questions about an assignment for five minutes without getting a single correct answer, an instructor hurls a pointer stick across the room and storms out.

Each of these situations illustrates the importance of attitude, a predisposition to action.

Attitudes are comprised of three components: feelings, beliefs, and behaviors. When an individual holds an attitude, he or she has feelings about it, perceives the world relative to it, and behaves in a way that is consistent with it. When facts run counter to attitudes, the individual experiences discomfort and will try to reduce the inconsistency by rationalization (making facts appear consistent), suppression (putting the facts out of mind), or some other method.

Attitudes about a job are important determinants of job satisfaction. Job dissatisfaction can result in increased turnover and absenteeism. Since turnover means training replacements and waiting until they reach a stage of socialization in which they can perform effectively, it is costly and lowers performance for the work group and organization. Absenteeism reduces productivity and can require expensive overstaffing. While there is only weak evidence that job satisfaction causes high performance and that high performance causes job satisfaction,[12] the greatest correlation between them can be found in white-collar occupations in which individual initiative is important in determining performance.[13]

When approaching a problem of individual performance, the HRD professional can ask several questions about attitudes. To what extent

- Do job methods depend on individual initiative?
- Do job outcomes depend on individual initiative?
- Are the person's attitudes favorable toward:
  a. the organization?
  b. the work group?
  c. the job?
  d. pay and reward practices?

If the answers to the first two questions are "to some extent" or "a great extent," then it is worthwhile to find answers to the third question. When dissatisfaction is high, the individual may need special counseling to identify the source of problems and work on solving them. Training, education, and development are only sometimes appropriate methods for dealing with problems of this kind.

Personality. As people mature, they acquire patterns or habits in the way they respond to the world around them. The wife who knows what her husband will say about something before he says it has mastered his habit pattern. In short, she knows his personality and his attitudes.

As people are socialized in an organization, they become similarly clued in to behaviors of others. Subordinates may know what their boss will say about a problem or event before he or she says it; a superior may be able to predict accurately the reaction of a subordinate or group of subordinates to a piece of news. This element of predictability stabilizes relationships.

It is entirely possible that individuals cannot be effective in roles that require them to behave in ways that run counter to their personalities or attitudes.[14]

When approaching a problem of individual performance, the HRD professional can ask several questions about personality. To what extent do job

- Methods call for particular kinds of uniform role behaviors from individuals?
- Outcomes depend on particular kinds of uniform role behaviors from individuals?

If answers to both questions are "to some extent" or "a great extent," then chances are good that a discrepancy between job requirements and the personality of the incumbent is the source of the problem.

Performance is not likely to be affected by personality when the job allows little latitude for individual expression—but performance can be seriously affected by personality when there is great latitude for expression. Personalities are not easily changed and, as the individual ages, become more difficult to influence. HRD efforts are rarely appropriate for trying to change personalities.

Learning. People change their perceptions, attitudes, and behavior through learning. Chapter 12 deals with this subject in depth, because performance change through organized learning is at the very heart of HRD.

Individuals differ in their styles of learning—that is, in how they prefer to approach a learning task. Some observers claim, rather simplistically, that individuals who are right-brained (i.e., rely heavily on the right hemisphere of the brain) learn intuitively while left-brained people learn logically. Actually, learning is more complicated, and research on learning styles is still in its infancy.

A few principles of learning are somewhat more useful. Generally, people learn

1. More quickly when they can participate and apply what they learn as they learn it.
2. Through repetition. For this reason, experience is a powerful teacher when it calls for repetition of what has been learned.
3. What they regard as useful to them.
4. Best when the learning environment closely matches the environment in which the learning will be applied.
5. To correct their errors through feedback—so prompt and concrete feedback facilitates effective transfer of learning.

How can these principles be applied to performance problems? When confronted with such a problem, HRD professionals can ask several questions. To what extent

- Are those who are trained for a task allowed to apply their learning immediately?
- Are people called on to perform repeatedly in ways that they have learned? Infrequent performance will lead to the gradual loss of some skills.
- Do people consider appropriate performance important to them? If they consider it unimportant, they will scarcely be motivated to learn.
- Does the environment in which a skill was learned match conditions where the skill is applied? The more the learning environment differs from actual job conditions, the less likely that people will be able to apply what they learned.
- Are people given concrete, specific feedback on their performance?

Answers to these questions can help to pinpoint the source of performance problems. Clearly, if the person has never learned how to perform or if past learning runs counter to present requirements, he or she is a candidate for HRD efforts.

Motivational Variables

Motivational variables include needs and expectations. A need is a deficiency, a lack of something the individual requires but does not possess. An expectation is the act of looking forward to something, often as an

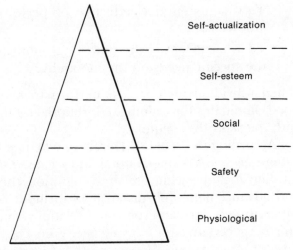

Self-actualization

Self-esteem

Social

Safety

Physiological

Figure 8.2 Maslow's hierarchy

outcome of behavior or performance. Motivation itself is that which impels behavior. Its source can be internal (a need, an expectation) or external (threats or compulsion).

There are two groups of theories about motivation: (1) *content* theories, which focus on what happens within people to motivate them, and (2) *process* theories, which focus on the means by which behavior is stimulated. Both are worth considering as they relate to job performance.

Two of the best known content theories of motivation are Maslow's Hierarchy and Herzberg's Motivation-Hygiene theory.

Maslow believed that human motives are complex and that needs form a hierarchy from basic to sophisticated. As each lower-level need is satisfied, it no longer motivates. In ascending order (see Figure 8.2) Maslow's hierarchy includes: *physiological needs,* those for food, water, sex, and sleep; *safety needs,* those for shelter and freedom from bodily harm; *love or social needs,* those for relationships with other people; *esteem needs,* those for respect from oneself and others; and *self-actualization needs,* those associated with a sense of achievement, self-satisfaction, and freedom to exercise creativity.

According to Maslow's Hierarchy, people are motivated to perform when they can satisfy their needs by doing so. When approaching an individual performance problem, HRD professionals need to consider such questions as:

- To what extent does effective job performance satisfy the individual's needs?

- To what extent is the individual motivated to perform by any of the specific needs on the hierarchy?

When individuals are unable to perform to meet a need, they are probably good candidates for training, education, and development to equip them with the skills they require.

According to Frederick Herzberg two major categories relate to motivation: *job satisfiers* (motivators) and *job dissatisfiers* (hygiene factors). Job satisfiers include: achievement, recognition, the work itself, responsibility, and advancement. Job dissatisfiers include: policy and administration, supervision, salary, interpersonal relations, and working conditions. For Herzberg, certain basic hygiene needs must be met to create the necessary *climate* for motivation. However, other factors are required to *induce* motivation.

In Herzberg's view, people are motivated only by achievement, recognition, the work itself, responsibility, and advancement. When considering individual job performance, the HRD professional should pose such questions as:

- To what extent does effective job performance inherently lead to job satisfiers as outcomes?

- To what extent does effective job performance, as it is accomplished, produce intrinsic satisfaction?

When individuals are unable to perform to take advantage of job satisfiers, there is good reason to believe that they are in need of training, education, or development. Individual performance can be increased when job satisfiers are maximized while the effects of dissatisfiers are kept stable.

The process theories of motivation show how people attempt to satisfy their needs. Two of them are known as *expectancy* theory and *equity* theory.

Expectancy theory contends that employees make decisions to take action based on their assessment of the probabilities that they will be rewarded and that they will value the reward. Expectancy is, essentially, an estimate of the odds for success. Human behavior is directed toward achieving certain goals that will serve to help satisfy needs (see Figure 8.3).

According to expectancy theory people will perform when they have the ability, when they believe they will be rewarded for performance,

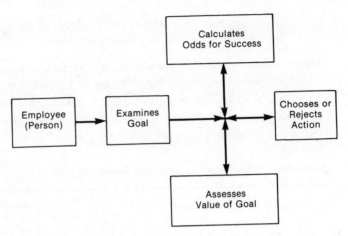

Figure 8.3   Expectancy theory

and when the reward itself is valued. When considering individual job performance, HRD professionals should pose such questions as:

- To what extent do people have the ability?
- To what extent do people perceive that they will be rewarded for appropriate job performance?
- To what extent do people value rewards they expect to receive from appropriate performance?

When the answers are "to some extent" or "a great extent," people will be highly motivated. If they cannot perform despite their motivation, they may be in need of training, education, and development.

Equity theory suggests that individuals compare their inputs (exertions) and outputs (pay, benefits, promotions) with those of other people (subordinates, peers, superiors). When the comparison produces a feeling of equity, the employee is motivated. However, if the comparison produces feelings of inequity, the employee may reduce inputs, try to increase work outputs, select someone different for comparison, or quit.

Thus, people are motivated to perform to the extent that they believe they are being treated equitably. When considering individual performance, the HRD professional should pose the following questions. To what extent

- Does the individual believe he or she is being treated equitably based on effort?
- Does the individual believe he or she is being treated equitably based on results of his or her effort?

• Is the person with whom the individual compares himself or herself an appropriate one for that purpose?

By considering these questions, HRD practitioners can detect sources of problems other than deficiencies in knowledge or skill.

Use the checklist shown in Figure 8.4 when addressing a performance problem. It summarizes all the questions described in this chapter and can be a helpful diagnostic tool.

Figure 8.4   Questions to consider when analyzing individual performance problems

		Check One (✓)				
Variable	*Questions*	*Very Great*	*Great*	*Some*	*Little*	*Very Little*
Physiological	1. To what extent is the person physically able to *a.* perform the job?					
	b. tasks in the job?					
	2. To what extent is the person mentally able to *a.* perform the job?					
	b. tasks in the job?					
	3. To what extent does the individual possess physical aptitudes that would improve present job performance if developed?					
	4. To what extent does the individual possess physical aptitudes that *might* improve future job performance if developed?					
	5. To what extent does the individual possess mental aptitudes that would improve present job performance if developed?					
	6. To what extent does the individual possess mental aptitudes that *might* improve future job performance if developed?					

Figure 8.4 (Continued)

Variable	Questions	Check One (√)				
		Very Great	Great	Some	Little	Very Little
Environmental	**7.** To what extent is the person likely to be aware of particular organizational expectations as a result of his or her *a.* Upbringing?					
	b. Social class?					
	c. Culture?					
	8. To what extent is the individual familiar with the organizational culture?					
Psychological	**9.** To what extent does the individual perceive the opportunity to perform?					
	10. To what extent has the person successfully perceived opportunities to perform in the past?					
	11. To what extent do job methods depend on individual initiative?					
	12. To what extent do job outcomes depend on individual initiative?					
	13. To what extent are the person's attitudes favorable toward: *a.* The organization?					
	b. The work group?					
	c. The job?					
	d. Pay and reward practices?					

Figure 8.4 (Continued)

Variable	Questions	Check One (✔)				
		Very Great	*Great*	*Some*	*Little*	*Very Little*
Psychological (Continued)	**14.** To what extent do job methods call for particular kinds of uniform role behaviors from individuals?					
	15. To what extent do job outcomes depend on particular kinds of uniform role behaviors from individuals?					
	16. To what extent are people called on to perform repeatedly in ways that they have learned?					
	17. To what extent are those who are trained for a task allowed to apply the training immediately?					
	18. To what extent do people consider appropriate performance important?					
	19. To what extent does the environment in which the skill was learned match conditions where the skill is applied?					
	20. To what extent are people given concrete, specific feedback on their performance?					
Motivational	**21.** To what extent does effective job performance satisfy the individual's needs?					
	22. To what extent is the individual motivated to perform by any of the specific needs on the hierarchy?					

Figure 8.4 (Continued)

Variable	Questions	Check One (✓)				
		Very Great	Great	Some	Little	Very Little
Motivational (Continued)	**23.** To what extent does effective job performance inherently lead to job satisfiers as outcomes?					
	24. To what extent does effective job performance, as it is accomplished, produce intrinsic satisfaction?					
	25. To what extent do people perceive that they will be rewarded for appropriate job performance?					
	26. To what extent do people value the rewards they expect to receive from appropriate performance?					
	27. To what extent does the individual believe he or she is being treated equitably based on exertions?					
	28. To what extent does the individual believe he or she is being treated equitably based on the results of his or her exertions?					
	29. To what extent is the person with whom the individual compares himself or herself an appropriate one for that purpose?					

Summing Up

Training, education, and development efforts are appropriate performance improvement strategies only when individuals:

- Lack abilities but possess aptitudes to perform.
- Lack awareness of organizational expectations and cultural norms.
- Have difficulty perceiving when to perform, but such perception is possible.
- Have never perceived when to perform in the past, but perception is possible.
- Are satisfied with their jobs when job methods or outcomes depend on individual initiative.
- Are capable of exhibiting necessary role behavior.
- Do not know how to perform because they never learned how.
- Are motivated to perform but cannot do so.

If the problem does not meet these conditions, then another approach to performance improvement will be necessary. Examples might include job redesign,[15,16] organizational redesign,[17] changes in reward systems,[18] and individual discipline.[19]

References

1. Gibson, J., J. Ivancevich, and J. Donnelly. *Organizations: Behavior, Structure, Processes*, 5th ed. Plano, TX: Business Publications, 1985.
2. Feldman, D. "A Practical Program for Employee Socialization." *Organizational Dynamics* (Autumn, 1976): pp. 64–80.
3. Feldman, D. "The Multiple Socialization of Organization Members." *Academy of Management Review* (July, 1981): pp. 309–318.
4. Feldman, D., and J. Brett. "Coping with New Jobs: A Comparative Study of New Hires and Job Changes." *Academy of Management Journal* (June, 1983): pp. 258–272.
5. Wanous, J. *Organizational Entry: Recruitment, Selection, and Socialization of Newcomers*. Reading, MA: Addison-Wesley, 1980.
6. Ibid.
7. Meier, T., and S. Hough. "Beyond Orientation: Assimilating New Employees." *Human Resource Management* (Spring 1982): pp. 27–29.
8. Pascale, R. "Fitting New Employees into the Company Culture." *Fortune* (May, 1984): pp. 28, 30, 34, 38–40.
9. St. John, W. "The Complete Employee Orientation Program." *Personnel Journal* (May, 1980): pp. 373–378.

10. Huse, E. *Management,* 2nd ed. St. Paul, MN: West Publishing, 1982.

11. Meckel, N. "The Manager as Career Counselor." *Training and Development Journal* 35 (1981) 7: pp. 64–69.

12. Greene, C. "The Satisfaction-Performance Controversy." *Business Horizons* (October, 1972): pp. 31–41.

13. Beach, D. *Personnel: The Management of People at Work,* 4th ed. New York: Macmillan, 1980.

14. Fiedler, F. *A Theory of Leadership Effectiveness.* New York: McGraw-Hill, 1967.

15. Hackman, J., and G. Oldham. *Work Redesign.* Reading, MA: Addison-Wesley, 1980.

16. Kelly, J. *Scientific Management, Job Redesign, and Work Performance.* London: Academic Press, 1982.

17. Galbraith, J. *Designing Complex Organizations.* Reading, MA: Addison-Wesley, 1973.

18. Stix, D. "Reward Management: The Integrating Process of Human Resources Strategy." In *Handbook of Wage and Salary Administration,* 2nd ed., M. Rock, ed. New York: McGraw-Hill, 1984.

19. Grote, R. "Discipline." In *Human Resources Management and Development Handbook,* W. Tracey, ed. New York: Amacom, 1985.

CHAPTER 9

Individual counseling and career planning.

One important role of the HRD practitioner is that of individual development counselor. This chapter describes the counseling process as a means of facilitating growth and dealing with performance or personal problems. It focuses on the HRD professional as coach, counselor, and consultant to managers. ■

The Role of Individual Development Counselor

According to *Models for Excellence,* the individual development counselor role consists of "helping an individual to assess personal competencies, values, and goals and to identify and plan development and career actions." To enact this role, the HRD professional must be able to exhibit:

- Counseling Skill
- Career-Development Knowledge
- Relationship Versatility
- Questioning Skill
- Feedback Skill
- Research Skill

- Intellectual Versatility
- Adult-Learning Understanding
- Competency-Identification Skill

These competencies are defined in Chapter 4 and in the Glossary. The first two are most critical.

According to *Models for Excellence,* typical work outputs of the role include:

1. "Individual career development plans."
2. "Enhanced skills on the part of the individual to identify and carry out his/her own development needs/goals."
3. "Referrals to professional counseling."
4. "Increased knowledge by the individual about where to get development support."
5. "Tools, resources needed in career development."

The counselor should be able to evoke new insights, be a sympathetic sounding board, and offer suggestions for dealing with job and career problems that individuals face or think they face.

The counseling process is depicted by the simple model in Figure 9.1. (A more sophisticated model can be found in the *Human Resources Management and Development Handbook.*[1]) This model is closely associated with performance coaching and is the basis for the discussion that follows.

Recognizing Problems and Opportunities

Three preconditions are essential if the counseling process is to be meaningful. Before people seek help (or are willing to accept it), they must first recognize that a problem exists or that an opportunity for improvement is available. Second, they must be motivated to seek more information. Finally, they must be willing and able to act on that information and on the problem.

Anybody can have a problem or can think of an opportunity. In the HRD context, a problem is simply something that impedes individual performance or adversely affects mental health. An opportunity is something that, if pursued, could lead to improved performance or greater satisfaction.

Personal problems stem from many sources, including:

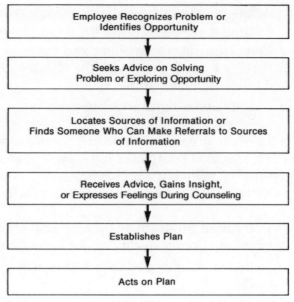

Figure 9.1   A simple model of the counseling process

1. *Physical and mental illness.* Such maladies as cancer and heart ailments can affect individual behavior and, through it, job performance. Mental illness, including alcohol and drug abuse, can also affect performance.

2. *Individual values, personality, and perceptions.* When people experience intrarole, interrole, or interpersonal conflict, their job performance can be adversely affected.

3. *Family matters.* What happens off the job can easily affect how one performs on the job.

4. *Motivation.* People can experience problems when they are not motivated, are inadequately or improperly rewarded, or perceive themselves to be inadequately or improperly rewarded.

Supervisors can identify individual performance problems in their subordinates by being alert for these tell-tale signs:

- Overly inappropriate behavior (e.g., engaging in horseplay, sabotage, or vandalism).
- A dramatic, sudden decline in productivity (e.g., turning in shoddy work, missing deadlines).

- A loss of interest in the work (e.g., spending too much time on the phone, going to lunch for three hours).
- Complaints about anything and everything (e.g., "It's too cold in here"; "I don't know why the cheapskates in this company don't do something about this").
- Arguments or fights with other people.

While a single instance of these behaviors might not prompt supervisory concern, repeated occurrence indicates that an employee is experiencing a personal or job-related problem.

The results of personal problems can include:

- Decreasing productivity because of higher scrap rates, more down time, and poorer quality of goods produced or services offered.
- Increasing morale problems as shown by higher turnover and absenteeism.
- Increasing complaints from customers and other employees.

To deal with these problems, organizations can sponsor:

- Employee health and assistance programs to avert illness and increase mental and physical alertness.
- Efforts to improve interpersonal, intragroup, and intergroup relationships (Organization Development).
- Participative-management and quality-circle programs to help people improve organizational, group, and individual performance.
- Formal or informal counseling and coaching.

There are other ways to identify opportunities for improvement, including formal career programs and employee suggestion systems.

Supervisors can help to spot opportunities for their subordinates. For example, they can:

- Recognize special aptitudes worth developing (e.g., writing ability, facility in mathematics).
- Notice special interests (e.g., a hobby with obvious vocational applications).

- Observe interpersonal skills deserving of greater use (e.g., extraordinary ability to influence others shown by someone working with data or things rather than people).

Seeking Advice

Some problems cannot be solved and some opportunities cannot be pursued without additional information. An employee facing a problem should consult someone else when he or she:

1. Does not understand it very clearly but can describe it.
2. Wants more information before taking action.
3. Wants advice on what action to take.
4. Needs someone to stimulate thought, evoke insight, or provide a different perspective on the problem, opportunity, or contemplated action and the likely results stemming from it.

Locating Information Sources

Many sources of information are available to help in counseling people on problems or opportunities. They include: (1) peers, (2) superiors, and (3) third-party consultants. The appropriate source will depend on the nature of the problem or opportunity, the person experiencing it, and the expertise of the counselors.

Clearly, some problems are best referred to a corporate psychologist or outside professional. Highly personal matters—marital disputes, financial difficulties, legal problems, and drug or alcohol abuse—exceed the expertise of friends, co-workers, supervisors, or HRD practitioners. Many firms sponsor alcoholism programs because the problem is so pervasive—about 10 percent of the entire labor force can be classified as alcoholics and another 10 percent are on the borderline.[2]

The appropriate information source depends partly on the person seeking the advice. Individuals can seek help for themselves or for others. For instance, an alcoholic may want to get help, a family member may want to see that the person is helped, or a supervisor may seek advice on how to deal with a worker who is suffering from a special, perhaps sensitive, problem.

The best source of assistance also depends on the nature of the problem or opportunity. Some counselors specialize in certain types of problems, such as marital or financial matters; some treat many matters but with a uniform approach.

Though many firms have found it worthwhile to establish long-term relationships with special providers of counseling services, at least 90 percent of all individual problems can be handled by in-house counseling, according to Ramsey in *Human Resources Management and Development Handbook.*

Counseling

The counseling process can help people who need to:

- Express their feelings freely.
- Gain new insights or perspectives.
- Obtain specialized advice.

It is during this process, whether formal or informal, that the counselor exhibits the competencies associated with the role.

Any counseling event consists of several steps in which the counselor addresses the following questions:

1. What is the problem or opportunity?
2. How important is it?
3. What feelings are associated with it?
4. What can be done about it?
5. What approach will probably work best?
6. How will improvement be recognized?

In the first step, the counselor establishes rapport and identifies the issue prompting concern. At this point it is essential to show empathy through precisely the same skills critical to group facilitation: effective nonverbal behavior, active listening, effective paraphrase, and questioning skill. Showing empathy is perhaps the key skill of a counselor. Begin the conversation by picking up cues from the other person.

When the issue is finally raised, ask the person needing help to describe it. Ask such questions as:

- What is the problem (or opportunity)?

- How did you recognize it?
- How is it affecting you? How has it affected you?
- What actions have you taken so far? On what assumptions were your actions based?

These and similar questions should help to clarify what has prompted the visit. They will enable the counselor to pinpoint the nature of the issue and may evoke new insights for the person discussing it.

In the second and third steps, the counselor collects additional information. Ask such questions as:

- How important is this issue to you now? For what reasons?
- Has this problem (or opportunity) been important to you in the past?
- What feelings are you experiencing at this moment? How do you feel when you experience the problem first-hand (or think of the opportunity)?

These questions are intended to bring out how the problem (or prospect of an opportunity) affects the individual. During this process, provide feedback regularly to clarify for yourself and your client what has been and is being felt about the issue.

In the fourth and fifth steps, the counselor provides advice and/or stimulates thought on what should be done and on what results will be achieved. It is best to generate a series of alternatives, leaving the choice of which one to pursue up to the client.[3] The counselor serves as a catalyst, one who prompts thinking. If the counselor is a supervisor and the problem affects job performance, he or she may stimulate action simply by establishing guidelines about what will happen if a problem capable of being solved is not acted on.[1]

Establishing a Plan

The counselor helps the client to establish a plan to solve a problem or pursue an opportunity.

Such a plan can be:

- *Informal.* The individual reaches his or her own decision about what to do, when to do it, and how to do it.

• *Formal.* The individual agrees to write out a contract stipulating action steps. As an alternative, a log can be used to record feelings and outcomes while the individual grapples with the change process.

The nature of the plan depends on the problem, the preferences of the individual with the problem, and advice by the counselor.

Taking Action

The final step in counseling is action: the individual attempts to solve the problem or take advantage of an opportunity. He or she may wish to consult periodically with the counselor during this process, though that is not always essential. If an action plan is successful, no further counseling is necessary.

Training Supervisors to Be Counselors

HRD people frequently serve as third-party consultants on organizational and individual performance problems or improvement opportunities. They may also counsel employees on career issues (a topic addressed in the next section of this chapter). In doing so, they will use the skills and competencies associated with the role.

However, an alternative approach—or at least a strategy that can be used in addition—is to train supervisors in counseling skills. Such skills can be useful in motivating subordinates and coping with individual performance issues. Moreover, supervisors are likely to be the first to notice effects of an employee's personal problem or an opportunity for individual development.

A very effective approach to training supervisors is *behavior modeling.* A behavior modeling course can be designed as follows:

1. Survey supervisors about the kinds of individual problems they encounter and how much of each kind they see.
2. Tell supervisors that if they are interested in counseling they can volunteer to attend the course.
3. Structure the course as follows:

  a. Describe the results of the survey. Cite company statistics on problem behaviors, if available.

b. Give an overview of issues affecting individual performance.
c. Cover problem diagnosis. How does the supervisor decide when a problem (or opportunity for improvement) exists?
d. Provide a model of the process. What are the steps in coaching employees?
e. Provide skill practice. Show participants videotapes of good and bad examples of how counseling skills are used. Role plays and case studies may also give participants an opportunity to build their skills.
f. Give supervisors the chance to counsel real people experiencing real problems.
g. Provide feedback on how well participants used counseling skills.

The approach is called behavior modeling because participants quite literally model (imitate) behaviors which they have observed.

Career Planning and Counseling

Some large organizations employ full-time professional psychologists and counselors to advise employees on personal problems. In this case, HRD practitioners devote most of their time to counseling supervisors confronted with special problems and individuals faced with career issues. Many employees are interested only in planned learning events as a means of career advancement. This means that individual development counselors must be aware of career planning theories and techniques—as well as ways to facilitate career development in an organizational setting.

Career Planning Terminology

Several terms are of special importance in any discussion of career planning and counseling:

- A *career* is a series of jobs that are related in some way. A career includes not only the work itself but also training, education, and development intended to improve how a job is done currently or to prepare the individual for future advancement.

- *Career development* is a structured process of interaction between a representative of the organization and the individual in which mutual expectations are discussed and negotiated.

- *Career planning,* a subcomponent of career development, is performed by individual employees. It is a conscious, deliberate process of identifying and exploring career opportunities, setting goals, establishing direction, and choosing the means by which to attain goals.

- *Career management,* another subcomponent of career development, is performed by organizations. It is a systematic, ongoing process to facilitate individual career planning and help individuals attain career goals.

- *Career paths* are formal, detailed descriptions of interrelationships between jobs in an organization, expressed in terms of the training, education, experience, and behaviors required for promotion or transfer from one to another.

- *Life planning* is an individual process that encompasses career planning but transcends it. In fact, it is the process of establishing goals and direction for one's entire life, including such personal matters as when and how to choose a mate, establish a family, and plan retirement.

- *Career counseling* is simply a process of helping individuals plan their careers.

Career Planning Theories

Numerous theories of career planning have been proposed. They are important because knowledge of theory can guide the actions of career counselors, so HRD professionals should be familiar with them. Career theories can be classified into seven major groups:

1. Economic
2. Rational
3. Existential
4. Sociological
5. Psychological
6. Dimensional
7. Developmental

Each is based on a unique view of human nature; each suggests a different approach to career counseling.

Economic Theory. This career theory is based on the assumption that people are rational and will select occupations in which they can make the most money. Individuals will change career goals if there is an economic incentive for doing so. From this perspective, human nature is driven by a desire to take advantage of labor market demand.

Economists stress the importance of forecasting this demand during the career counseling process. People should:

1. Determine which occupations are most in demand now or are likely to be in the future.

2. Assess personal skills and abilities.

3. Select what promises to be the most lucrative occupation, based on a match between labor market demand and individual skills.

The implications for career counseling are apparent. Counselors can help by providing:

- Accurate information on labor market demand in the future—for example, from projections found in the *Occupational Outlook Handbook*.

- Tools and instruments to facilitate assessment of skills and abilities as well as information about how much they are used in various occupations (e.g., as found in the *Dictionary of Occupational Titles*).

- Opportunities to compare labor market demand and individual skills.

Economists have devoted most of their attention to external labor markets (outside firms or occupations), particularly to phenomena such as discrimination and school-to-work transitions that sometimes impede the free flow of supply and demand. They have generally devoted much less attention to internal labor markets (within firms or occupations), though many of the same principles apply.

Rational Theory. This career theory synthesizes separate beliefs of economists and psychologists on career planning. Advocates believe that human nature is highly rational and goal-oriented. Occupational choice depends equally on a firm sense of personal identity and good information about labor market demand. The goal of career planning is to maximize individual success. Career change occurs as a result of personal experience and/or environmental labor market conditions. Some of the best expressions of this theory can be found in the works of Bergland,[4] Gelatt,[5] Herr and Cramer,[6,7] Hershenson and Roth,[8] Katz,[9,10] and Krumboltz and Sorenson.[11]

For example, Gelatt sees individuals making career decisions by:

1. Recognizing a need for such a decision.
2. Collecting information about choices.
3. Using this information to develop alternative career strategies.
4. Estimating the probability of success for each alternative, relying heavily on personal values.
5. Selecting a career strategy or deciding to collect more information.

By facilitating these steps, career counselors can help people choose occupations and periodically re-evaluate career strategies.

Krumboltz and Sorenson see individuals making career choices by:

1. Working with peers to identify personal goals.
2. Establishing timetables for career decision-making.
3. Gathering career or occupational information systematically.
4. Estimating probabilities of individual success in different occupations and along different career paths.
5. Discussing alternatives with others.
6. Making a tentative decision.
7. Considering, over time, the validity of the decision.

For career counseling this theory can be applied particularly well in group settings, such as workshops and seminars, where people can share information and support each other.[12]

Existential Theory. This theory has not been widely applied to career planning, even though it appears to lend itself quite well to such use. Existentialists believe that the world lacks any inherent meaning, that people are totally—indeed, painfully—free to act, and that they are completely responsible for establishing their identities and realizing their potential.[13] In this context career issues are minor compared to such fundamental matters as:

1. Becoming aware of individuality.
2. Accepting responsibility for total freedom.
3. Preserving self-identity while interacting with other people.
4. Searching for meaning and purpose in life.
5. Experiencing the anxiety that results from not realizing one's potential.
6. Learning to deal with death, the certainty of an ending which gives every act in life importance.

Existentialists would thus see career decisions resulting from individual choice alone. People must learn to accept responsibility for the direction of their lives and their careers. Work, jobs, and careers have no meaning until it is given to them. Anxiety is a possible stimulant to growth that can challenge people to realize their capabilities.

The role of career counselor in this context is to help individuals learn to be more in touch with their feelings, establish personal identity and meaning, and accept total responsibility for career choices.

Sociological theory. Sociologists emphasize the crucial importance of such institutions as family, religion, and school in early career planning. Human nature is, in part, a function of socioeconomic conditions. Family members influence occupational preferences by shaping individual values about them.[14]

Upon entering occupations and organizations, individuals meet others who help them form new career expectations. Socialization becomes a guiding force in career decision-making.[15] Planning coincides with stages in socialization. Effective career counseling is best done informally and by those, like supervisors, with influence on the person making decisions.[16]

Psychoanalytical theory. This theory is often equated in career literature with the seminal work of the psychoanalyst Sigmund Freud. Generally speaking, Freud did not emphasize the importance of work or of occupational choice. Hence, the psychoanalytical view of career planning was not articulated until a study by Bardin, Nachmann and Segal.[17] After extensive research, they concluded that early childhood has a profound impact on subsequent career choice, work is really a sublimation of infantile impulses, lack of information can result in selecting a career that does not satisfy personal needs, and all occupations may be described in terms of needs they satisfy.

From the psychoanalytic view, the functions and roles of other people—particularly early childhood experiences with parents—are crucial in career choice. Individuals will change careers as their personalities grow enough to recognize their own needs and how to meet them in more satisfactory ways. In an organizational context, career planning is handled through extensive testing. Counseling is guided by the outcomes of such tests.

Dimensional Theory. This theory—sometimes called trait-and-factor theory—is one of the oldest in career planning. To its advocates it is simple enough: analyze the personality of individuals, analyze occupations, and then match them. Its name comes from classifying aspects—that is, dimensions—of personality. Since this theory is no longer widely accepted, it needs only brief mention.

To advocates of this theory, human nature is measurable and quantifiable. The individual has only one correct career choice in a lifetime, and the goal of career planning is to find that one best career. Tests are the quickest way to determine this choice. Individuals will change careers only if, by some accident, they did not make a correct choice to begin with. In an organizational context, career planning is handled best by developing tests to measure personality. The results are then compared with characteristics of various occupations.

Developmental Theory. Of all theories of career planning, developmental theory has had the widest acceptance and has stimulated the greatest attention. It includes theories devised by Ginzberg; Krumboltz, Mitchell and Gelatt; Roe; Schein; Super; Tiedeman and O'Hara; and others. It has been widely accepted by many HRD practitioners and deserves the most attention here.

Eli Ginzberg,[18,19,20] the prominent labor economist, is generally considered the first to consider occupational choice as developing in distinct life stages. Like the psychoanalytic theorists, Ginzberg stressed the importance of childhood; unlike those advocates, he extended personal and occupational development into adolescence. Briefly summarized, his research identifies three important stages in personal development:

Stage 1, occurring before age 11, in which play is gradually oriented more to work.

Stage 2, occurring between ages 11 and 17, in which the individual gradually discovers interests, abilities, values, and other factors important in occupational choice.

Stage 3, occurring from age 17 through the end of formal schooling, in which the individual becomes gradually committed to a career.

Ginzberg's early research led him to conclude that career choice is fixed, because people can never turn back the clock to the time when their interests and values are first programmed. He later reconsidered this view, but continued to stress the importance of early life stages both in career choice and in subsequent career success.

Psychologist Erik Erikson [21] articulated classic developmental theory. He extended the assumptions of Freud, who first stressed early childhood as the period when personality is formed. Erikson believed that individual development really stretches throughout an individual's life span. While not a career theorist, Erikson profoundly influenced subsequent career and learning theory. He classified human development into eight stages, each of which is dominated by a central *life crisis* that must be resolved before the individual can progress to the next stage. They are:

Stage 1: Infancy. The central crisis is between trust and mistrust of others.

Stage 2: Early childhood. The central crisis is between establishing independence and remaining dependent on others.

Stage 3: Preschool. The central crisis is between activity and passivity, between a sense of individual competence and a sense of guilt.

Stage 4. School. The central crisis is between adequacy and inadequacy, the ability or inability to establish and act on personal goals.

Stage 5: Adolescence. The central crisis is between identity and diffusion, between establishment of self-concept and over-reliance on others without a clear sense of self.

Stage 6: Young adulthood. The central crisis is between intimacy and isolation, between establishment of close personal relationships and an inability to form close ties with others.

Stage 7: Middle age. The central crisis is between personal growth and stagnation. Growth involves a sense of creativity stemming from work, leisure, and family life. Stagnation is a feeling of tragic unfulfillment, sometimes called a midlife crisis.

Stage 8: Old age. The central crisis is between fulfillment and lack of fulfillment. Those satisfied with their lives feel fulfillment; those unsatisfied feel despair over that which was lost.

Erikson thus maintained that personal development does not cease with the end of childhood—and it is this central assumption that characterizes developmental theory. Occupational choice and learning continue throughout life and are influenced by the individual's stage in the life cycle. Erikson's work has been popularized by later writers, such as Gail Sheehy.[22]

Krumboltz, Mitchell, and Gelatt [23] have based their thinking about career planning on social learning theory. Learning is seen as the primary influence on career choice throughout life. Although influenced by heredity, environment, and learned skills, individuals are most influenced by instrumental learning (that is, direct observation of others) and associative learning (perceptions based on observation). Career choice is the product of learned skills and occurs in developmental stages over time. Success throughout life is closely tied to accurate information sources and decision-making ability.

Ann Roe's [24] theory of career planning is heavily indebted to Maslow's Hierarchy of Needs. Occupational choice is made in an attempt to satisfy personal needs, which change over time as individuals develop. As one need is satisfied, others arise and may lead to occupational change. However, early childhood influences will have a major impact on initial career choice. Occupational life is the single greatest determinant of personal lifestyle.

Edgar Schein [25] adopted Erikson's model of adult development. He views occupational choice and entry as a process of maturation. Both personal and environmental factors affect choice and subsequent growth in a given career.

Donald Super [26,27,28] has also based his scheme of career planning and development on the work of Erikson. Though not calling himself a theorist, Super has made a major contribution to career planning by formalizing certain stages of vocational development and by classifying career patterns. He maintains that individuals pass through the following stages:

Stage 1: Crystallization. Between the ages of 14–18, the individual formulates a career plan.

Stage 2: Specification. Between 18 and 21, the individual makes more specific efforts to implement the plan.

Stage 3: Implementation. Between 21 and 24, the individual completes formal schooling and enters an occupation.

Stage 4: Stabilization. Between 24 and 35, the individual becomes established in a career and experiences increasing security.

Stage 5: Consolidation. Between 35 and 65, the individual seeks career advancement.

A drawback of Super's theory is his assumption that an early occupational choice blossoms into a lifetime career with little interruption. The fact is that many adults change their careers—sometimes many times.

According to developmental theorists, individuals are continually growing, learning, and developing. Career decisions arise from, and are influenced by, central crises occurring during the individual life cycle. To be effective, counseling and instruction should take these crises into account.[29]

Career Management

Individuals bear the responsibility of planning their own careers. The initiative is theirs. However, organizations bear a responsibility for identifying future HR needs and for helping individuals realize their potential.

Identifying Future HR Needs. Before people can offer career advice, they must first have some sense of the future HR needs of the organization. In many organizations, the original impetus for career management programs came from a desire to promote from within. Such a desire suggests that some effort has been made to identify future HR needs.

There are two ways to identify these needs:

1. Through human resources planning efforts.
2. Through career paths.

Since the first of these ways has been covered in Chapter 7, we will focus here on career paths.

As defined earlier, career paths are formal, detailed descriptions of interrelationships between jobs in an organization, expressed in terms of the training, education, experience, and behaviors required for promotion or transfer from one to another. In effect, all jobs are placed on a continuum much like that of a series of college courses of increasing difficulty. To extend this analogy, some jobs may require specific prerequisite experience—and perhaps even specific psychological characteristics.

The traditional expectation in American culture is that career paths lead upward. That need not necessarily be true. People can move up through promotion, down through demotion, sideways through transfer, out of the organization completely into something similar or completely new, or remain where they are and acquire increasing expertise.

There are several ways to think of career paths:

• Job progression ladders link positions requiring common educational backgrounds. For example, a recent college graduate is hired

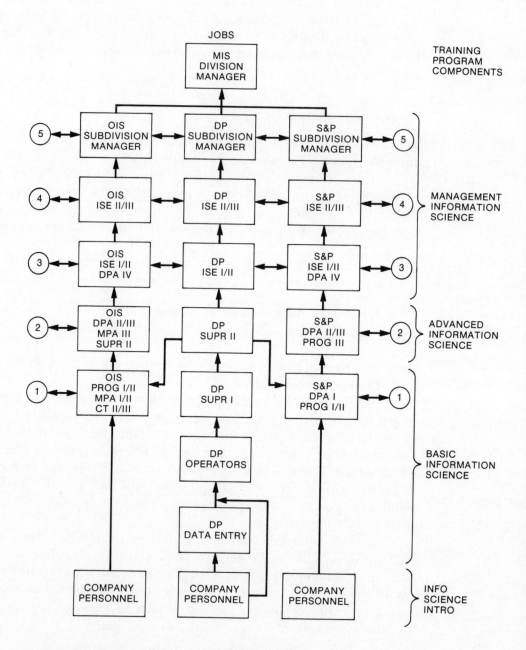

Figure 9.2 A job progression ladder linked to training requirements by level.
(*NOTE: Above abbreviations refer to job titles or unit titles.*)

onto the first rung of the ladder and moves up. Figure 9.2 illustrates such a ladder.

- A suspension bridge links positions with different kinds of tasks that may require different educational preparation and experience. A first-line supervisor who decides to make a move into computer programming, for example, may make a move over or down.
- A job with high visibility outside an organization acts as a spring-board that frequently leads to moves out and up in related firms. For example, an Air Force general working with a defense contractor on a multibillion-dollar weapons system may, upon retirement from the military, make a move out and up into the contracting firm.

The more explicit an employer makes career paths, the greater the likelihood that employees can establish realistic career goals and work toward them systematically. Training provides them with skills to do their present jobs better; education prepares them for moves along career paths; and development systematically rotates them through a series of jobs.

Helping Individuals Realize Their Potential. There are four ways by which an organization can deliver career management opportunities.[30]

1. Self-directed individual activities.
2. Supervisory counseling and coaching.
3. Professional career counseling given individually.
4. Group activities.

Each has distinct advantages and disadvantages.

Self-directed individual activities are prepared by the personnel or training department—or purchased from external vendors—to help employees in career planning. Examples include programmed instructional packages, in print or on the computer, which people work through at their own pace. These packages usually provide an overview of steps in career planning and a series of exercises. The advantage is that results are confidential and need not be shared with others by those who might feel threatened by doing so. The disadvantage is that there is little chance for feedback from co-workers or superiors unless it is specifically requested.

There are two types of self-directed individual activities: those geared to one organization or those that are more general. The first type is based on career paths connecting various jobs in a single firm. For example: planning for a move from market research to computer programming. The second type is geared toward establishing career plans in any organization.

Supervisory career coaching and counseling are normally handled by an immediate superior. They are similar to job or personal counseling, described earlier in this chapter. The idea is a simple one: supervisors offer advice and make themselves available for discussion.[31] A major advantage of this approach is that supervisors are best positioned to observe individual behavior, identify unique talents, and offer helpful suggestions. A big disadvantage is that they may lack adequate counseling skills and career planning knowledge.

Several methods can be used to formalize supervisory coaching: employee performance appraisals, formal mentoring, and training for supervisors on career planning.

Employee appraisals can stimulate discussions about an individual's long-term and short-term prospects—as well as help in making decisions about compensation, transfer, discharge, layoff, training needs, and human resources plans. Formal mentoring systems reinforce the responsibility of the supervisor or other mentor, who guides people over organizational and role socialization hurdles and along the career path they have chosen. (For more on mentoring, see Clawson;[32] Kram;[33] Johnson;[34] Meckel;[35] and Sikula and McKenna.[36]) Training for supervisors on career planning is often needed, even when they play no part directly. (For more on this subject, see Leibowitz and Schlossberg.[37]) Of course, it is crucial when they do play the part of counselor, which requires supporting skills different from those needed for directing or controlling. (See Carkhuff;[38] Egan;[39] and Meckel.[35])

Professional in-house career counseling, distinct from employee assistance programs, was rare until recently. It is now on the rise as government agencies and companies work together to retrain people left jobless because of plant shutdowns or relocations. Professionals in this field emphasize personal feelings as an important component in the career planning process, the need to supplement workshops with individual counseling, and the crucial issue of individual differences that may be overlooked by counselors lacking professional training. There are distinct advantages to using professionals: There can be a more objective approach than might be used by supervisors; the focus is on confidential, professional guidance; and sensitive matters like organizational culture need not be overlooked. Disadvantages include: the comparatively high cost; possibility of greater turnover; and the difficulty of finding trained professionals who are attuned to the special norms and culture of one organization.[40]

Group activities include career planning and development seminars, workshops, or counseling sessions. They are often the first step taken in an organization to address career matters and are frequently followed by self-directed individual activities and formalized supervisory counseling efforts. (Figure 9.3 illustrates topics covered in a typical workshop.) Workshops are advantageous in that they provide: a clear structure for addressing careers; an opportunity for people to share experiences, support, and perceptions of others; and an opportunity to discuss the policy of the organization on career matters and the nature of individual responsibility for career development.[41] They are disadvantageous in that they: ignore individual differences; may not be compatible with organizational realities; may build unrealistic expectations; are not necessarily the best place for individuals to explore different options for which additional information may be needed; and may give a false impression that career planning is a one-shot affair that needs no follow-up.

There are several possible approaches to group activities:

- An open forum without an agenda.
- A seminar on general career planning or about specific career planning in one organization.
- A workshop of short lectures followed by individual and group activities to build planning skills.
- Group career counseling sessions.

In an open forum, people meet to brainstorm on individual and organizational career planning. The leader should be a skilled group facilitator, capable of stimulating thought and raising consciousness.

A seminar has more structure. It focuses on building specific career planning skills and providing information about the process itself. It should be led by an instructor capable of making an effective presentation.

In a workshop, attention is divided equally between building career-planning skills and practicing those skills individually or in small groups. The leader alternates between roles as instructor, group facilitator, and individual development counselor.

Finally, group career counseling sessions meet periodically over many weeks or months, usually with fewer than 12 participants. They mutually

Figure 9.3 Topics in a career planning workshop

I. Day One

    A. Morning Session (9:00 A.M.–12 Noon) Overview of Career Development

        1. Participant introductions

        2. Sharing of expectations

        3. Overview of career development/career planning process

        4. Discussion of why career planning is needed

        5. Review of program content and objectives

        6. Introduction to organization's career philosophy

    B. Afternoon Session (1:00–5:00 P.M.) Initial Self-Assessment

        1. Who am I? What Do I Want to Do?

            a. Self-concept

            b. Values clarification

            c. Personality characteristics/personal style

            d. Motivational patterns

            e. Occupational interests

            f. Personal preferences

        2. Where Have I Been?

            a. Personal/educational background

            b. Work history/experience

            c. Key accomplishments/successes

            d. Peak experiences

            e. Significant life decisions

            f. Satisfying/dissatisfying experiences

II. Day Two

    A. Morning Session (9:00 A.M.–12 Noon) Completion of Self-Assessment

        1. Where Am I Now? What Can I Do?

            a. Analysis of current job

               —Behavioral demands

               —Importance of various job elements

               —Likes/dislikes

            b. Valued skills and abilities

               —Professional/technical

               —Managerial

               —Personal

Source: *Organizational Career Development: State of the Practice* by T. Gutteridge and F. Otte. American Society for Training and Development, 1983.

explore their personal feelings on career issues and serve as a support and resource group. This approach can be effective when people share something in common—such as the job search following a plant shutdown. The leader serves as instructor, group facilitator, and individual development counselor.

Outcomes of Career Planning, Management, and Counseling

The results of career planning, management, and counseling efforts coincide with many of the work outputs of the individual development counselor role. Individuals acquire skills to plan for their careers and learn to accept responsibility for them. They also know when they need more information, ways to go about getting it, and how to assess its usefulness.

Other major outcomes of career planning and management include people who:

1. Are self-directed and know who they are and where they are going.

2. Can appreciate the value of training, education, and developmental activities in helping them and others realize their potential and their career aspirations.

3. Are willing to help others as they were helped by serving as formal or informal mentors or counselors in the future.

References

1. Ramsey, K. "Counseling Employees." In *Human Resources Management and Development Handbook*, W. Tracey, ed. New York: Amacom, 1985.

2. Nathan, P. "Failures in Prevention: Why We Can't Prevent the Devastating Effect of Alcoholism and Drug Abuse." *American Psychologist* (April, 1983): pp. 459–467.

3. Wagner, W. "Assisting Employees with Personal Problems." *Personnel Administrator* (November, 1982): pp. 59–64.

4. Bergland, B. "Career Planning: The Use of Sequential Evaluated Experience." In *Vocational Guidance and Human Development*, E. Herr, ed. Boston: Houghton Mifflin, 1974.

5. Gelatt, H. "Decision-Making: A Conceptual Frame of Reference for Counseling." *Journal of Counseling Psychology* 9 (1962) 3: pp. 240–245.

6. Herr, E., and S. Cramer. *Career Guidance Through the Life Span.* Boston: Little Brown, 1984.

7. Herr, E., and S. Cramer. *Career Guidance Through One Life Span.* Boston: Little Brown, 1979.

8. Hershenson, D., and R. Roth. "A Decisional Process Model of Vocational Development." *Journal of Counseling Psychology* 13 (1966) 3: pp. 368–370.

9. Katz, M. *Decisions and Values.* New York: College Entrance Examination Board, 1963.

10. Katz, M. "A Model of Guidance for Career Decision-Making." *Vocational Guidance Quarterly* 15 (1966) 1: pp. 2–10.

11. Krumboltz, J., and D. Sorenson. *Career Decision Making.* Madison, WI: Counseling Films, 1974.

12. Kinnier, R., and J. Krumboltz. "Procedures for Successful Career Counseling." In *Designing Careers: Counseling to Enhance Education, Work, and Leisure,* N. Gysbers & Associates, eds. San Francisco: Jossey-Bass, 1984.

13. Shaffer, B. *Humanistic Psychology.* Englewood Cliffs, NJ: Prentice-Hall, 1978.

14. Blau, P., J. Gustad, and R. Jessor. "Occupational Choice: A Conceptual Framework." *Industrial Labor Relations Review* 9 (1956): pp. 531–543.

15. Borrow, H. "Occupational Socialization: Acquiring a Sense of Work." In *Designing Careers: Counseling to Enhance Education, Work, and Leisure,* N. Gysbers & Associates, eds. San Francisco: Jossey-Bass, 1984.

16. Hall, R. "Theoretical Trends in the Sociology of Occupations." *Sociological Quarterly* 24 (1983): pp. 5–23.

17. Bardin, E., B. Nachmann, and S. Segal. "An Articulated Framework for Vocational Development." *Journal of Counseling Psychology* 10 (1963): pp. 107–116.

18. Ginzberg, E. "Career Development." In *Career Choice and Development,* D. Brown and L. Brooks, eds. San Francisco: Jossey-Bass, 1984.

19. Ginzberg, E. *Career Guidance.* New York: McGraw-Hill, 1971.

20. Ginzberg, E., S. Ginsburg, S. Axelrod, and J. Herman. *Occupational Choice.* New York: Columbia University Press, 1951.

21. Erikson, E. *Childhood and Society.* New York: Norton, 1963.

22. Sheehy, G. *Passages: Predictable Crises of Adult Life.* New York: Bantam, 1976.

23. Krumboltz, J., A. Mitchell, and H. Gelatt. "Applications of Social Learning Theory of Career Selection." *Focus on Guidance* 8 (1975): pp. 1–16.

24. Roe, A. "Perspectives on Vocational Development." In *Perspectives on Vocational Development,* J. Whiteley and A. Resnikoff, eds. Washington, D.C.: American Personnel and Guidance Association, 1972.

25. Schein, E. *Career Dynamics: Matching Individual and Organizational Needs.* Reading, MA: Addison-Wesley, 1978.

26. Super, D. "Vocational Development Theory: Persons, Positions, and Processes." In *Perspectives on Vocational Development,* J. Whiteley and A. Resnikoff, eds. Washington, D.C.: American Personnel and Guidance Association, 1972.

27. Super, D. "Career and Life Development." In *Career Choice and Development,* D. Brown and L. Brooks, eds. San Francisco: Jossey-Bass, 1984.

28. Super, D. "Perspectives on the Meaning and Value of Work." In *Designing Careers: Counseling to Enhance Education, Work, and Leisure,* N. Gysbers & Associates, eds. San Francisco: Jossey-Bass, 1984.

29. Burack, E. "The Sphinx's Riddle: Life and Career Cycles." *Training and Development Journal* 38 (1984) 4: pp. 52–61.

30. Bowen, D., and D. Hall. "Career Planning for Employee Development: A Primer for Managers." *California Management Review* (Winter, 1977): pp. 29–30.

31. Gilley, J., and H. Moore. "Managers as Career Enhancers." *Personnel Administrator* 31 (1986) 3: pp. 51–60.

32. Clawson, J. "Is Mentoring Necessary?" *Training and Development Journal* 39 (1985) 4: pp. 36–39.

33. Kram, K. "Improving the Mentoring Process." *Training and Development Journal* 39 (1985) 4: pp. 40–43.

34. Johnson, M. "Mentors—The Key to Development and Growth." *Training and Development Journal* 34 (1980) 7: pp. 55–57.

35. Meckel, N. "The Manager as Career Counselor." *Training and Development Journal* 35 (1981) 7: pp. 64–69.

36. Sikula, A., and J. McKenna. "Individuals Must Take Charge of Career Development." *Personnel Administrator* (October, 1983): pp. 89–97.

37. Leibowitz, Z., and N. Schlossberg. "Training Managers for Their Role in a Career Development System." *Training and Development Journal* 35 (1981) 7: pp. 72–79.

38. Carkhuff, R. *The Art of Helping.* Amherst, MA: Human Resource Development Press, 1972.

39. Egan, G. *The Skilled Helper: A Model for Systematic Helping and Interpersonal Relating.* Monterey, CA: Brooks-Cole, 1975.

40. Gutteridge, T., and F. Otte. *Organizational Career Development: State of the Practice.* Washington, D.C.: American Society for Training and Development, 1983.

41. Ibid.

For More Information

Brown, A. "Career Development 1986." *Personnel Administrator* 31 (1986) 3: pp. 44–55.

Brown, D., and L. Brooks & Associates. *Career Choice and Development.* San Francisco: Jossey-Bass, 1984.

Burack, E., and N. Mathys. *Career Management in Organizations.* Lake Forest, IL: Brace-Park, 1980.

Connolly, P. *Promotional Practices and Policies: Career Building in the '80s.* New York: Pergamon Press, 1985.

Dickman, F., and W. Emener. "Employee Assistance Programs: Basic Concepts, Attributes, and an Evaluation." *Personnel Administrator* 27 (1982) 8: pp. 55–62.

Gardner, J. *Self-Renewal: The Individual and the Innovative Society.* New York: Harper and Row, 1964.

Gysbers, N. "Major Trends in Career Development Theory and Practice." In *Designing careers: Counseling to enhance education, work, and leisure,* N. Gysbers & Associates, eds. San Francisco: Jossey-Bass, 1984.

Healy, C. *Career Development Counseling Through Life Stages.* Boston: Allyn & Bacon, 1982.

Kellogg, M. *Career Management.* New York: American Management Association, 1972.

Loughary, J., and T. Ripley. *Career and Life Planning Guide.* Chicago: Follett Publishing, 1976.

Miller, A. "Learning Theory and Vocational Decisions." *Personnel and Guidance Journal* 47 (1968): pp. 18–23.

Lewis, J., and M. Lewis. *Counseling Programs for Employees in the Workplace.* Monterey, CA: Brooks/Cole, 1986.

Myers, D. *Establishing and Building Employee Assistance Programs.* Westport, CT: Quorum Books, 1984.

Osipow, S. *Theories of Career Development,* 3rd ed. New York: Appleton-Century-Crofts, 1983.

Parsons, G., and J. Wiftil. "Occupational Mobility as Measured by Holland's Theory of Career Selection." *Journal of Vocational Behavior,* 5 (1974): pp. 321–330.

Patterson, C. *Theories of Counseling and Psychotherapy,* 2nd ed. New York: Harper and Row, 1973.

Randolph, B. "Managerial Career Coaching." *Training and Development Journal* 35 (1981) 7: pp. 54–55.

Robbins, P. *Successful Midlife Career Change.* New York: Amacom, 1978.

Rothwell, W. "Thinking Strategically." *Training News* (May, 1984): pp. 19–20.

Sommers, D., and A. Eck. "Occupational Mobility in the American Labor Force." *Monthly Labor Review* 100 (1977): pp. 3–19.

Spenner, K., L. Otto, and V. Call. *Career Lines and Careers.* Lexington, MA: Lexington Books, 1982.

Stockard, J. *Career Development and Job Training.* New York: Amacom, 1977.

Strauss, A. *Professions, Work and Careers.* New Brunswick, NJ: Transaction Books, 1975.

Walker, J. *Human Resource Planning.* New York: McGraw-Hill, 1980.

Walker, J., and T. Gutteridge. *Career Planning Practices.* New York: Amacom, 1979.

5

The HRD department—its strategy and management.

The HRD department is a distinct component of many organizations, and the manager of the department has responsibilities similar to those of other managers: planning, directing, controlling, and staffing the department. However, the HRD department is unique in that its efforts call for management skills somewhat different from those needed to manage other facets of organizational activity. How are long-range strategic plans for an HRD department prepared? How is the department itself managed? This part addresses these questions and thus focuses on the HRD department as the vehicle for coordinating formal employee training, education, and development in an organization.

CHAPTER 10

Managing HRD at the strategic level.

This chapter discusses the HRD professional as strategist, defining this role as well as its associated competencies and work outputs.

Managing HRD at the strategic level involves developing a long-range plan for the training department. This plan must take into account present strengths and weaknesses and likely future opportunities and threats affecting the department. Preparing this plan does not differ markedly from strategic planning for the organization itself (described in Chapter 6). However, it does require additional steps that take into account plans of the organization, its human resources activities in general, and known career aspirations of individual employees. ■

The Role of Strategist

According to *Models for Excellence,* the strategist role consists of "developing long-range plans for what the training and development structure, organization, direction, policies, programs, services, and practices will be in order to accomplish the training and development mission." To enact this role the HRD practitioner must be able to exhibit:

- Futuring Skill
- Organization Understanding
- Personnel/HR-Field Understanding
- Training-and-Development-Field Understanding
- Intellectual Versatility
- Data-Reduction Skill
- Organization-Behavior Understanding
- Industry Understanding
- Cost/Benefit-Analysis Skill
- Model-Building Skill

Of these competencies (described in Chapter 4), the first four are most important and require the greatest expertise of any HRD role.

According to *Models for Excellence,* typical work outputs of the strategist include:

1. "[The] Training and Development strategy included in the broad human resources strategy of the client organization."
2. "Identification (written/oral) of long-range T&D strengths, weaknesses, opportunities, threats."
3. "Descriptions of the T&D function and its outputs in the future."
4. "Identification of forces/trends (technical, social, economic, etc.) impacting T&D."
5. "Guidelines/plans for implementing long-range goals."
6. "Alternative directions for T&D."
7. "Cost/benefit analyses of the impact of T&D on the organization."

This role is very highly correlated with that of manager (treated in Chapter 11) but negatively correlated with those of instructor and program administrator.

HRD strategists are, of course, leaders in the strategic planning process of the department. Though almost anyone can propose plans for the department, ultimate responsibility for strategy rests with the highest-level decision-maker in much the same way that corporate strategy ultimately rests with the CEO and Board of Directors. Together with those from inside and outside the department, the highest-level decision-maker in HRD sets out to:

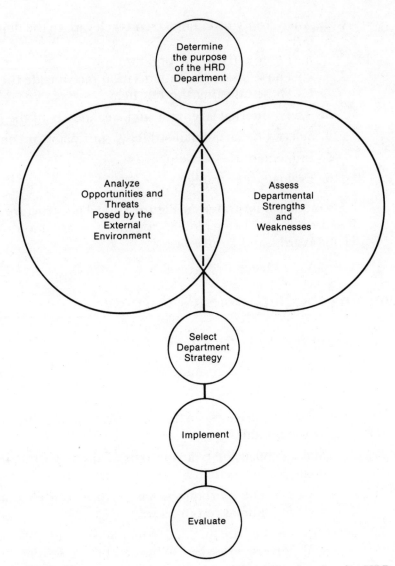

Figure 10.1 A simplified model of strategic planning for the HRD department

1. Determine the purpose of the department, particularly as it relates to:
   a. Organizational strategic plans
   b. Human resources plans
   c. Individual career plans

2. Analyze environmental trends relevant to the department, particularly:
   a. Those outside the organization
   b. Those inside the organization but outside the department
   c. Those affecting the HR field
3. Assess internal strengths and weaknesses of the department.
4. Select a departmental strategy—but plan for contingencies.
5. Implement the strategy.
6. Evaluate the strategy.

This model is illustrated in Figure 10.1. The structure of this chapter is based on parts of this model. For more information on this subject see Hall,[1] Ward,[2] and Zemke.[3]

Determining the Department's Purpose

Asking the Right Questions

It is important to determine the purpose of the department in order to:

- Avoid duplication of effort and overlapping duties with other parts of the organization.
- Make explicit the contributions of the department to the purpose, goals, and objectives of the organization.
- Ensure that important work is performed while unimportant efforts receive minimal resources.
- Provide the basis for departmental strategy, because accountability and purpose must be established before setting direction.

In addition, a statement of purpose provides a starting point for allocating responsibilities to units and work groups within the department. For example, it would be difficult to specify the role of management training when that of the department itself is unclear.

Several questions are particularly important to consider in determining departmental purpose.

First, what role is (and should be) enacted by the department relative to training, education, and development? Individual managers do bear primary responsibility for ensuring the best use and development of their human resources.[4] Individual employees bear responsibility for self-development. How, then, does the role of the HRD department relate to these managerial and individual responsibilities? How should it contribute over time? Should priority be given to short-term training, intermediate-term education, long-term development efforts—or what combination of them?

Second, whose needs are given most attention and through what products or services? Who are the primary clients or consumers and how are they to be served? The HRD department may deal with an assortment of groups—new employees, first-line supervisors, middle managers, top managers, company customers, and even representatives of suppliers, distributing wholesalers, and many others. Should the client be considered the trainee who receives services directly, the trainee's superior whose support is crucial, the organization as a whole that benefits, or some combination? Which clientele is of first importance? second? third? How are the needs of this clientele to be met: classroom instruction? individualized instruction? job aids? which delivery methods are most important? why?

Third, what is the intended relationship between the HRD department and the organization's internal and external environments? To what extent is the department's major role to routinize interactions and procedures inside the organization? To what extent, on the other hand, is its major role to help prepare the organization for changes created by external pressures?

Fourth, what is the role of the department relative to other potential sources of training and education? What does the HRD department do that cannot be performed by universities, community colleges, professional societies, and external consultants? What part do they play in the overall scheme of the organization's HRD efforts? Why?

Fifth, what is the role of the department concerning special issues that affect professions or occupations within the organization? In some fields—accounting and nursing, for example—the trend is toward mandatory continuing professional education for practitioners in order to renew licensure. How important is it for the HRD department to help individuals comply with such requirements? To what extent does this purpose supersede others—such as training people how to do their jobs better in one organizational setting?

Sixth, how should the HRD department contribute to organizational strategic plans? As noted in Chapter 6, pursuit of strategy sometimes requires new knowledge, skills, and abilities. But how and when are they to be acquired? Through what means: recruitment? training? education? development? other HR activities? Clearly, what the HRD department does should be integrated with other HR activities and departments. Such initiatives also influence individual career planning by specifying, from the organization's standpoint, appropriate career management efforts.

These issues—and many others—should be considered when determining the purpose of the HRD department. Of course, this purpose can be influenced by the sometimes conflicting expectations of various top managers and others in the organization. It can also be influenced by changes in corporate strategy or in how the department is placed in the organizational structure.

Methods for Determining Department Purpose

Several methods can be used to determine or review the purpose of the HRD department:

1. The top HRD executive can make decisions and then issue them formally in writing or informally in meetings. This method operates from top down. It may be appropriate when the department is new or when the organizational culture is authoritarian.

2. The top HRD executive and his or her immediate subordinates can meet to discuss and consult on the department's formal mission or purpose statement. Subordinates can offer their opinions, but the executive makes the final decision. This consultative method is appropriate when the department has been in operation for some time, subordinates are experienced in the organization, and the HRD director wants to gain their commitment to the mission statement.

3. The top HRD executive establishes a structure—a committee, a series of meetings, or an open forum—to deal with the issue of purpose, but does not influence outcomes. It is appropriate when the department is highly professional; when members know the HRD field, the organization, the department, and the industry; and when the organization encourages a bottom-up approach to strategy-making.

Undoubtedly, other approaches can be used. Variations of the above approaches could include representatives of line management, professional groups served, or others with special interests in the process of establishing or reviewing the purpose and direction of the HRD department.

The checklist appearing in Figure 10.2 should be helpful in making

Figure 10.2 A checklist for determining the purpose of the HRD department

In Considering the Purpose of the HRD Department, have you Addressed the Following Issues:	*Yes* (✔)	*No* (✔)	*N/A* (✔)	*How did you Answer the Question?*
1. The role of the department relative to:				
a. Training?	( )	( )	( )	
b. Education?	( )	( )	( )	
c. Development?	( )	( )	( )	
2. What relationship exists between the role of the department and:				
a. The responsibility of each supervisor to train and develop subordinates?	( )	( )	( )	
b. Individual responsibility for self-development?	( )	( )	( )	
3. What relative priorities should be associated with:				
a. Short-term instructional efforts? (training)	( )	( )	( )	
b. Intermediate-term instructional efforts? (eduation)	( )	( )	( )	
c. Long-term instructional efforts? (development)	( )	( )	( )	
4. The clients who are				
a. Of first importance?	( )	( )	( )	
b. Of second importance?	( )	( )	( )	
c. Of third importance?	( )	( )	( )	

Figure 10.2 (Continued)

In Considering the Purpose of the HRD Department, have you Addressed the Following Issues:	Yes (✔)	No (✔)	N/A (✔)	How did you Answer the Question?
5. Which products or services are *a.* Of first importance?	( )	( )	( )	
b. Of second importance?	( )	( )	( )	
c. Of third importance?	( )	( )	( )	
6. Which means of delivering products or services are *a.* Of first importance?	( )	( )	( )	
b. Of second importance?	( )	( )	( )	
c. Of third importance?	( )	( )	( )	
7. What is the desirable relationship between the HRD department and *a.* The external environment?	( )	( )	( )	
b. The internal environment?	( )	( )	( )	
8. The role of the HRD department relative to external providers of training and education?	( )	( )	( )	
9. The role of the HRD department relative to special issues affecting professions or occupations in the organization?	( )	( )	( )	
10. How the HRD department contributes to organizational strategic plans?	( )	( )	( )	
11. How the HRD department contributes to human resources (staffing) plans?	( )	( )	( )	
12. How the HRD department contributes to individual career plans?	( )	( )	( )	

sure that the most important issues are considered in determining the HRD department's purpose.

Benefits of Establishing Department Purpose

Determining the purpose of the department should result in:

- A description of its guiding philosophy, priorities, and role.
- A better understanding among those who participated in the process of grappling with problems facing the department.
- Commitment to fulfilling the purpose on the part of the department and the whole organization.

The process of grappling with the issue of departmental purpose is as important as the results achieved. It provides an opportunity for team-building and for collecting views of many groups about the appropriate role of the department. The outcomes—and, indeed, the process—will reveal much about the culture of the organization and values of key decision-makers.

Though the department's purpose need not be stated formally in writing, there are distinct advantages in doing so. A written purpose statement can:

1. Help those outside the HRD department better understand its role.
2. Help those inside the department understand how it contributes to the organization and to employees.
3. Focus thinking about possible new initiatives.

A simple purpose statement might read:

> The purpose of the HRD department in the XYZ Company is to provide for the most efficient, effective, yet humanistic utilization of people in the company through:
>
> 1. Training geared to jobs people now hold.
> 2. Educating people for future jobs in the company.
> 3. Developing individuals through long-term planned experience.

Analyzing Environmental Trends

What Factors to Consider

The purpose statement of the HRD department helps to clarify its stance relative to the organization's environment. There are four possible stances, illustrated in Figure 10.3:

1. A Type 1 department has very few, if any, independent transactions with the external environment. Information is filtered through the organization, and the HRD strategist is dependent on other people such as line managers for the assessment of organizational needs.

2. A Type 2 department has some independent transactions with the external environment, but they are limited. Although most information about learning needs is filtered through the organization, it is also available from such external sources as consultants, vendors, or customers.

3. A Type 3 department has substantial dealings outside the organization. Equal amounts of information about external conditions are available internally and externally.

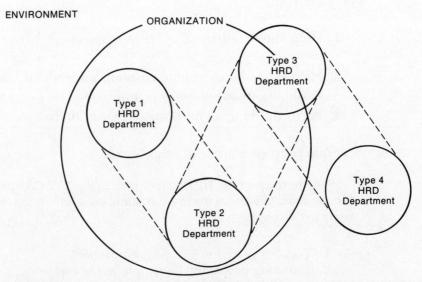

Figure 10.3 Four different ways an HRD department can relate to its environment

4. A Type 4 department is autonomous, transacting business more with those outside than inside the organization—for example, a department funded solely by sales of training packages and consulting services to company customers.

The more autonomous the department, the more likely it is to (1) develop a base of information sufficient for setting its own direction, perhaps independent of the client organization, and (2) acquire valuable data about the external environment that can be used in establishing organizational strategy.

Several different environments affect an HRD department. The most important ones include:

- That outside the organization, but influencing it.
- That inside the organization but outside the department.
- That of the general HR or personnel management field.
- That of the HRD field specifically.

Conditions in each environment can pose future threats and opportunities to the department in the enactment of its role.

First, the HRD strategist should consider trends in the organization's environment. For example, how will changes in each of the following factors influence the organization and, through it, the HRD department:

1. Economic conditions?
2. Governmental and legal conditions?
3. Competitive conditions?
4. Suppliers?
5. Distributors?
6. Social conditions?
7. Demographic conditions?

There are many others that could be considered. Each external trend can create pressure on an organization to change. In many instances, such change calls for new knowledge, skills, and abilities that can be supplied in whole or part through HRD initiatives sponsored by the department.

Second, the HRD strategist should consider trends inside the organization but outside the HRD department. How will changes in each of the following influence the HRD department:

1. Key leadership positions?
2. Organization policies?
3. Structure and reporting relationships?
4. Methods for measuring individual performance and allocating rewards?

Each change may create unique learning needs, which will in turn pose opportunities or threats for the HRD department.

Third, the HRD strategist should consider trends affecting human resources. How will changes in each of the following influence the HRD department:

1. Selection and staffing policies and practices?
2. Compensation and benefits?
3. Employee assistance programs?
4. Union/labor relations?
5. Organization development?
6. Personnel research and information systems?
7. Organization and job design?

As noted in Chapter 7, a change in any of these areas may create learning needs and thus exert pressure on the department for action.

Fourth, the HRD strategist should be sensitive to changes in the HRD field itself. For example, what trends or issues can be identified relative to:

1. Training content?
2. Training delivery systems?
3. Training resources?
4. Managing the training function? [5]

The first question affects all others, because it involves the problems and concerns of line managers, top managers, trainees, and other groups interested in HRD. The second question directs the strategist to look at how instruction is being offered. The third question asks the strategist to consider what resources—time, money, staff—will be made available in the future. Finally, the fourth question directs attention to issues of likely future concern to managers of the HRD function, such as the possibility of increased regulation.[6]

The process of analyzing environments calls for Futuring Skill, the single most important competency of the strategist. When applied to the inner workings of the organization outside the HRD department, this competency becomes synonymous with that of Organization Understanding. When applied to trends affecting human resources, it is synonymous with Personnel/HR-Field Understanding. When applied to trends in HRD itself, it is synonymous with Training-and-Development-Field Understanding.

What Methods to Use

Methods for environmental analysis of an HRD department need not differ markedly from techniques used for an organization. They include:

- *Unstructured expert opinion,* in which representatives of key groups are asked open-ended questions about trends likely to affect the department.
- *Structured expert opinion,* in which representatives of key groups are involved in surveys, Delphi procedures, or Nominal Group Technique.
- *Scenarios,* in which short descriptions of future situations are used in trying to predict their effects.
- *Trend extrapolation,* in which past issues are projected into the future to see what effect they will have.

Any of these approaches—and others [7,8]—can be applied to most of the environments described in the previous section.[9]

Figure 10.4 can help in organizing the environmental analysis process.

What Are the Results?

The results of environmental analysis should include:

1. Descriptions, written or oral, of opportunities and threats facing the HRD department.

Figure 10.4 Environmental analysis for HRD

DIRECTIONS: For each subject listed in Column 1 describe in Column 2 what kinds of changes are expected *in three years,* what kind of learning needs they might create for people in your organization in Column 3, and how those needs will pose threats or opportunities for the HRD department in Column 4.

Column 1 *Subject*	*Column 2* *What Kinds of Changes are Expected in Three Years?*	*Column 3* *What Learning Needs Might be Created by this Change?*	*Column 4* *How will these Needs Pose Threats or Opportunities for the HRD Department?*
1. Economic conditions outside the organization.			
2. Governmental and legal conditions affecting the organization.			
3. Competitive conditions faced by the organization.			
4. Suppliers of the organization's key inputs.			
5. Distributors of the organization's products or services.			
6. Social conditions affecting the organization.			
7. Demographic conditions affecting the organization.			
8. Changes in key leadership positions in the organization.			
9. Changes in organizational policies.			
10. Changes in organization structure.			
11. Changes in methods for measuring individual performance.			

Figure 10.4 (Continued)

Column 1 *Subject*	*Column 2* *What Kinds of Changes are Expected in Three Years?*	*Column 3* *What Learning Needs Might be Created by this Change?*	*Column 4* *How will these Needs Pose Threats or Opportunities for the HRD Department?*
12. Changes in selection and staffing practices.			
13. Changes in compensation/benefits.			
14. Changes in employee assistance programs.			
15. Changes in union/labor relations.			
16. Changes in organization development activities.			
17. Changes in personnel research and information systems.			
18. Changes in job design.			
19. Trends in training content.			
20. Trends in training delivery systems.			
21. Trends in training resources.			
22. Trends in managing the training function.			
23. Other trends.			

2. Descriptions of forces and trends that are likely to create learning needs in the organization.

3. Information of potential value for inclusion in organizational strategic and human resources plans.

4. Information of value for long-range instructional (i.e., curriculum) planning.

Environmental analysis should enable the HRD department to anticipate—not just react to—organizational problems.

Assessing Departmental Strengths and Weaknesses

Questions to Ask

Establishing the purpose of the HRD department provides a starting point for judging its strengths and weaknesses. To some extent such judgments are influenced by the life-cycle stage of the department. A life cycle refers to predictable stages of development over time. Individuals develop through a life cycle, described in the previous chapter. Organizations can also be said to pass through life cycles.[10]

An HRD department goes through at least four life-cycle stages.[11]

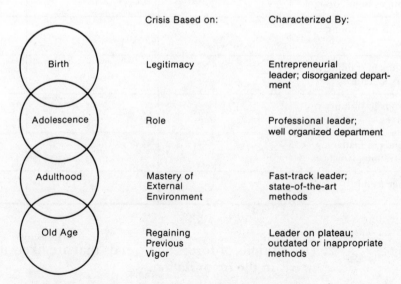

	Crisis Based on:	Characterized By:
Birth	Legitimacy	Entrepreneurial leader; disorganized department
Adolescence	Role	Professional leader; well organized department
Adulthood	Mastery of External Environment	Fast-track leader; state-of-the-art methods
Old Age	Regaining Previous Vigor	Leader on plateau; outdated or inappropriate methods

Figure 10.5 Life-cycle stages of an HRD department

Each is typified by a central conflict that must be resolved before passage to the next stage (see Figure 10.5).

During infancy, the department is poorly organized. The entrepreneur manager who undertakes start-up takes advantage of obvious problems and needs of line managers. The central crisis concerns legitimacy—that is, acceptance of the department by others. Failure leads to elimination.

During adolescence, the department becomes better organized. The leader is an HRD professional, perhaps a specialist in the field. The central crisis has to do with defining the department's role—that is, finding a niche and a clientele. Failure here also leads to elimination.

During adulthood, the department has mastered the internal environment of the organization and may begin dealing with the world outside. Methods are state-of-the-art. The central crisis involves mastery of the external environment.

During old age, the department loses vitality. The leader may have reached a plateau and could be unhappy about it. The central crisis involves regaining previous vigor.

Every HRD department has specific strengths and weaknesses, some influenced by what life-cycle stage it is in. In assessing these strengths and weaknesses the HRD strategist can ask the following questions: [12]

1. To what extent does the department have the ability to *research* and *prepare* instruction to match identified learning needs in the future?

   This question concerns the department's potential for assessing learning needs and designing instruction based on that assessment. If the need is important but expertise does not exist within the department, then it may be necessary to have a consultant carry out this phase of an important project. Though it is customary to think of hiring consultants from outside the organization, that is not always necessary. There may be those within the firm but outside the department whose skills could be borrowed for a short time.[13]

2. To what extent does the department possess the ability to *market* instruction to meet identified learning needs in the future? Consider cost of materials and labor, productivity of the department, and motivation of staff.

This question concerns the marketing of instruction. If the HRD Department can design learning experiences but cannot gear them to the unique concerns of special groups, then it is unlikely that a learning need can be met with in-house resources; rather, alternative strategies will have to be used. Examples include relying on external consultants, sending people to outside courses, or sending a staff member out to build the skills needed to offer instruction later internally. The cost of materials and staff, the amount of time available, and other relevant factors should be considered.

3. To what extent is the department able to *deliver* instruction to meet identified learning needs in the future? Consider the work loads of staff, their familiarity with areas in which instruction is to be offered, and methods of delivery available.

   This question deals with delivering instruction. It does little good to undertake a project when work loads are already excessive, trainers know very little about the area in which instruction is to be offered, and there is little chance of reaching all who might have the need.

4. To what extent does the department have *funding* (or a good chance of obtaining it) to deliver instruction to meet identified learning needs in the future?

   This question focuses on financing. If a learning need is worth addressing, somebody should be willing to pay. It is a test of commitment to obtain funding if it is not already available.

5. To what extent does the department have the ability to *manage* the instructional process? Consider such issues as departmental purpose, values of managers and staff, and turnover.

   This final question focuses on management. How well does an identified learning need match up to the purpose of the department? How well does it match up to values of departmental decision-makers? Will there be consistent perspective over the duration of the project, or is turnover so high that a long-term effort is unrealistic?

The process of assessing departmental strengths and weaknesses calls for organization understanding, the second most important competency of the HRD strategist. When applied to the HRD effort in one setting, it is closely associated with such other competencies as understanding of personnel/HR and of the training and development field.

Methods for Assessing Strengths and Weaknesses

Information about strengths and weaknesses of the HRD department can come from outside the department, inside, or both. Any number of specialized methods can be helpful, including:

1. Using unstructured expert opinion much as it is used in environmental analysis. Representatives of important groups inside and outside the HRD department are asked open-ended questions about its strengths and weaknesses.

2. Using structured expert opinion. Representatives of key groups participate in specialized surveys, Delphi panels, or other formal processes. They are asked to consider structured questions about the HRD department.

3. Using training department audits that focus on the programmatic outcomes of the department [14]—or on how well results match intentions or departmental objectives.

Any of these approaches—and such others as cost-benefit analysis [15] and portfolio analysis [16]—can be applied to departmental projects as well as to the department as a whole.

Try assessing strengths and weaknesses yourself, using the exercise in Figure 10.6.

Assessment Results

An assessment of HRD department strengths and weaknesses should produce information about its present status relative to possible future opportunities and threats. This information will provide the basis for comparisons that can help in determining departmental strategy.

Selecting, Implementing, and Evaluating Departmental Strategy

Issues to Consider

Selecting strategy for the HRD department should be based on a comparison of environmental threats and opportunities with internal strengths

Figure 10.6 Assessing departmental strengths and weaknesses

DIRECTIONS: Use this exercise to continue the process begun in Figure 10.4. In Column 5, describe how well the department is presently prepared to design instruction to meet the learning need identified in Column 3 (Figure 10.4). In Columns 6, 7, 8, and 9, describe how well the department is presently prepared to market, deliver, fund and manage instruction to meet each learning need identified in Column 3.

Column 5	Column 6	Column 7	Column 8	Column 9
How Well-Prepared is the HRD Department to Design Instruction?	*How Well-Prepared is the HRD Department to Market Instruction?*	*How Well-Prepared is the HRD Department to Deliver Instruction?*	*How Well-Prepared is the HRD Department to Fund Instruction?*	*How Well-Prepared is the HRD Department to Manage Instruction?*

Add paper as needed, but be sure to use this exercise in conjunction with Figures 10.4, 10.7, 10.8, and 10.9.

and weaknesses. Implementation, not treated at length here, is synonymous with management (see Chapter 11). Evaluation occurs before, during, and after implementation and helps reveal the relative success of the strategy selected.

There are three issues to consider in the selection process:

1. What strategy can take maximum advantage of departmental strengths while minimizing departmental weaknesses?
2. How accurate is the information on which the strategy is based?
3. What should be done in the event of unexpected environmental change?

The first question addresses actual selection of strategy; the second, confidence in the choice; and third, contingency plans.

Strategy selection is a key to the entire planning process for the department. Selection is:

- Partly rational in that the strategist, much like an entrepreneur, looks for environmental trends that stimulate learning needs and enable the department to have maximum impact on the organization.
- Partly political in that successful implementation, following strategy selection, will depend on support from others.[17] Most strategy-making is informal.[18] This makes it essential to give others—particularly those outside the department—participation in the selection process so that they will support implementation.

Information used in strategy selection will seldom be highly accurate. It is important to keep in mind that environmental analysis and assessments of strengths and weaknesses can provide guidance for, but never certainty about, future initiatives. Strategists never have enough information, though the more they have the more accurate the resulting predictions and decisions.[19]

To be ready for unexpected environmental change, some contingency planning is desirable. What if events do not turn out as expected? Should department strategy be abandoned? Not at all. The idea is to predict, as much as possible, likely alternative events and departmental reactions to them. Examples of such events include: an unexpected merger, acquisition, or takeover; the entrance of a major competitor; or sudden deregulation (or increased regulation) of the industry or HRD practice. In each case, the impact on the department can influence strategy. What is the likelihood of these and other such changes? What learning needs will they create in the organization, and how can the department respond?

During implementation, HRD strategists should bear in mind such issues as:

1. What specific outcomes are expected?
2. What risks are involved?
3. What resources are needed, including
   a. funds?
   b. staff?
   c. time?
4. How does the department's position in the organization's reporting structure affect strategy?
5. How should the department be structured to support implementation of plans?

Some of these questions are addressed in the next chapter.

During evaluation, HRD strategists should consider:

1. To what extent are results likely to match expected outcomes?
2. To what extent *are* results matching expected outcomes?
3. What are the aggregate:
   a. costs of departmental efforts?
   b. benefits resulting from departmental efforts?

Evaluation occurs before, during, and after implementation. Evaluation need not always focus on specific outcomes of single courses or other learning events; rather, it can focus on aggregate outcomes—that is, the total impact of the HRD department on the organization it serves.

Methods for Selecting Strategy

Selecting the strategy of the HRD department is not significantly different from that of selecting organizational or HR strategy, with one exception: pains must be taken to ensure that there is no inherent conflict between initiatives of the department and those of other parts of the organization. Indeed, it is preferable that HRD be part of an overall, integrated strategy

Figure 10.7 Selecting HRD department strategy

DIRECTIONS: Use this exercise to continue the process begun in Figure 10.4. First, review Columns 1–4 and 5–9. Then for each subject (in Column 1, Figure 10.4) identify in Column 10 what the department should do. In Column 11, consider the accuracy of the information on which the strategy is based. In Column 12, consider one or more alternative strategies in the event the environment changes.

Column 10	*Column 11*	*Column 12*
What Strategy can take Maximum Advantages of Departmental Strengths While Minimizing Weaknesses? (Identify what to do)	*How Accurate is the Information on Which the Strategy is Based?*	*What Should be Done—That is, What Alternative Strategy Should be Used—in the Event of Unexpected Environmental Change?*

Add paper as needed, but be sure to use this exercise in conjunction with Figures 10.4, 10.6, 10.8, and 10.9.

Figure 10.8 Implementing department strategy

DIRECTIONS: Use this exercise to continue the process begun in Figure 10.4. In Column 13, identify what results are expected; in 14, what risks are involved; in 15, what resources are needed for implementation; in 16, how departmental placement may affect implementation; in 17, how the department should be structured.

Column 13	Column 14	Column 15			Column 16	Column 17
		What Resources are Needed?				
		A	*B*	*C*		
What Specific Outcomes are Expected from the Strategy?	*What Risks are Involved?*	*Funds*	*Staff*	*Time*	*How does the Department's Placement in the Organization Affect Strategy?*	*How Should the Department be Structured to Support Strategy?*

Add paper as needed, but be sure to use this exercise in conjunction with Figures 10.4, 10.6, 10.7, and 10.9.

Figure 10.9 Evaluating department strategy

DIRECTIONS: Use this exercise to continue the process begun in Figure 10.4. In Column 18, evaluate before strategy is implemented; in 19, evaluate periodically during implementation; in 20, evaluate at the point when departmental strategy will be changed.

Column 18	Column 19	Column 20	
		What are the Aggregate	
To What Extent are Results Likely to Match Expected Outcomes?	To What Extent are Results Matching Expected Outcomes?	Costs of Efforts?	Benefits Resulting from the Efforts?

Add paper as needed, but be sure to use this exercise in conjunction with Figures 10.4, 10.6, 10.7, and 10.8.

to which the HRD practitioner has contributed.[20] That does not mean that departmental strategy must be driven by that of the organization, but the two strategies should be compatible and even synergistic.[5]

Any of the methods appropriate for selecting organizational or HR strategy can be used in selecting HRD department strategy (see Chapters 6 and 7). Bear in mind that, while selection itself can be made rationally—with due consideration of departmental strengths, weaknesses, opportunities and threats—subsequent implementation is likely to be successful only when line managers and trainees have had a say in the direction of the HRD department and its activities.

Use Figures 10.7, 10.8 and 10.9 to continue the process begun in Figure 10.5. If you prefer a different approach, rate how well your own department supports organizational strategy by completing the short quiz in Figure 10.10.

Figure 10.10   Rate HRD planning in your organization

	No. of Points
1. Does your HRD plan link directly to the corporate planning process? Are HRD plans clearly assisting the corporation to achieve specific objectives? If yes, strongly—10 pts. If somewhat—5 pts. If very loosely—2 pts. If not at all—0 pts.	_____
2. Is HRD planning systematic and routinely done? Do you have a formal timetable for planning and are plans for specific periods? If yes, very much—10 pts. If somewhat—5 pts. If not—0 pts.	_____
3. Does your HRD plan have both short-range (1 year or less) and long-range (3 years or longer) elements? if both—10 pts. If just short-range—5 pts. If just long-range—2 pts. If neither—0 pts.	_____
4. Does your HRD planning process have provisions for routinely modifying the plan at fixed points? Does the plan allow for flexibility, emergencies and routine changes? If yes—10 pts. If somewhat—5 pts. If very little—2 pts. If not at all—0 pts.	_____
5. Does your HRD plan tie to the budget in a specific and direct way? Are resources estimated and tied specifically to the plan so that costs are clear and tied to outcomes? If yes, strongly—10 pts. If somewhat—6 pts. If very loosely—3 pts. If not at all—0 pts.	_____
6. To what extent is your planning process routinely tied to specific data? Do you have sufficient data upon which to make HRD program decisions? Do you have an HRD Management Information System (MIS)? If yes, very much—10 pts. If yes, somewhat—6 pts. If yes, but not very much—3 pts. If no, it's entirely subjective judgment—0 pts.	_____

Figure 10.10 (Continued)

	No. of Points

7. Does your HRD plan make provisions for a close linkage to manage-ment activity to carry it out? Does it lead to assigning work and/or objectives to the staff? To setting timetables and schedules for activ-ity? Is it the reference point for all major activity in the HRD pro-gram? If yes—10 pts. If somewhat—5 pts. If little—0 pts.   _____

8. Is your planning process autocratic or participative? Are staff mem-bers involved? Are their suggestions used? Is the process truly a group effort? If yes—10 pts. If somewhat—5 pts. If no, it's a one-person operation—0 pts.   _____

9. To what extent is your plan evaluated and used in the next planning cycle? Is the plan reviewed at the end of the planning period? Are outcomes reviewed? Is the data from the evaluation of this plan recycled into the next plan? If yes—10 pts. If somewhat—5 pts. If only informally—2 pts. If not at all—0 pts.   _____

10. If you have read every word in this survey and have faithfully scored your program, give yourself 10 pts. If you have skimmed this survey but have not scored it—5 pts. If this is the first question you have read, you get 0 pts.   _____

Scoring

100–90 POINTS	Excellent— You have a sound planning system.
89–80 POINTS	Good—But there are some basic points that can be im-proved upon in your planning system.
79–70 POINTS	Weak—But with some changes you could have a good planning system.
69 and BELOW	Poor—It's a question of whether any planning you are doing is worth the effort.

Source: "Effective Planning for Human Resource Development," by L. Harvey. Reprinted from the October, 1983 issue of *Personnel Administrator*, copyright 1983, The American Society for Personnel Admin-istration, 606 North Washington Street, Alexandria, VA 22314, $40 per year.

Outcomes of Strategy Selection

Desirable outcomes of strategy selection include:

- A plan for the HRD department.
- A sense of direction among department staff members.

• Support for this direction from managers in other parts of the organization.

Each outcome is crucial for success in the role of HRD strategist.

References

1. Hall, D. "Human Resource Development and Organizational Effectiveness." In *Strategic Human Resource Management,* C. Fombrun, N. Tichy and M. Devanna, eds. New York: Wiley, 1984.

2. Ward, L. "Eight Steps to Strategic Planning for Training Managers." *Training* 19 (1982) 11: pp. 22–29.

3. Zemke, R. "Strategic Thinking for HRD." *Training* 18 (1981) 4: pp. 24–34.

4. Nininger, J. *Managing Human Resources: A Strategic Perspective.* Ottawa: The Conference Board of Canada, 1982.

5. Vaill, P. "Strategic Planning." In *Organization Development: Managing Transitions,* E. Pavlock, ed. Washington, D.C.: American Society for Training and Development, 1982.

6. Mager, R., and D. Cram. "The Regulators Are Coming!" *Training* 22 (1985) 9: pp. 40–46.

7. Hulett, D., and J. Renjilian. "Strategic Planning Demystified." In *Organization Development: Present Practice and Future Needs,* S. Sherwood, ed. Washington, D.C.: American Society for Training and Development, 1983.

8. Utterback, J. "Environmental Analysis and Forecasting." In *Strategic Management: A New View of Business Policy and Planning,* D. Schendel and C. Hofer, eds. Boston: Little Brown, 1979.

9. McLagan, P. *Strategic Planning for the HRD Function.* St. Paul, MN: McLagan & Associates, 1981.

10. Kimberly, J., and B. Miles, eds. *The Organizational Life Cycle.* San Francisco: Jossey-Bass, 1980.

11. Rothwell, W. "The Life Cycle of HRD Departments." *Training and Development Journal* 7 (1983) 11: pp. 74–76.

12. Rothschild, W. *Putting It All Together: A Guide to Strategic Thinking.* New York: Amacom, 1976.

13. Kobel, T., and A. Faron. "Poof—You're a Trainer!" *Training and Development Journal* 39 (1985) 1: pp. 106–107.

14. Olivas, L. "Auditing Your Training and Development Function." *Training and Development Journal* 34 (1980) 3: pp. 60–65.

15. Spencer, L. "Calculating Costs and Benefits." In *Human Resources Management and Development Handbook,* W. Tracey, ed. New York: Amacom, 1985.

16. Ryans, J. and W. Shanklin. *Strategic Planning: Concepts and Implementation.* New York: Random House, 1985.

17. Schein, V. "Strategic Management and the Politics of Power." *Personnel Administrator* 28 (1983) 10: pp. 55–59.

18. Linkow, P. "HRD at the Roots of Corporate Strategy." *Training and Development Journal* 39 (1985) 5: pp. 85–87.

19. LeBell, D., and O. Krasner. "Selecting Environmental Forecasting Techniques from Business Planning Requirements." *Academy of Management Review* (July, 1977): pp. 373–383.

20. Rothwell, W. *Management Training in Support of Organizational Strategic Planning in Twelve Illinois Organizations.* Unpublished doctoral dissertation. University of Illinois, 1985.

For More Information

Biles, G. and R. Schuler. *Audit Handbook of Human Resource Management Practices.* Alexandria, VA: American Society for Personnel Administration, 1986.

DeChambeau, F. and F. MacKenzie. "Intrapreneurship." *Personnel Journal* 65 (1986) 7: pp. 40–45.

Douglas, J., S. Klein, and D. Hunt. *The Strategic Managing of Human Resources.* New York: Wiley, 1985.

Feuer, M. "From Environmental Scanning to Human Resource Planning: A Linkage Model Applied to Universities." *Human Resource Planning* 6 (1983) 2: pp. 69–82.

Fombrun, C., M. Devanna, and N. Tichy. "The Human Resource Management Audit." In *Strategic Human Resource Management,* C. Fombrun, N. Tichy, and M. Devanna, eds. New York: Wiley, 1984.

McConnell, J. *How to Audit the Human Resources Department.* New York: Amacom, 1986.

Prager, A., and M. Shea. "The Strategy Audit." In *The Strategic Management Handbook,* K. Albert, ed. New York: McGraw-Hill, 1983.

Sheridan, J., and J. Monaghan. "Environmental Issues Scanning." *Human Resource Planning* 5 (1982) 1: pp. 57–68.

CHAPTER 11

Managing the HRD department.

T his chapter focuses on the HRD professional as manager and discusses the key competencies and work outputs of this role.

The HRD manager translates broad strategy into operating objectives—and then uses these objectives to estimate financial and other resources needed to carry out department activities. The structure of the department and its work units increases efficiency of operation and provides a useful framework for allocating work.

In small or medium-sized departments, the HRD manager can play many roles, including most or all of those described in *Models for Excellence.* As the department grows larger and jobs become more specialized, the manager performs fewer roles. In the largest organizations the role of HRD manager is enacted in its purest form. ■

The Role of HRD Manager

According to *Models for Excellence*, the manager role consists of "planning, organizing, staffing [and] controlling training and development operations or training and development projects and of linking training and development operations with other organizational units." To enact this role, the HRD practitioner must be able to exhibit:

- Organization-Behavior Understanding
- Delegation Skill
- Cost/Benefit-Analysis Skill
- Intellectual Versatility
- Feedback Skill
- Data-Reduction Skill
- Presentation Skill
- Relationship Versatility
- Industry Understanding
- Organization Understanding
- Futuring Skill
- Group-Process Skill
- Negotiation Skill
- Training-and-Development-Field Understanding
- Adult-Learning Understanding
- Computer Competence
- Career-Development Knowledge
- Personnel/HR-Field Understanding

Of these competencies (described in the Glossary), the first four are most important and the last four least important for the HRD manager.

According to *Models for Excellence*, typical work outputs of this role include:

1. "Training and development department or project operating objectives."
2. "Training and development budgets developed and monitored."
3. "[A] positive work climate in the training and development function or project group."
4. "Department/project staffing."
5. "Training and development standards, policies, and procedures."
6. "Outside suppliers/consultants selected."

7. "Solutions to department/project problems."
8. "Training and development actions congruent with other HR and organization actions."
9. "Related information exchanged with clients/departments (internal/external)."
10. "Staff evaluated."
11. "Staff developed."

This role is very highly and positively correlated with those of HRD strategist and marketer; it is negatively correlated with those of evaluator, instructional writer, needs analyst, task analyst, and theoretician.

The HRD manager plays the key role in the process of managing the department. A simple model of this process is shown in Figure 11.1.

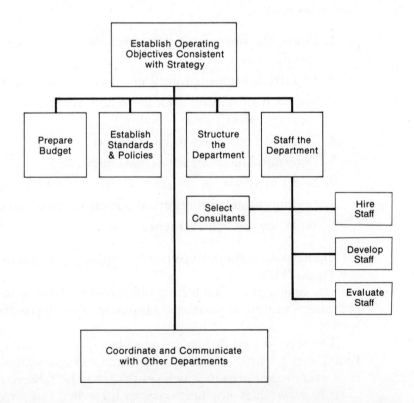

Figure 11.1 A simplified model of managing the HRD department

Establishing Operating Objectives

Once the strategic plan of the department has been prepared, the next step is to implement it. Operating objectives, defined as statements of results desired, are useful for this purpose. Research on objective-setting suggests that individuals who are assigned specific but difficult goals and receive feedback on how well they have done will outproduce those who do not receive such goals or feedback.[1] The same principle could well hold true for the manager of a department.

Eight Key Steps in Setting Objectives

The process of establishing operating objectives has aroused substantial interest ever since Peter Drucker coined the term Management by Objectives (MBO) in 1954. Though theorists differ in their descriptions, the basic idea is to:

1. Define the purpose of the organization, its departments, and even specific positions.
2. Identify the most promising areas in which to devote resources.
3. For each promising area identified, select some way by which to measure effectiveness.
4. Negotiate outcomes to be achieved.
5. Determine methods for achievement.
6. Select methods for overseeing effective achievement of objectives.
7. Communicate with others about means and ends.
8. Work toward achievement.

As an alternative, these steps can be rephrased as a series of questions—see Figure 11.2.

The first step in establishing objectives is identical to that in strategic planning: defining departmental purpose. This step is discussed in Chapter 10.

The second step in establishing objectives is to identify action areas. Based on departmental purpose, the manager and staff of the department rank every major area in which results are to be achieved. The important word is *major:* it is not necessary to list every task or activity. Rather, the focus is on key outcomes or results to which time, money, effort,

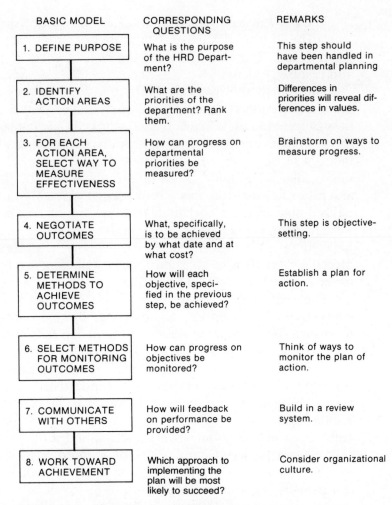

BASIC MODEL	CORRESPONDING QUESTIONS	REMARKS
1. DEFINE PURPOSE	What is the purpose of the HRD Department?	This step should have been handled in departmental planning
2. IDENTIFY ACTION AREAS	What are the priorities of the department? Rank them.	Differences in priorities will reveal differences in values.
3. FOR EACH ACTION AREA, SELECT WAY TO MEASURE EFFECTIVENESS	How can progress on departmental priorities be measured?	Brainstorm on ways to measure progress.
4. NEGOTIATE OUTCOMES	What, specifically, is to be achieved by what date and at what cost?	This step is objective-setting.
5. DETERMINE METHODS TO ACHIEVE OUTCOMES	How will each objective, specified in the previous step, be achieved?	Establish a plan for action.
6. SELECT METHODS FOR MONITORING OUTCOMES	How can progress on objectives be monitored?	Think of ways to monitor the plan of action.
7. COMMUNICATE WITH OTHERS	How will feedback on performance be provided?	Build in a review system.
8. WORK TOWARD ACHIEVEMENT	Which approach to implementing the plan will be most likely to succeed?	Consider organizational culture.

Figure 11.2 The objective-setting process

and other resources will be committed. They can be categorized according to their impact on different environments: (1) that outside the organization (e.g., community relations); (2) that outside the department but inside the organization (e.g., design, delivery, and evaluation of training); and (3) that in the HRD field (e.g., level of contribution to the profession). One way to approach this task is to first list priorities of the prior year based on expenditures of time and/or money and then set those for future years. Another way is to list future opportunities and threats posed by the external environment and then establish objectives for dealing with them.

The third step is to select methods for measuring organizational problems to be addressed, such as the number of employee promotions following training. The idea is to find the best fit between priorities, actions, and results.

The fourth step is to establish specific operating objectives. At this point, action areas (identified in Step 2) and ways of measuring effectiveness (selected in Step 3) are formally linked. Each objective should focus on only one result, describing maximum cost and a date by which achievement is to be expected. Objectives should be challenging, though not impossible, and should be mutually negotiated by the HRD manager and his or her subordinates. From departmental objectives, more individualized objectives for each staff member can be negotiated.

The fifth step is to determine methods to achieve outcomes. Methods have to do with means, while objectives only address ends. For each objective, a plan is established that describes necessary actions and the order in which they should be taken.

The sixth step is to select methods for monitoring outcomes. To control progress toward achievement of objectives, ways must be devised to ensure that corrective action will be taken before something actually goes wrong.

The key is to anticipate what will probably go wrong and then plan for it ahead of time. Performance standards, defined as measures of how well objectives are being achieved, can be used as control devices. Examples include: people trained, number of organizational units contacted, complaints about HRD efforts, amount of savings, new ideas accepted, and projects completed. These standards furnish yardsticks by which to monitor how much progress is being made on objectives. They can provide, in addition to control, tools for individual staff evaluation and incentives for performance. They are established by negotiation between the HRD manager, his or her subordinates, and often the manager's superior.

The seventh step focuses on communication. It is pointless to have performance standards and objectives if they are not used. Feedback is necessary:

- *On a regular basis.* At some pre-established time (monthly, quarterly) the HRD manager meets with staff collectively or individually to discuss progress.
- *When there is a problem or unexpected event.* If barriers to progress are created by an unanticipated problem or event, the HRD man-

ager and his or her staff can meet collectively or individually to grapple with the matter.

• *During appraisals.* If a Management by Objectives employee appraisal system is used for HRD staff, it is a good time to discuss individual contributions and difficulties.

Feedback on performance is essential to improvement, making it important to formalize how and when it will be provided.

The eighth and final step is implementation.

The HRD manager must simply decide how best to go about implementing the operating objectives in his or her organization. It is not necessary for the organization to adopt MBO for the HRD manager to do so. The manager can:

1. Adopt MBO unilaterally without asking others.
2. Apply the principles with a few key subordinates but not with everybody.
3. Implement MBO in the HRD department and thereby serve as a model to emulate for others in the organization.

The culture of the organization may provide clues to what approaches might work. However, the HRD manager wanting to adopt a full-scale, formal MBO program should give careful thought to the following questions before taking any action:

1. What opinions about MBO does the HRD staff already have?
2. Has the system been attempted before in the organization? If so, how was it done? With what results?
3. To what extent does the manager's own superior support the idea?
4. How is the climate of the department? Are staff open and trusting or closemouthed and guarded?
5. Will the MBO approach receive genuine commitment—or will it be only so much window dressing?

As an aid in establishing operating objectives—or considering it—a worksheet is provided in Figure 11.3. Though not intended to be complete, it can serve as a starting point to generate thought and discussion.

Departmental objectives are potentially important work outputs of the HRD manager's role. If properly handled, they can contribute to a

DIRECTIONS:	Work through the questions on this worksheet by yourself or (even better) with your staff. Add more detailed questions if necessary. Use more pages if you wish.

QUESTIONS	ANSWERS
1. What is the purpose of the HRD department?	

2. What are the priorities of the department?
   a. List them.
   b. Prioritize them.	

3. How can progress on departmental priorities be measured?	

4. What results are to be achieved
   a. by what dates?
   b. with what cost limitations?	

5. How will each objective (specified in question 4) be achieved?
   a. In what steps?
   b. In what sequence?
   c. Over what time?	

6. How can progress on objectives be monitored over time? (Describe performance standards.)	
7. How will feedback on performance be provided? (Describe feedback mechanisms.)	
8. What approach to implementing plans is most likely to succeed?	

Figure 11.3 Worksheet for establishing operating objectives

288

positive work climate by providing clear direction to the work of everyone in the department. Further, they are potent for evaluating staff performance and for negotiating individual development plans in line with departmental needs. However, successful application of a formal MBO approach requires understanding of organizational behavior, intellectual versatility, the ability to give feedback, and the ability to apply data-reduction skill.

Structuring the HRD Department

Structure can be defined as the formal make-up of the organization. It refers to the grouping of departments, divisions, work groups, jobs, and individuals. The process of establishing structure is called organizational design.

Theorists have long been aware that structure affects performance. The reasons are simple enough:

- For individuals, structure affects who reports to whom, creates a basis for interaction with others, and influences roles by creating expectations about what tasks should be assigned to (or expected of) those in specific jobs.
- For work groups, structure affects the amount and kind of communication, openness to innovation, and the psychological closeness of people.[2]
- For organizations, structure constrains choice of strategy by determining who participates at the highest levels of formulation and implementation. One of the most common reasons that strategy fails is that organizational structure is inadequate to support implementation.

Establishing an effective structure is not easy. There are two basic aspects to consider when dealing with the structure of the HRD department:

1. Its placement in the whole organization.
2. Its internal organization.

Where Is the HRD Department Positioned?

HRD managers cannot always influence placement of their departments in the reporting structure of the organization. There are, of course, several possibilities. The HRD department can be:

- Autonomous, directed by a Vice President (or equivalent) who reports directly to the Chief Executive.
- Part of the personnel or HR function, directed by a manager who reports to a Vice President of Personnel (or equivalent).
- Part of the Office of Chief Executive, directed by an individual who reports to the CEO.
- Part of an Office of Planning, directed by an individual who reports to a Vice President of Planning (or equivalent).
- Part of an operating department (such as marketing, production, finance, or data processing).
- Segmented into specialized parts or units in operating departments or regions with a separate corporate HRD department.

There are some advantages and disadvantages to each placement. If the department is autonomous, the manager is likely to have considerable authority and departmental priorities will be centered on HRD. The HRD manager possesses this authority as an immediate subordinate of the CEO. He or she is likely to receive desired funding, hear first-hand about major problems, and have a say in strategy-making. The only possible disadvantage is that the HRD manager will be associated with those in power, a position sometimes commanding more fear than genuine respect.

It is common to place HRD in the personnel department. A substantial percentage of people entering HRD positions do so from personnel. Unfortunately, placing HRD in a "staff" capacity like personnel tends to reduce information flow from "line" functions. Even worse, this placement will often mean that promotions go to those who develop personnel—not HRD—skills. As both Leonard Nadler [3] and Dugan Laird [4] have pointed out, personnel tends to want to put people in "boxes" on the organization chart. HRD activities conflict with this process of limitation by assuming that people will not necessarily remain in their present "box" but that they can move to different ones, change existing ones, or even create new ones.

If HRD is placed with the Chief Executive, the HRD manager is associated with the power and prestige of the highest office. While the authority that goes with this placement will probably bring much cooperation from others, the value depends considerably on the expectations and skills of the CEO. When the CEO understands the uses and limitations of HRD, the position of the HRD department can be ideal.

If HRD is placed with the Vice President of Planning, it may become an adaptive function intended to anticipate future problems. To the extent that planning is perceived by others in the organization as useful and worthy of commitment, HRD will probably be perceived in the same way. The fate of the department may thus depend less on what it does and more on what planners do.

If HRD is placed in an operating department, it gains the advantage of proximity. People in the department will be more willing to approach HRD practitioners with their problems and action can be taken more quickly. The major disadvantage is that, as a subordinate of a line manager, the HRD manager can be overruled on decisions and priorities in a way that would not happen to a staff officer of equal rank.

The last possibility is to create two or more different HRD departments—with one placed in a staff capacity and one or more in line departments. The advantage of this arrangement is that practitioners can specialize in what they do best. Line practitioners are on the firing line and can detect problems quickly; staff practitioners can devote more time, money, and effort to specific issues. By combining forces, the two types of practitioners maximize advantages and minimize disadvantages.

Designing the Department's Internal Structure

How should the HRD department be organized? To answer this question, the HRD manager should ask four questions:

1. How will the tasks, duties, and responsibilities of the department be divided?
2. How much authority will be delegated
   a. to whom?
   b. on what matters?
3. How many positions will report to each supervisor?
4. How will jobs be grouped?

The first question focuses on division of labor; the second, on authority; the third, on span of control; and the fourth on departmentalization.[5]

Division of labor refers, quite literally, to the way work is divided. There are two ways to think of it: (1) by difficulty of tasks or duties, and (2) by number of tasks and duties. A series of trade-offs are involved in dividing up work. For instance, jobs containing

- Few tasks require little training. People are easily replaced. However, such jobs do not command much interest and can breed dissatisfaction.
- Many tasks require more training. People are not easily replaced. If there are too many tasks for an individual to handle, dissatisfaction (and subsequent turnover) can result.
- Few challenging tasks are said to be impoverished. There is little opportunity for individual growth.
- Many challenging tasks are said to be enriched. There is much opportunity for individual growth.

The goal is to strike a balance between the efficiency that comes from specializing and the effectiveness that comes from loading a job with the right number and types of tasks.

Authority refers to the degree of individual decision-making that is allowed without approval by higher authority. Again there is a trade-off. The greater the degree of individual decision-making that is allowed:

1. The greater the probability that people can be developed to their full potential.
2. The less the capability of exerting control over what they do.

People who are allowed to make decisions can learn from experience. At the same time, the cost may be mistakes that a higher authority could have prevented. The question is: how much is it worth to develop people? If a high value is placed on development, give each staff member maximum authority for what they do; if a low value is placed on development, delegate little authority.

Span of control refers simply to the number of people reporting to one superior. The central question is: how many interpersonal transactions will take place? An HRD manager who refuses to delegate authority may find that even a few subordinates will be an overload, because each

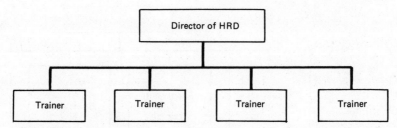

Figure 11.4 An entrepreneurial structure

one may have to consult with the superior frequently. On the other hand, a manager who delegates much authority may find a large span of control (eight or more people) comfortable. The greater the need for contact between supervisor and subordinate and the more complicated the jobs of subordinates, the smaller the span of control should be.

Finally, departmentalization refers to the ways jobs and work groups are organized.[6] Common approaches include: entrepreneurial, functional, divisional, project, and matrix.

In an entrepreneurial structure (see Figure 11.4), one person is in charge of the HRD department. It can be a one-person department or a few employees reporting to a single supervisor. Job specialization is low, because each person plays several parts.

In a functional structure (see Figure 11.5), the HRD department is specialized by (1) activities, such as needs assessment, instructional writing, instruction and evaluation, or (2) types of training such as executive training, management training, technical training, and others. A supervisor is in charge of each function.

In a divisional structure (see Figure 11.6), the HRD department is organized by location or division in addition to function. Supervisors are responsible either for functional duties, geographic duties, or some combination of the two. This complex structure helps the department cope with greater environmental uncertainty.

In the most complex structures (see example in Figure 11.7), supervisors are placed in charge of HRD projects in addition to functions and locations. The most dynamic external environments call for such structures. In some cases, people from outside the department may be temporarily assigned to project teams to prepare training as part of an integrated campaign to create a new market or service. A matrix structure is much like that of the project structure, except that project managers

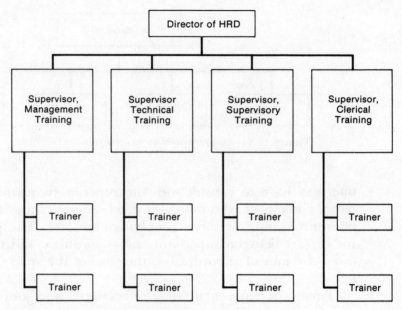

Figure 11.5 A functional structure

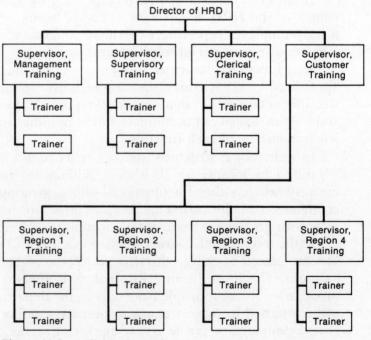

Figure 11.6 A divisional structure

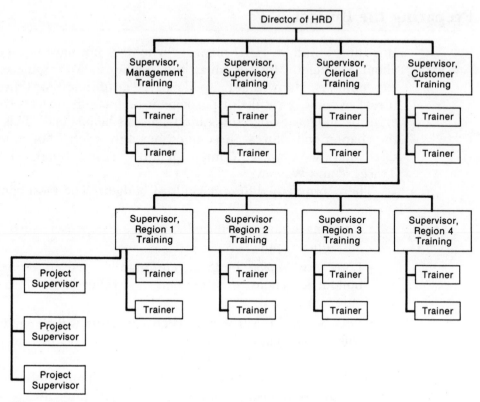

Figure 11.7 A project structure

in a matrix design are at the same level as divisional supervisors, while in a project structure divisional supervisors have higher status. Thus, in a matrix structure, an HRD staff person may be reporting to both a divisional supervisor and a project supervisor.

The structure of the HRD department is crucially important. It should be reviewed periodically against strategic plans and operating objectives, because structure is a control for making sure that nothing falls through the cracks and is forgotten. Like the process of establishing departmental objectives, examining structure calls for such skills as organization-behavior understanding and intellectual versatility. An effective structure can contribute to a positive work climate and adequate flow of information.

Preparing the Budget

It is rare to find an HRD manager who does not have to be concerned about a budget. Most organizations require at least some estimate of expenditures. Many would also like to see justification for those expenditures beyond the results of participant evaluations or test scores. What types of budgets exist? How can HRD costs be justified? This section of the chapter will address these questions only briefly. For more detailed discussions, see Clark & Perlman,[7] Jenness,[8] Laird,[4] Sheppeck & Cohen,[9] Tracey[10] and Warren.[11]

There are many different kinds of budgets. The most common are:

- *Operating* budgets itemized by specific expenses, such as salaries and office supplies.
- Long-term *capital* budgets, customarily used in requesting new buildings, expensive equipment, and other large items subject to amortization.
- *Cash* budgets that forecast when payments will be made and bills will be due. They ensure that cash is on hand when needed.

In HRD, most attention is usually focused on operating budgets.

Warren distinguishes between two budget categories: *support costs,* which include such items as staff, materials, equipment, travel expenses, consulting fees, and state-of-the-art (train-the-trainer) expenses; and *specific activity costs* which include costs for analysis, development, delivery, and evaluation. Laird considers such cost categories as production, trainees, conducting programs, and evaluation. Benchmarks on how much various organizations are budgeting for HRD can be found in Feuer.[12] For detailed worksheets on how to cost out a budget, consult these other sources and see Figure 11.8.

To justify a budget, it helps to have sound information on problems that HRD efforts will be directed to solving. In fact, the budget should be based on that information to demonstrate that there will be a solid return on investment for every dollar allocated to training, education, and development.[13] Cost-benefit analysis is useful for this purpose.

Many have proposed methods for placing economic value on training efforts, among them Cascio,[14] Flamholtz,[15] Gilbert,[16] Kearsley,[17] Phillips,[18] Spencer,[19] and Weinstein.[20] Most would probably agree that the process involves answering four basic questions:

1. What units of poor performance can be identified?
2. What is the estimated cost of each unit?
3. How many such units have there been (or how many are there expected to be)?
4. What is the total cost of these units (reached by multiplying the number of units by the cost per unit)?

Figure 11.8 Cost of training

Activity		Cost
CREATION OF TRAINING MATERIALS		
Staffing	Number of staff × average salary × hours.	$_____
Consulting	Cost of hiring consultants and paying expenses.	$_____
Traveling	Direct cost of travel plus per diem expenses.	$_____
Other	1. Standard overhead.	$_____
	2. Materials (rent or create films, videotapes, etc.).	$_____
PRESENTATION OF MATERIALS		
Staffing	1. Number of participants x average salary × hours.	$_____
	Number of participants × fringe benefits × hours.	$_____
	2. Number of presenters × hours × salary.	$_____
	3. Number of hours of lost production or service per participant × number of participants.	$_____
Traveling	1. Number of participants × cost of travel plus expenses.	$_____
	2. Number of presenters × cost of travel plus expenses.	$_____
Equipping	1. Number of student handouts × cost each.	$_____
	2. Number of trainer materials × cost each (includes rental of equipment and facilities.	$_____

Figure 11.8 (Continued)

	Activity	Cost
EVALUATION OF MATERIALS		
Staffing	1. Number of researchers × average salary × hours in designing, conducting, analyzing, and reporting evaluation.	$_____
	2. Number of participants × average salary × number of hours spent on assisting in evaluation.	$_____
Traveling	1. Number of researchers × cost of travel plus per diem expenses.	$_____
	2. Number of participants × cost of travel plus per diem expenses.	$_____
Equipping	1. Number of evaluation instruments × cost each.	$_____
Other	Itemize any additional costs	$_____

See Figure 11.9 for a worksheet using more specific descriptions.

Compare results of this process to the total cost of providing training. If the cost of training is estimated to be less than that of the performance

Figure 11.9   Cost of not training

Activity	Cost
1. Assess production/service levels per employee per hour on average	_____ units
2. Identify highest performer and calculate the difference between his/her average output × number of employees in work groups and total present output.	_____ units
3. Assess the value of total units or services lost less expenses at present.	$_____
4. Assess the *historical* value of total units or services lost less expenses (specify time period).	$_____
5. Project the value of total units or services lost less expenses in a specified time period if the deficiency is not corrected.	$_____
6. Add 4 and 5. **TOTAL**	$_____

problem, there is a cost-benefit advantage to offering instruction. If training costs exceed those of the problem, then some other solution to the problem should be sought.

A unit of poor performance can include mistakes in processing, loss of customers, lost time, money, or effort of other kinds. The problem is less in quantifying what Gilbert calls performance improvement potential than in convincing others of its accuracy. The most persuasive figures are likely to come from quizzing line managers familiar with the problem, according to Phillips. When they accept the figures and when HRD efforts do help to improve performance, training budgets are less likely to be cut first during financial austerity.

In a very real sense, a budget activates operating objectives and long-term plans. Managers who budget effectively are skilled in organization-behavior understanding and cost-benefit analysis.

Establishing Policies, Procedures, and Standards

Policies

Policies are simply broad descriptions of preferred actions intended to ensure coordination within a department or between departments. Procedures are related to policies, but are more specific. They describe precisely how a task is to be done or how activities should be handled. Standards are broad statements of desirable professional practice. (They should not be confused with performance standards—which are more specific.) All three tools—policies, procedures, and standards—can help to implement organizational and departmental plans and objectives.

Many policies are important to the HRD manager. They include those imposed by higher management, those imposed by special staff functions (e.g., internal audit), and those created to regulate activities within a large HRD department. For examples, see Tracey.[21] However, the most important is program policy. As Newman explains:

> When an agency or company has a program policy, then the issues of training, of reimbursement of training, of who is eligible for training, of the purpose of training are all placed on a standard and impersonal basis.[22]

In this way, personal favoritism is minimized. When the policy is written and communicated, everyone understands what the department does—and why.

According to Newman, a comprehensive policy should have at least these seven components:

1. A statement of department purpose.
2. Basic objectives.
3. The philosophy that guides practice.
4. General practices (e.g., scheduling, evaluation).
5. Use of facilities.
6. Budgeting methods.
7. Record-keeping.

Other issues may also be addressed, including:

- The respective responsibilities of the HRD department and of individual managers in employee development.
- The relationship between HRD and organizational plans.
- The relationship between HRD and career management.
- The relationship between HRD and other HR activities.

Basically, a program policy should state concisely why the HRD department is needed and for what it is accountable.

Typically, HRD program policy is prepared together with managers in other departments, who provide their own suggestions. By allowing or encouraging participation, the HRD manager builds support for the function while raising awareness of it. In one sense, giving others a say is a way of taking the pulse of decision-makers on what they want. For this reason, periodic updates and revisions are worthwhile.

Procedures

For many subjects in the policy it is also appropriate to have corresponding procedures. Some examples include how to:

- Request attendance at an internal course.
- Request assistance for college tuition.
- Request payment of fees for short workshops.
- Check out materials on loan.
- Schedule use of a classroom or other meeting site.

There are many more possible procedures—all of which should describe a process step by step.

Standards

Standards, which may be included in policy, are short and concise statements of broad import. Like policies, they are directives for action. A substantial number of general standards for HRD, useful for self-evaluation, can be found in Morrisey [23] and Tracey.[24] Some general examples are:

- Training should contribute to improvements in employee knowledge, skills, attitudes, or abilities.
- Training should indicate the amount of knowledge, level of skills, and type of attitudes or abilities that participants should have before they attend the training.
- Training should indicate the amount of knowledge, level of skill, and type of attitudes or abilities that the participants should exhibit following the training experience.
- Training should be designed by people competent both in the subject and in principles of training.
- Training materials should be tested before they are used.
- Training materials should be critiqued by third-party experts on the subject matter and experts on the principles of training.
- Trainees should be informed about training objectives and other necessary information before the training experience.
- Instructors should be competent in the subject matter and the instructional methods used.
- Training directors or sponsors should screen participants to ensure that only those with necessary prerequisite knowledge, skills, and other qualifications will attend sessions.

Policies, procedures, and standards are important devices for controlling HRD activities, as well as for implementing long-term plans and operating objectives. Developing them calls for such competencies as organizational-behavior understanding, relationship versatility, organization understanding, negotiation skill, and training-and-development-field understanding.

Staffing the HRD Department

Staffing is the process of establishing selection criteria and recruiting, socializing, using, developing, and evaluating people. It can also include selection of outside consultants and part-time HRD staff from outside the department. Obviously, the caliber of people working in the HRD department will influence what it can do and how well it can do it. Staff members serve as marketing tools in their own right because the image they project to the organization, HRD field, and community are important in establishing and maintaining department credibility.

Establishing Selection Criteria

The first question to ask about staffing is: What kind of job is being filled, and what kind of person should fill it?

Too often this question is forgotten in the process of advertising, collecting and sorting resumés, and interviewing applicants. Yet it is crucial—in fact, really what the staffing process in its initial stages is all about.

There are three ways of thinking about this issue:

1. What are the basic job requirements?
2. How is the job being done by present incumbents?
3. What are probable future job requirements, and what skills are needed in higher-level positions in the department?

The first question should help identify basic, minimum requirements; the second, how the job has been changed by incumbents; and the third, expectations for the future based on departmental plans, operating objectives, and career paths.

Information for addressing basic requirements is available in most organizations. Personnel departments conduct job analysis and evaluation studies to prepare job descriptions, which literally describe general tasks and responsibilities of a class or group of jobs, and specifications, which outline minimum education, experience, and other qualities essential for a newcomer. An additional step is to prepare a "person description" of skills, abilities, knowledge, education, and background that characterize the individual who will be selected. This provides a profile of the ideal candidate before the recruitment process begins.

It is rare for a job description to weight importance of tasks or responsibilities or to furnish more than a sketchy outline of experience, education, and other essential attributes. It is up to the hiring HRD manager to remedy this lack of information. One method is to select from *Models for Excellence* a list of key competencies associated with the job and then weight them according to their importance. For more on staffing, see Lee,[25] Aldrich,[26] Brinkerhoff,[27] and Chaddock.[28]

The second question concerns the job as it is actually being done. After working in a job for a while, an employee will personalize it to some extent. The job will be subtly transformed to reflect the unique talents of the incumbent. This personalization is an unimportant factor in highly structured jobs allowing little room for discretion in performing duties. However, it does become an issue in creative jobs with latitude for innovation. HRD is a field in which personalization can be of concern. The problem usually manifests itself when the manager starts looking for a clone of the present incumbent or, after hiring, when someone tells the newcomer that "Mary wouldn't have done it that way." While some attributes may be essential, not all are. Using the approach described in the paragraph above can help to minimize effects of personalization on basic entry requirements.

The third question concerns future job requirements—and it is here that most selection procedures are very weak.[29] In too many cases, the interviewer is interested only in someone who can do one job—the criteria for which are past-oriented. Little thought is given to such matters as: (1) How will the job change in the short-term and intermediate-term? (2) How well will a candidate be suited during and after the change? (3) How will a given candidate do at subsequent points along the career path of the department—that is, to what extent does he or she exhibit the skills (or motivation to learn them) of higher-level jobs? After all, technical skill (knowing how to apply the technology of HRD) is critical only at entry. Supervisory jobs call for more interpersonal skill (knowing how to deal with people) and cultural skill (knowing how to operate within norms of the organization). At the highest level, cultural skill is critical. To address the third question the hiring manager must add to the list of skills needed of a successful candidate.

Recruiting

Recruiting is the process of attracting qualified applicants for existing or anticipated job openings. There are two sources of such applicants:

internal and external. External recruitment utilizes outreach programs, cooperative education, internships, and other sources.

Employees within the organization are targets for internal recruitment. They are reached through:

- *Job posting:* Employees learn of openings in other departments through bulletin boards or company publications.
- *Skill inventories:* Individuals with desired skills are located through manual or automated directories.
- *Referrals:* People aware of openings spread the word to qualified colleagues or subordinates—or tell the HRD manager about someone they think has the necessary skills.
- *Career literature:* Career paths through the HRD department are described.

Recruitment from within has advantages: applicants have already been socialized in company culture and have (one hopes) acquired useful skills in the process. They may have even participated as trainees in HRD department-sponsored events. Promotion from within boosts morale and builds bridges with other parts of the organization; transfer provides the opportunity to learn about a new part of the firm.

There are disadvantages as well: internal candidates might not be as qualified as external ones; insiders may have learned company culture too well so that their potential for innovation is lost in norms and tradition.

In some organizations, part-time trainers are loaned temporarily to the HRD department, because of their special expertise in the subject area. The process of locating them is quite similar to that of other internal recruitment. Advantages of using part-timers are that they hold down staff costs, can be used temporarily in peak periods, are attuned to company methods and culture, are a source of potential full-timers, and can build support for the HRD department in other quarters.[30,31] Disadvantages of using them are that they may not be good presenters and may not be available when needed because of conflicting job assignments.

People from outside the organization are targets for external recruitment. They are reached through:

- Advertising in newspapers and trade publications.
- College recruitment, internship, and outreach efforts.

- Employment agencies and search firms.
- Referrals from incumbent employees.
- Walk-ins.

Choosing the appropriate method or combination of methods depends largely on the nature of the opening. Entry-level jobs should probably be advertised through national publications in the HRD field and through specialized search firms. In addition, college recruitment efforts (e.g., participation in career fairs), internships, and outreach programs (e.g., an HRD manager who teaches college courses) are especially good sources of potential entry-level candidates.

Recruitment from outside is advantageous in that it attracts new talents and fresh outlooks, and generally stimulates the department. It is disadvantageous in that a newcomer faces socialization not only to the job but also to the organization.

The process of selecting external consultants resembles that of hiring from outside. The steps in both cases are the same: the HRD manager must first decide what skills are needed and then search out those with those skills. In general, external consultants should be used when there is a need to:

- Make progress quickly.
- Use specialized talents not available internally.
- Ensure objectivity of approach.
- Take advantage of a consultant's relative immunity from the internal authority structure of the organization.

In all other respects, the steps in locating a consultant, discussing company problems, checking references, and negotiating contractual arrangements are very similar to those involved in hiring staff. For more information, see Kennedy,[32] Parry & Ribbing,[33] and Zawacki.[34]

Hiring

Hiring should result in selecting the best applicant. It includes compiling a list of final candidates from an initial list, examining work samples, conducting and scoring screening tests, conducting employment interviews, choosing the successful candidate, and following up with those who were unsuccessful.

If the manager has prepared a composite of the kind of person needed to do the job, sorting out resumés should not be difficult. Though resumés are seldom assembled on a competency basis (what the person can do rather than past education and experience), it is relatively easy to determine from an applicant's background whether he or she is likely to possess the needed skills.

Once candidates have been screened initially, the most promising ones are usually interviewed. At that time they can be asked to furnish work samples if they are experienced or demonstrate basic knowledge and skills if inexperienced. This step will narrow the list of candidates.

During a more lengthy, in-depth assessment of final candidates, managers may want to ask them to:

- Demonstrate their skills—for example, give a short presentation or write up a short lesson plan.
- Go through an assessment center geared to HRD (if the organization has such facilities).
- Answer questionnaires intended to assess their previous experience relative to the job opening.
- Take employment exams.

Some managers may prefer to handle some or all of these matters during initial screening, though this could be prohibitively expensive. Selection testing is also a sensitive area, perhaps the most vulnerable to litigation. Valid tests are difficult, time-consuming, and expensive to develop.[35]

Most HRD managers will find that structured interviews, using a prepared list of questions asked of all applicants and based on job competencies, will serve their purposes. Though interviews are prone to special problems, structured interviews conducted by trained people will be more reliable than either unstructured ones or those conducted by untrained interviewers. To increase reliability, a series of interviews conducted by those trained in the requisite skills can be used.

After the selected candidate has accepted an offer, it is advisable to follow up with those who did not get the job. Though reasons for the final choice probably should not be revealed, it is only courtesy—and good public relations—to let people know the final decision on their application. The applicant who is turned away today could later turn out to be the ideal candidate for a different job.

Other Steps in Staffing

The remaining steps in staffing include socializing, using, developing, and evaluating employees in the HRD department. Socialization experiences begin with recruitment and hiring. That is the time to build realistic expectations about the new job, work group, department, and organization. Upon hiring, newcomers can be assigned "peer mentors"—people at the same level—to show them around, introduce them to others, and generally orient them.

Developing and evaluating the staff will pose no problems if performance standards are used to identify individual strengths and weaknesses. *Models for Excellence* provides an excellent tool for planning HRD staff development and, indeed, for evaluating staff performance. Though it may need to be adapted to the organization's (and department's) culture, it can serve as a useful starting point.

The staffing process requires most of the competencies associated with the manager of HRD. The results should include a positive department climate and effective staff development and evaluation. The role is important, since leadership is a crucial factor in organizational—and departmental—success.

References

1. Locke, E., K. Shaw, L. Saari, and G. Latham. "Goal Setting and Task Performances: 1969–1980." *Psychological Bulletin,* (July, 1981): p. 129.

2. Pearce, J., and F. David. "A Social Network Approach to Organizational Design and Performance." *Academy of Management Review,* (July, 1983): pp. 436–444.

3. Nadler, L. *Developing Human Resources,* sec. ed. Austin, TX: Learning Concepts, 1979.

4. Laird, D. *Approaches to Training and Development,* 2nd. ed. Reading, MA: Addison-Wesley, 1985.

5. Gibson, J., J. Ivancevich, and J. Donnelly. *Organizations: Behavior, Structure, Processes,* 5th ed. Plano, TX: Business Publications, 1985.

6. Johnson, R. "The Organization and Management of Training." In *Training and Development Handbook,* 2nd ed., R. Craig, ed. New York: McGraw-Hill, 1976.

7. Clark, G., and J. Perlman. "Budgeting for Human Resources Systems." In *Human Resources Management and Development Handbook*, W. Tracey, ed. New York: Amacom, 1985.

8. Jenness, J. "Budgeting and Controlling Training Costs." In *Training and Development Handbook*, 2nd ed., R. Craig, ed. New York: McGraw-Hill, 1976.

9. Sheppeck, M., and S. Cohen. "Put a Dollar Value on Your Training Programs." *Training and Development Journal* 39 (1985) 11: pp. 59–62.

10. Tracey, W. "The HRD Manager." In *Human Resources Management and Development Handbook*. W. Tracey, ed. New York: Amacom, 1985.

11. Warren, M. *Training for Results*. Reading, MA: Addison-Wesley, 1979.

12. Feuer, D. "1985 Training Budgets: Running Steady." *Training* 22 (1985) 10: pp. 28–44.

13. Bell, C. "How Training Departments Win Budget Battles." *Training and Development Journal* 37 (1983) 9: pp. 42–49.

14. Cascio, W. *Costing Human Resources*. New York: Van Nostrand Reinhold, 1982.

15. Flamholtz, E. *Human Resources Accounting*, 2nd ed. San Francisco: Jossey-Bass, 1985.

16. Gilbert, T. *Human Competence: Engineering Worthy Performance*. New York: McGraw-Hill, 1978.

17. Kearsley, G. *Costs, Benefits and Productivity in Training Systems*. Reading, MA: Addison-Wesley, 1982.

18. Phillips, J. *Handbook of Training Evaluation and Measurement Methods*. Houston, TX: Gulf Publishing, 1983.

19. Spencer, L. "Calculating Costs and Benefits." In *Human Resources Management and Development Handbook*, W. Tracey, ed. New York: Amacom, 1985.

20. Weinstein, L. "Collecting Training Cost Data." *Training and Development Journal* 36 (1982) 8: pp. 30–38.

21. Tracey, W. *Managing Training and Development Systems*. New York: Amacom, 1974.

22. Newman, K. "Guidelines on Developing Program Policy." *Training and Development Journal* (July, 1980): pp. 20–23.

23. Morrisey, G. "Establishing HR Program Standards." In *Human Resources Management and Development Handbook*, W. Tracey, ed. New York: Amacom, 1985.

24. Tracey, W. *Human Resource Development Standards*. New York: Amacom, 1981.

25. Lee, C. "How to Hire the Right Trainer." *Training* 21 (1984) 8: pp. 22–24; 26–27; 29–32.

26. Aldrich, J. "Staffing Concepts and Principles." In *Human Resources Management and Development Handbook,* W. Tracey, ed. New York: Amacom, 1985.

27. Brinkerhoff, D. "The HR Professional Staff." In *Human Resources Management and Development Handbook,* W. Tracey, ed. New York: Amacom, 1985.

28. Chaddock, P. "Selection and Development of the Training Staff." In *Training and Development Handbook,* 2nd ed., R. Craig, ed. New York: McGraw-Hill, 1976.

29. Mandt, E. "The Failure of Business Education—and What to Do About It." *Management Review* 71 (1982) 8: pp. 47–52.

30. Fabian, B., and B. Mink. "Line Managers as Learning Facilitators at an Equipment Manufacturer." In *Andragogy in Action: Applying Modern Principles of Adult Learning,* M. Knowles & Assoc., eds. San Francisco: Jossey-Bass, 1984.

31. Kobel, T., and A. Faron. "Poof—You're a Trainer!" *Training and Development Journal* 39 (1985) 1: pp. 106–107.

32. Kennedy, J. *Directory of Management Consultants.* Fitzwilliam, NH: Consultants News, 1986.

33. Parry, S., and J. Ribbing. "Using Outside Training Consultants." In *Training and Development Handbook,* 2nd ed., R. Craig, ed. New York: McGraw-Hill, 1976.

34. Zawacki, S. "Contracting for Training Support Services." In *Human Resources Management and Development Handbook,* W. Tracey, ed. New York: Amacom, 1985.

35. Brown, A. "Employment Tests: Issues Without Clear Answers." *Personnel Administrator* 30 (1985) 9: pp. 43–57.

For More Information

Andrews, J. "Is There a Crisis in the Personnel Department's Identity?" *Personnel Journal* 65 (1986) 6: pp. 86–93.

Arvey, R. *Fairness in Selecting Employees.* Reading, MA: Addison-Wesley, 1979.

Feldman, M. "Eight Steps to Clarify a Training Philosophy for You and Your Department." *Training* (August, 1982): pp. 48–51.

Gordon, J. "What They Don't Teach You about Being a Training Manager." *Training* 23 (1986) 6: pp. 22–27, 29–32, 34.

Marsh, N. "Training Records and Information Systems." In *Training and Development Handbook,* R. Craig, ed. 2nd ed. New York: McGraw-Hill, 1976.

McMurry, R. *Tested Techniques of Personnel Selection,* 3rd ed. Chicago: Dartnell Corp, 1978.

Otto, C., and R. Glaser. *The Management of Training.* Reading, MA: Addison-Wesley, 1970.

Pace, R. *Organizational Communication: Foundations for Human Resource Development.* Englewood Cliffs, NJ: Prentice-Hall, 1983.

"Personnel Department Profile." *Training* 23 (1986) 8: p. 69.

Reid, P. *The Employer's Guide to Avoiding Job-Bias Litigation.* New York: Random House, 1986.

"A Self-Development Process for Training and Development Professionals." *Training and Development Journal* 33 (1979) 5: pp. 6–13.

Ward, L. "Eight Steps to Strategic Planning for Training Managers." *Training* 19 (1982) 11: pp. 22–29.

White, T. "Increasing Your Effectiveness as a Training and Development Professional." *Training and Development Journal* 33 (1979) 5: pp. 3–13.

Zemke, R. "In Search of a Training Philosophy." *Training* 22 (1985) 8: pp. 93–102.

6

The HRD program—how learning is planned.

If HRD efforts are to bring about individual learning, then HRD practitioners must be able to apply what is known about learning theory. Indeed, if there is a single area in which the practitioner must be expert, it is this one. How do individuals learn? How, in turn, should learning experiences be conducted? In what ways can learning be planned? Part Six addresses these questions.

CHAPTER 12

Theories of learning and instructing.

This chapter describes the role of the HRD professional as theoretician and discusses important theories of learning and instructing.

As theoretician, the HRD practitioner develops a theory of learning that guides instruction. Since HRD itself consists of organized learning experiences, it makes sense for practitioners to understand the nature of learning. This is not simple, for there are many theories of learning and of instruction. This chapter describes them, as well as discussing unique characteristics of adult learners. ■

What Is the Role of Theoretician?

According to *Models for Excellence,* the role of HRD theoretician consists of "developing and testing theories of learning, training and development."

To enact this role the practitioner must be able to exhibit such critical competencies as:

- Adult-Learning Understanding
- Intellectual Versatility

- Model-Building Skill
- Data-reduction Skill
- Writing Skill
- Research Skill
- Futuring Skill

Of items on this list, the first three are most important and the last one is least important.

According to *Models for Excellence,* typical work outputs of this role include:

1. "New concepts and theories of learning and behavior change."
2. "Articles on Training & Development issues/theories for scientific and trade publications."
3. "Research designs."
4. "Research reports."
5. "Training models and applicatons of theory."
6. "Existing learning/training theories evaluated."

This role is positively correlated with such others as instructional writer and program designer and negatively correlated with those of group facilitator, manager, marketer, program administrator, and transfer agent.

The Nature of Theories

Theories and models are key terms when discussing the role of theoretician. A theory can be understood as a plausible principle or group of principles offered to predict and explain facts, observations, or events. Theories are abstract because they seek to explain reality through such media as language or symbols. Theories are explanatory in that they assert underlying causes that affect or give rise to a phenomenon. Finally, theories are predictive because they imply that manipulating variables or conditions will result in different but foreseeable outcomes.

Theory development can range on a continuum from empirically-based methods to intuitively-based methods. Typically, the process begins with exploration, then advances through concept development, hypothesis generation, and hypothesis testing. This process of cycling and recycling between theory development and testing is how disciplines progress through scientific (sometimes called positivistic) methods.

According to Turner,[1] the building blocks of theory consist of 1) definitions; 2) principles; 3) variables; 4) hypotheses; and 5) formats (see Figure 12.1). *Definitions* identify certain key terms or ideas about which there should be uniform meaning. *Principles* are built from definitions and point to some belief about an existing phenomenon. *Variables* are special principles that either label phenomena or point to differences between phenomena. *Hypotheses* state how phenomena are related to each other, and *formats* consist of a series of interrelated hypotheses.

Theories differ by type. The physical sciences—including physics, biology, and astronomy—evolve through the testing of theories about the nature of the world in which we live. For example, a physicist may speculate on the existence of meson particles based on prior experimentation and observation. But the social sciences—including psychology, sociology, economics, education, communication, and management—devise and test theories that are less certain and more akin to philosophical views. Theories about human beings are simply less reliable than those

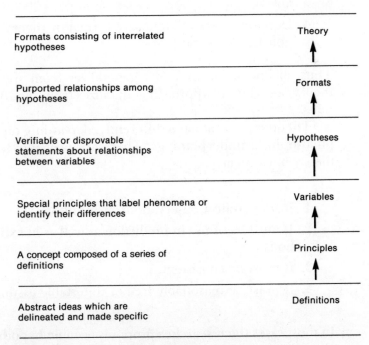

Figure 12.1 The building blocks of theory

of the physical sciences because people, unlike objects, can change their behavior when they know they are being studied.[2]

Theories may be *deductive* and/or *inductive,* according to the type of logic used in developing and testing them. Although distinctions are sometimes blurred in practice, deductive theorizing usually includes these steps:

1. Propose a theory based on intuition or past experience.
2. Propose definitions, variables, and hypotheses for testing.
3. Test the theory by describing or manipulating variables.
4. Tentatively confirm or negate hypotheses and/or theory itself.

Inductive theorizing, on the other hand, works this way:

1. Observe phenomena.
2. Develop definitions, variables, and hypotheses to describe phenomena.
3. Test hypotheses, usually through controlled manipulation of variables.
4. Develop a general, tentative format or theory to explain interrelationships of hypotheses.

Thus, an inductive approach generalizes from specific observations to theory; a deductive approach generalizes from theory to specific observations.

Theories are evaluated differently, depending on their form and their philosophical underpinnings. There are probably four criteria that any theory must meet:

1. It must reflect observations or intuition.
2. It must be of use in prediction as well as in explanation of observations.
3. It must be consistent.
4. It must be reasonably free of untestable assumptions.

In most cases the researcher proposes testable hypotheses based on prior observations, collects information to prove or disprove hypotheses, and publishes findings. (For more on theories, see: Bernstein,[3] Blalock,[4] Dubin,[5] Gibbs,[6] Hage,[7] Mullins,[8] Reynolds,[9] Shutz,[10] Stinchcombe,[11] and Zetterberg.[12])

The Nature of Models

A model is a simplified representation of an object, process, or phenomenon. It can only be proven accurate and cannot, like theory, be proven wrong with finality.[13] It dramatizes key features of that which it depicts but cannot, like theory, explain underlying causes. In short, a model can help to conceptualize a phenomenon but can rarely help to explain why it occurs.

Just as there are different formats for theory, there are different kinds of models. Two kinds are the *ideal* and the *constructed*.[14] An ideal model exaggerates certain features of what it represents, usually for comparative purposes. Max Weber used ideal models of religion and capitalism in his classic comparison of them. Most writers espousing training as a tool for implementing organizational strategy have relied on ideal models of the process. Products of imagination only, these models usually describe ideal relationships.

Constructed models are closer to reality. They are created from compilations of real events, conditions, situations, or variables—though not necessarily occurring in one setting. Some cultural anthropologists have used constructed models to compare societies. As a simple example, the griffin—a constructed model—is a mythical animal that is half-lion and half-eagle. In contrast, the dragon—also a mythical animal but not based on anything found in nature—is an ideal model. The limitation of an ideal model is that it is not based on anything that really exists; the limitation of a constructed model is that it can only be compiled from what does exist and has been observed. Here is an example of a constructed model:

1. (Based on the smaller manufacturer) Strategists should conduct an annual strategic planning meeting or retreat each year to
   a. Assess future environmental conditions relative to the organization's present strengths and weaknesses.
   b. Re-assess current long-term strategy in light of expected changes in the environment which were not apparent when the strategy was initially formulated.

c. Re-assess current strategy in light of how well strategic objectives were met during the past year as part of a multi-year plan.

2. (Based on the smaller service firm) During the strategic planning meeting, top managers should compare the strategy with assessments of the knowledge and abilities of managers in charge of organizational components. They should ensure that there are no fundamental mismatches.

   a. (Based on the larger manufacturer) The personnel department should project replacement needs resulting from expected retirement or turnover.

   b. (Based on the smaller financial firm) The personnel department should update succession charts for key management positions in light of strategy.

3. (Based on the smaller manufacturer) During the strategic planning meeting, strategists should identify management training initiatives most likely to support plans over the next year.

4. (Based on the smaller financial firm) The senior management trainer should separately interview top managers/strategists during the strategic planning meeting—but in a setting separate from it—to identify their individual assessments of management training initiatives supportive of plans.[15]

Preparing a model is a creative activity. The modeler is free to borrow parts from different theories and exclude whatever might be irrelevant to the purpose. For this reason, models are usually only partial representations of reality. For more on models, see Bunge,[16] Buzzell,[17] Casstevens,[18] and Love and March.[19]

It is possible to model almost anything through a picture (iconic models), words and pictures (verbal-pictorial models), comparison of two objects or ideas otherwise unlike (analog models) or by three-dimensional representation (symbolic models). A flight simulator is a three-dimensional model of an airplane cockpit; a comparison of the classic Shannon and Weaver Communication model to steps in the strategic planning process is an analog model.

Both theories and models are useful for organizing thinking and focusing on steps in a process, such as performing a job task. They can help HRD practitioners in providing information, stimulating creativity, and illustrating ideas economically. Practitioners should base their actions on a model or theory of human performance so that they understand how instruction will help improve it.[20] Models also can be used to describe competencies needed to do a job or perform a role.[21,22]

It is important for the HRD theoretician to have research skills because the process of building models and theories and then testing them makes it possible to:

- Describe conditions necessary for efficient and effective job performance.
- Identify skills associated with performance.
- Separate training from nontraining needs.
- Promote advances in the HRD field generally, through articles, books, and reports about theories and models that can help to explain or predict human performance.

Some HRD observers believe that the starting point for any performance analysis is theory-building and testing.[23] This belief may help to account for growing interest in research skills for HRD practitioners.[24]

Theories of Learning

Although some would disagree, theories of learning are not as advanced nor as detailed as theories in disciplines such as physics or biology. In many cases they represent merely philosophical beliefs—supported by some research—about the nature of learning. Writers in this area have proposed different means of classifying such theories:

1. Learning as a process of giving or receiving information. Sometimes called pedagogy, it is more a theory of instructing than of learning.
2. Learning as an association of a series of stimuli and accompanying responses. This is called behaviorism.
3. Learning as a result of insight, perception, and other internalized phenomena. This is called cognitivism.
4. Learning as a means of meeting human needs. This is called developmentalism.

Theories within each of these groups are based on different assumptions about the nature of human beings, the definition of learning, the role of trainee, and the role of instructor. They serve as foundations for different applications of HRD.

Pedagogy: The Manipulation of Environment

Pedagogy is not a formal theory of learning at all; rather, it is an informal philosophy about teaching that can be traced to the instructional practices of medieval universities.[25] However, it has had a profound impact on modern educational practice. Based on assumptions about human learning, it is pervasive enough to deserve treatment as a formal theory of learning.

Advocates of pedagogy assume that learning occurs through exposure to subject matter. In a university, the pedagogical environment is the "major," the sequence of subjects within a discipline through which learners must progress to graduate.

Learning, to pedagogues, consists of increasingly sophisticated awareness of bodies of knowledge. The purpose of learning is to absorb information. The learner is a passive receiver; the instructor is an active sender of information. In pedagogy, learning is a linear, one-way process of communication and change.

To foster learning, the instructor places heaviest emphasis on organizing information from least to most difficult, from previously known to unknown, and from past to present.

This theory views learning as the awareness of a discrete body of knowledge, such as a discipline or academic major, with the role of instructor being crucial in planning logically arranged information. Learners need high tolerance for ambiguity until instructors choose to reveal the purpose of prearranged instruction.

Behaviorism: Learning as Conditioning

Behavioral theory has had a lasting impact on learning theory and on organizational training practices. The word *behaviorism* was coined in 1913 by John B. Watson. Advocates use rigorous psychological research to derive principles that explain and predict relationships between stimuli (i.e., the means to induce behavior), behavior (i.e., observable actions that are presumably in response to stimuli), and consequent conditions (i.e., rewards or punishments for action). Sometimes called Second Wave psychology, behaviorism—or behavioralism—stresses the importance of external, environmental influences on specific, observable, and measurable human behavior. To behaviorists, thinking and feeling have relatively little to do with learning because they are internal, and thus unobservable and only indirectly measurable.

As a school of psychology, behaviorism encompasses a wide range of different viewpoints. However, advocates do share three primary assumptions:

1. The focus should be on present behavior, not on past determinants of it.
2. The focus should always be on the external and observable.
3. Behavioral goals or objectives of learning should be specified prior to instruction and should be measurable.

Behaviorists have been sharply attacked for fostering a mechanistic, manipulative view of learning. Under the force of such attacks, some behaviorists have modified their classic view that human beings are mere products of environment shaped completely by its myriad stimuli. Indeed, some have argued that behavioral change can arise from learner as well as from instructor/trainer and that such change leads to environmental adaptation. The result: individuals who are more satisfied with their world.[26]

Early behavioralistic learning theorists included Ivan Pavlov (1849–1936), John D. Watson (1878–1958), Edwin Guthrie (1886–1959), and Edward Thorndike (1874–1849). Pavlov is the grandfather of behaviorism. His experiments demonstrated that when dogs received food after a buzzer was sounded, they came to associate the buzzer with food. Food is an *unconditioned stimulus;* salivation in anticipation of food is an *unconditioned response.* When the buzzer is sounded just before feeding it becomes a *conditioned stimulus* that will lead to salivation, a *conditioned response.* This is called *signal learning,* since a conditioned stimulus (the buzzer) literally signals an unconditioned stimulus (food).

As the father of behaviorism, Watson built his work on Pavlov's. He argued that all differences between human beings result from learning. To demonstrate his belief, Watson used an 11-month-old boy in a series of experiments. Pairing a loud noise and a white rat, Watson taught the boy to fear the rat through association.

Edwin Guthrie [27] made at least one major contribution to learning theory. He rejected Watson's assertion that learning is improved through practice. He contended instead that a connection between stimulus and response is formed when they are first paired. In other words, no amount of practice improves performance of a behavior; rather, when a stimulus is repeated, the learner will tend to repeat the same response time and again.

To change a conditioned response, Guthrie suggested three techniques: 1) tiring the learner by repeatedly presenting the stimulus; 2) replacing the response by varying the degree to which the stimulus is presented; and 3) presenting the stimulus under conditions in which the response cannot take place. Simple examples should illustrate these three techniques. To break the habit of smoking, a smoker can: 1) be forced to smoke too much; 2) be given tobacco that is increasingly weaker; or 3) be given access to tobacco only in strictly enforced "no smoking" areas.

Edward Thorndike has had a profound influence on learning theory. Founder of *connectionism*, he believed that learning occurs through formation of a bond between stimulus and response. Unlike his predecessors, he accepted the notion that learning—synonymous with bonding—is improved through practice. He further believed that bonding between a stimulus and a response is improved through vigor (i.e., a strong response and a strong stimulus and frequency of occurrence). His so-called laws of learning include:

- *The Law of Effect.* A response is strengthened to the extent that it is followed by satisfaction but weakened to the extent that it is followed by annoyance.
- *The Law of Readiness.* A response is satisfying when the agent (i.e., learner) is predisposed to act; an inability to respond is annoying when an agent is predisposed to act; a forced response is annoying when an agent is not predisposed to act.
- *The Law of Exercise.* The bond between stimulus and response is strengthened when used but weakened when unused.
- *The Law of Multiple Response.* When a response to a stimulus does not lead to satisfaction, the agent will try other responses.
- *The Law of Prepotency.* An agent will selectively perceive the stimulus to which a response will be made.
- *The Law of Analogy.* An agent will respond to a new stimulus based on analogy with responses to similar but known stimuli.
- *The Law of Associative Shifting.* An agent can be taught to make a connection between a stimulus and response even when the stimulus is not presented. From a given connection, the researcher gradually

withdraws the stimulus but the agent still makes the association in the new situation.

Thorndike's major influence on modern learning theory is probably his Law of Effect.

Subsequent behaviorists have built on the foundations constructed by their predecessors. They include Clark Hull, Kenneth Spence, and B. F. Skinner. Each contributed to the gradual development of learning theory.

Hull [28] was a true behaviorist in the tradition of positivism. Not content with vague theorizing, he stated over 100 hypotheses about learning and tried to verify them through controlled experimentation in the laboratory. Like his forerunners, he believed all learning was essentially the result of a stimulus-response connection. Inspired by systems theory, he called the stimulus by a new name: the *input*. The response he called *output*. Hull postulated the existence of a third set of variables—*intervening* ones—which are the effects on an individual of a stimulus from the environment.

Although Hull's theory is quite complex, it can be summarized in one statement: the response potential of a given stimulus is the result of multiplying such intervening variables as *habit strength* (i.e., the number of previous and reinforced pairings of a stimulus and a response), *drive* (i.e., the need to meet certain requirements of the body), *stimulus dynamism* (i.e., the strength of a stimulus), and *incentive* (i.e., the strength of a reward that will meet body requirements).[29] A simple example should serve to clarify Hull's theory. A rat will learn to master a maze provided that previous efforts to do so have been reinforced (i.e., rewarded), that the reinforcement met the rats' needs, that the rat recognizes the relationship between the maze and the reward resulting from mastering it, and that the reward is sufficiently worthwhile to induce effort.

Kenneth Spence [30] built on Hull's work and modified it. His major contributions include:

- *A re-examination of habit strength.* Contrary to Hull, Spence concluded that it was solely a function of pairing stimulus and response.

- *A re-examination of the basic relationship between habit strength, drive, stimulus dynamism, and incentive.* Spence defined their relationship as additive, not multiplicative.

In most other respects their theories are basically similar.

B. F. Skinner [31] challenged mainstream behaviorism and substituted his own thinking. In doing so, he left a major imprint on learning theory. Earlier theorists believed that responses are always elicited by a stimulus, a view called *classical conditioning*. But Skinner believed that some responses are made without reference to a specific stimulus. If such responses are reinforced, they are more likely to be repeated. This view is called *operant conditioning*. While Skinner did not utterly reject classical conditioning, he did assert that its value was limited in explaining human learning. Instead, he emphasized the importance of reinforcement. Primary reinforcers satisfy basic needs, such as those for food, water, and sex; secondary reinforcers are learned through association with primary reinforcers. There are two types of reinforcers: positive and negative. A positive reinforcer will increase the likelihood of a response when provided; a negative reinforcer will increase the likelihood of a response when removed. Punishment differs from a negative reinforcer, because punishment does not provide an indication of what behavior should be.

As conceptualized by mainstream behavioristic learning theorists, human nature is primarily reactive. People respond to stimuli. Hence, observable and measurable behavior is the means by which learning occurs. A change in external behavior will result in changed internal attitudes, beliefs, and values. Human beings are shaped by their surroundings.

By extension, the role of learners is dependent. They are products of environmental stimuli contrived by instructors and other people. Reinforcement through various rewards is used to shape desired behavior. Learning itself is largely external—that is, it begins with behavior.

Social learning theory bridges behaviorism and another major tradition—cognitivism. The term "social learning" is linked closely with "socialization"—that is, adaptation to a cultural environment. Appropriate behaviors vary across cultures, depending on norms regulating interaction whenever the individual is introduced to a new role or new environment.

For social learning advocates, most learning results from *observation* and *imitation*. The individual observes behaviors of others and the resulting outcomes, later imitating what was rewarded. The stimulus may be vicarious in that an observer can form an association between a response and a reward or reinforcer. The response may also be a means of meeting primary or secondary needs. Repeated observations of a model—that is, a representation of behavior—may have the same effect as repeated performance of a behavior by learners themselves. Behavioral change occurs when learners perceive some benefit from imitating acts performed or even suggested by others.

For social learning theorists, human nature is highly imitative and is shaped by behaviors appropriate to the unspoken norms of a culture. The role of learner thus consists of imitating behaviors demonstrated by others; the role of the instructor is to provide a model to be imitated. Learning occurs when behavior is demonstrated and reinforced.

Cognitivism: Learning as Insight

Unlike behavioralism, cognitive learning theory is concerned with such internal phenomena as insight and understanding. Its focus is on the internal and the personal, not on the external and impersonal influences of stimuli and responses. For the most part, cognitivists reject the behavioralistic assumption that people are mere products of their environment; rather, they see people as major influences on the environment itself. Although the Gestalt school of psychology contributed most to the development of cognitive learning theory, Edward Tolman (1886–1959) and Kurt Lewin (1890–1947) can be viewed as its major exponents.

Cognitive theory began with the work of Gestalt psychologists at about the same time as behaviorism. Pavlov's early experiments laid the foundations of behaviorism; Wolfgang Kohler's observations of apes laid the foundations of cognitivism. Stranded on a tropical island at the beginning of World War I, Kohler occupied his time with experiments. He placed a bunch of bananas just out of reach of some caged apes. He noticed that they were clever enough to move boxes—and even place one on top of others—in order to reach the food. In another experiment they used a stick to knock down the bananas. He concluded that learning is a result of *insight,* a sudden recognition of relationships between discrete parts of a larger problem.

Kohler was a Gestalt theorist (as used in psychology, the German word *Gestalt* refers to a system or pattern of phenomena). Gestalt theorists attack behaviorism for reducing elements of learning to such separate parts as stimuli and responses while ignoring the larger pattern of relationships between them. The pattern, not the parts, is important. Indeed, the whole (the pattern) is greater than the sum of its parts (specific stimuli and responses). Gestalt theorists emphasize the uniquely personal side of learning, since it is essentially a process of individuals discovering relationships. Individual change results from acute awareness; hence, Gestalt theorists emphasize *perception* as fundamental to learning.

Gestalt psychology has proposed certain principles about the nature of perception:

- *The Principle of Direction.* Stimuli that appear to be meaningful and form a pattern will stand out against a neutral background. Observers will perceive the pattern.

- *The Principle of Contiguity.* Stimuli that are close together tend to be perceived as grouped together.

- *The Principle of Embeddedness.* A large figure with a great number of stimuli will stand out from small figures with lesser numbers of stimuli.

- *The Principle of Likeness.* Similar objects will tend to be perceived together.

- *The Principle of Joint Destiny.* Objects that move together will tend to be perceived together.

- *The Principle of Closure.* The mind will tend to perceive as complete otherwise incomplete experiences or patterns.

These general principles are essentially an outgrowth of the Gestalt belief that every psychological event—that is, every experience—tends to be perceived as meaningful and complete.

Edward Tolman is considered by some another major adherent of cognitive learning theory. Although he shared many views with behaviorists he differed from them in his belief that behavior is *purposive*—that is, directed toward achieving some purpose. Since behavior is goal-directed, expectations (i.e., the *cognitive*) play a crucial role in learning.

Tolman's theory of learning was based, like so many others, on experimentation with rats. He released rats in a maze with more than one way to the exit. After giving the animals sufficient opportunity to learn how to get through the maze, he then blocked several routes. He hypothesized that the rats, finding that the shortest route through the maze was blocked, would next try the second shortest. Results of the experiment confirmed his expectations, leading to his so-called *sign theory*. The sign is the stimulus.

In essence, Tolman found that learning occurs through development of *cognitive maps*, meaning internalized associations between a goal, a behavior (or series of behaviors), and an awareness of the environment in which the goal is located. Learning occurs when expectations are aroused in connection with some behavior. Aroused expectations are called *significates* and are associated with a sign.

Unlike behaviorists, Tolman did not view learning as a result of many stimuli-response relationships; rather, he viewed learning as composed of large units of behavior unified in their perceived relationship to a purpose or goal. To him, cognition is an expectation of good performance within the context of a unique environment.

Kurt Lewin's theory of learning shares important features with those of Tolman and the Gestalt theorists. His work has had a major impact on HRD. He was influenced by phenomenology, the belief that people interpret experience and that interpretation is central to existence.

For Lewin [32,33] individuals exist in a life space that consists of everything affecting their behavior. At the center of the life space is the individual as perceiver of environment. The environment itself has no inherent meaning; rather, the way it is perceived is crucial to understanding individual behavior.

The life space can be considered in terms of *valence,* a word Lewin used to mean the relative attractiveness of a goal to the individual. A *barrier* is a perceived difficulty or drawback in achieving a goal. Life space varies as individual goals change.

Like Tolman, Lewin believed that human behavior is essentially purposive, and oriented toward goals with strong valence in a given life space. Unlike Tolman, however, he did not emphasize cognitive mapping. Lewin's work is important as the foundation of experiential learning: the act or transfer of learning through personal experience. In addition, his work is the basis of action research—the essence of Organization Development—which suggests that group learning occurs through unfreezing old beliefs, restructuring those beliefs, and then refreezing (i.e., accepting new beliefs).

Jerome Bruner [34,35] is classified as a cognitive theorist because he prefers to emphasize the internalized nature of learning. For him, human learning is not a function of stimulus-response as it is for behaviorists. Instead, human development corresponds to the evolution of the species: the child progresses through periods in which the focus is on the amplification of motor abilities, sensory abilities, and intellectual facility. In the same way the human race evolved from enhancements to motor abilities (e.g., tool and weapon making), sensory abilities (e.g., the telescope and microscope), and finally intellectual facility (e.g., the computer).

Human learning occurs through *categorization,* the classification of objects or ideas that are similar. Categories are based on *attributes,* qualities that objects must have to be classified as stimuli. A *coding system* is a hierarchy of categories in which the most general category (e.g., human being) is more generic than those below it (e.g., men and women). To learn is to form or attain an inference between categories (or concepts) within the coding system. *Concept formation* involves an inference that two objects belong in the same category; *concept attainment* involves a discovery of attributes that are useful in helping to distinguish between objects that do or do not belong in the same category.

According to Bruner, the ability to create a coding system depends on such individual qualities as:

1. *Set.* A readiness to perceive.
2. *Need.* A motivation to learn based on drives.
3. *Specifics.* The more a learner already knows about objects in a possible generic coding system, the easier it will be to create a coding system.
4. *Diversity.* The more widely an object or event is experienced, the easier it will be to relate it to other objects or events.

Concept attainment resembles the creation of categories. Bruner suggests four general approaches to concept attainment:

1. *Complete scanning.* Attempting to generate all possible relationships between categories.
2. *Partial scanning.* Developing a hypothesis and testing it to see if it holds true.
3. *Conservative scanning.* Accepting the first attribute observed between two categories.
4. *Gambling.* Changing attributes to see if categories still appear similar.

Based on experimentation, Bruner concluded that people do indeed adopt such learning strategies in the process of concept attainment.

To cognitive learning theorists, human nature is more complex than it is to behaviorists. They see human beings as highly adaptive to their environment but capable of changing it. The role of learner is active because all learning is uniquely personal and experiential. The role of instructor is to create an environment that will lead to learning, a quintessentially individualized matter.

Developmentalism: Learning as Need Fulfillment

Developmental learning theory is a descriptive term encompassing the work of such modern writers as Jean Piaget, Carl Rogers, and Malcolm Knowles. Influenced by cognitive theory, their ideas represent a rejection of behaviorist assumptions about the nature of human beings. They prefer an emphasis on human freedom rather than on determinism and share deep faith in the human capacity to act on the environment rather than merely react to it.

Jean Piaget (1896–1980) devised a theory of learning based on stages of a child's development. He did not consider the stages of individual development as a reflection of human evolution. In fact, his view of childhood development is somewhat similar to that of Sigmund Freud.

Piaget [36,37] has been widely influential in U.S. and European education. He started out with two simple questions: how are children able to adapt to their environment and how can stages of childhood development be conceptualized? In answering the first question, he concluded that children play, imitate, and combine play and imitation. Play is a means of using objects for activities that have already been learned. It is a process of reinforcing the known. Imitation is a means of modifying behavior to that which was previously unknown. It is through imitation that children internalize the world, developing cognitively.

In answering the second question, Piaget concluded that children (from birth to age 15) develop through four stages: in the first (birth to age 2), they master language, come to understand objects, and discern cause-and-effect relationships; in the second (ages 2 to 7) they learn to solve problems through intuition; in the third (ages 7 to 11) they learn that it is possible for objects to retain the same bulk or space despite optical illusions; in the fourth (ages 11 to 15) they learn to compare actual to hypothetical conditions.

Based on Piaget's work and the countless research studies it has spawned, teachers have attempted to gear instruction to the child's stage of development (see Athey & Rubadeau; [38] Ginsberg and Opper [39]). More important for HRD practitioners, Piaget's work has directed attention to the efforts of Erik Erikson and others to show developmental stages beyond childhood. [40] Even Piaget believed that adults adapt to their environment through the same two basic techniques as children—that is, *assimilation* (repetition of activities already learned) and *accommodation* (change in behavior resulting from environmental pressure).

Carl Rogers [41] is seldom classified as a learning theorist, since he was a clinical psychologist by vocation. His writings have had a profound and revolutionary impact on teachers, trainers, and learning theorists. Beginning with the assumption that psychological counseling is essentially a learning experience, he proposed five hypotheses of learning:

1. Learning is entirely internal. For this reason, teaching is impossible because only the learner governs what is learned.

2. People will learn only that which they perceive as worthwhile to themselves.

3. People will resist learning experiences that are perceived as posing a potential for change in self-concept.

4. Self-concept becomes more rigid when threatened. Hence, significant learning is fostered in a supportive climate.

5. Learning occurs most effectively in a supportive climate in which the learner is encouraged to explore answers to questions.

For Rogers, people learn in order to satisfy their needs. They are inclined to seek greater freedom and to strive to become what they are capable of becoming. An exponent of Maslow's theoretical hierarchy of needs, Rogers revolutionized psychology and ushered in a new era in learning theory as well.

Malcolm Knowles [21,25,42] argues that adults learn in ways different from children, so that instruction geared to adults must take into account their special needs. As a leading exponent of the so-called adult education movement, he summarizes the theory of andragogy as follows:

- Learning is a result of self-direction. People have a need to function with greater autonomy as they age.

- Learning is intimately influenced by individual experience. Adults have an intense need to participate actively in learning rather than function as passive sponges of information.

- Learning is influenced by the timing of the experiences. Adults are most willing to learn when faced with specific life problems to which they seek answers.

- Learning is problem-oriented. Adults learn solely to meet needs.

For Knowles, as for Rogers, human beings have a deep drive to become more of what they are capable of becoming. Learning is strictly internal and influenced by human developmental stages. Instructors only facilitate learning. Individuals are self-actualizing, willing to learn in settings that are problem-centered.

To sum up, developmental learning theorists are often more cognitive than behavioral in their orientation to learning. For them learning is internal; the instructor's role is to help learners; the learner's role is crucial; learning is natural; and, human nature is essentially growth-oriented.

Figure 12.2 summarizes key points of the four primary theories of learning.

Major Theories of Instruction

Instruction refers to what an instructor does to guide or facilitate learning. In contrast, learning refers to changes in knowledge, skills, and

Figure 12.2 Major learning theories

	Pedagogy	*Behavioral*	*Cognitive*	*Developmental*
Theorists	None	John B. Watson Ivan Pavlov Edwin Guthrie Edward Thorndike Clark Hull Kenneth Spence B. F. Skinner Albert Bandura	Wolfgang Kohler Edward Tolman Kurt Lewin Jerome Bruner	Jean Piaget Carl Rogers Malcolm Knowles
Definition of Learning	General awareness of knowledge; information received	Conditioning	Development of internal classification schemes	Problem-solving; influenced by stages of development
Human Nature	Passive, reluctant learners	Influenced by the environment	Influenced by individual interpretations of external events	Active, eager learners
Role of the Instructor	Crucial	Model	Provides environment suitable to learning	Facilitator
Role of Learner	Unimportant	Shaped by environment	Crucial	Crucial

attitudes of an individual. Though intended to promote learning, instruction is capable of stifling it; likewise, instruction need not be planned for learning to occur.[43,44]

Logically, theories of instruction are based on theories of learning. There are thus what might be called four general theories of instruction:

1. *The subject-centered.* Based on pedagogical principles, it focuses on what will be taught.

2. *The objectives-centered.* Based on behaviorism, it focuses on observable and measurable outcomes of instruction.

3. *The experience-centered.* Based on cognitivism, it focuses on what learners experience during instruction.

4. *The opportunity-centered.* Based on developmentalism, it focuses on matching individual needs to appropriate instructional experiences.

These theories are not mutually exclusive and within each one there are alternative approaches.

Subject-Centered Instruction

What general principles are useful for instruction based on a subject-centered approach?

Although there is no one spokesperson for the theory, Malcolm Knowles [25] has summarized it while describing his own developmental theory. Advocates believe instructors should:

- Plan instruction carefully, sequencing information according to the logic of the material.
- Ignore or discount the value of learner experiences.
- Assume learners will understand that what they learn will have future uses not readily apparent to them now.
- Assume that the learner is dependent on the instructor for guidance.
- Use strong discipline to force learning when students lack motivation.
- Be expert on the subject to be taught, not necessarily on facilitating learning.

Pedagogues often reach such conclusions based on their own prior classroom experiences. Social learning theorists would say they imitate behaviors modelled by former instructors whose methods they observed.

Objectives-Centered Instruction

What general principles are useful for instruction based on an objectives-centered approach? How would learning theorists of the behavioral school deal with instruction?

For Pavlov, the instructor will attempt to pair a neutral object or subject (what is to be learned) with another already viewed positively (wealth, beauty, prestige). John Watson would employ similar methods. Based on Thorndike's views, the instructor should:

- Reward learners for correct performance and correct them promptly when performance is incorrect.
- Encourage repetition of acts performed correctly.
- Give frequent examinations to gather feedback on learning progress.
- Emphasize ways to elicit numerous correct responses from learners.

Based on Guthrie's views, the instructor should:

- State objectives clearly in advance. The instructor should know what responses should be elicited from what stimuli.
- Provide many different variations of the same stimuli, because each stimulus-response bond is unique.

Based on the views of Hull, the instructor should:

- Create an atmosphere of anxiety for learners, to provide an incentive to learn.
- Vary subjects so that learners do not become fatigued.
- Arrange subjects in disjointed order to increase learner attention span.

To Hull, learning will only occur when the learner wants something, must do something, and sees learning as a way of achieving that which he or she wants. Spence would largely agree with these views.

Based on the views of Skinner, the instructor should:

- Use such secondary reinforcers as praise, grades, and challenging assignments to encourage learning.
- Define, in behavioral terms, what learners will be able to do after instruction.
- Reinforce learner behavior 100 percent of the time after the first few responses but then gradually switch to partial reinforcement.
- Make learning experiences as individualized as possible—for example, utilize programmed instruction instead of lectures.
- Avoid punishment. Simply ignore or fail to reinforce inappropriate behaviors.

Based on the views of Bandura, the instructor should:

- Illustrate models of behaviors being taught.
- Establish clearly defined objectives for behavioral change.
- Gain commitment of learners to strive for achievement of those objectives.
- Devise ways to record or measure the extent of behavioral change.
- Allow learners to establish their own reward systems for successful achievement of objectives.

Generally, instructors using a behavioristic learning orientation should:

- Keep learners active, since repetition of appropriate responses is generally important to behaviorists.
- Reinforce appropriate responses.
- Encourage practice.
- Motivate learners by making explicit the link between learning and achieving goals.[45]

Objectives-centered instruction has had a lasting impact on organizational training practices, perhaps because it stresses the measurement of learning that is so important in justifying organizational expenditures on HRD activities. This approach, though requiring specialized expertise in instructional design, is widely used in many organizations.

Experience-Centered Instruction

What general principles are useful for instruction based on an experience-centered approach? How would learning theorists of the cognitive school deal with instruction?

Based on Gestalt theory, instructors should:

- Emphasize learner understanding more than behavioral change.
- Present a model of the whole first and then relate parts to the whole. The model can be of a work process or of the learning experience.
- Help learners solve problems, because unsolved problems create uncomfortable ambiguity for learners.

Based on the views of Tolman, instructors should:

- Provide learners with opportunities to test hypotheses and solutions to problems.
- Serve as consultants to learners engaged in problem-solving activities or exercises.
- Expose learners to a variety of interpretations and viewpoints so that these views may be tested in the relative safety of the learning environment.

Based on the views of Lewin, instructors should:

- Encourage "unfreezing" of learner stereotypes and inappropriate predispositions.
- Encourage "restructuring" of views so that the learner is more open to new experience and is more critical.
- Encourage "refreezing" of views learned through the restructuring process.

Based on the views of Bruner, the instructor should:

- Encourage the human predisposition to learn.
- Structure information so that it can be more readily understood by learners.
- Sequence instruction in "concept hierarchies."
- Provide reinforcement for student learning.

Generally, the instructor who has accepted a cognitive orientation to learning should:

- Structure learning problems so that learners perceive the most important features first.
- Emphasize the meaningfulness of the learning event and its importance in achieving desired goals.
- Provide frequent feedback to learners to confirm appropriate responses or correct inappropriate ones.
- Allow learners to establish or participate in establishing instructional goals.[46]
- Encourage creative thought as much as—or even more than—logically correct thought or appropriate performance.

This approach has had a substantial influence on HRD practitioners and has been widely used in Organization Development.

Opportunity-Centered Instruction

What general principles are useful for instruction based on an opportunity-centered approach? How would learning theorists of the developmental school deal with instruction?

Based on the views of Piaget, the instructor should:

- Be aware of the learner's stage of development and cultural background.
- Provide challenging learning experiences that will allow both assimilation and accommodation.
- Make instruction as individualized as possible.

Based on the views of Carl Rogers, the instructor should:

- Provide a supportive climate for individuals and/or groups.
- Help learners clarify their own needs.
- Encourage students to think for themselves through diligent but reflective questioning.

Based on the views of Malcolm Knowles, the instructor should:

- Encourage learner self-direction and autonomy.
- Provide groups of learners with every opportunity to pool individual experiences and insights.
- Assess the readiness of individuals to learn by analyzing problems that learners are facing in their careers or work at present.
- Pose instruction in the form of problems, rather than just transmit information.

This approach to instruction has had a major impact on organizational training practices. It has prompted greater attention to individual life and career planning, since life and career stages provide a cluster of needs to which instruction can be geared.

Factors Affecting Instruction

Theories of learning and instruction differ in their orientation to certain key factors that could influence learning and thereby influence effective instruction. They include memory, motivation, conditions, and rates of learning. Although these factors are complicated, HRD practitioners should at least be aware of them.

Research on memory suggests that there are really two kinds: short-term (lasting up to 20 seconds) and long-term. Short-term memory is ongoing as we interact in the world, and is easily disrupted by competing stimuli. Long-term memory is unlimited in capacity, a result of physiological change in the human brain, and subject to some distortion over time unless recalled and tested periodically.

Memory is crucial to all theories of instruction. For the subject-centered instructor, the student must be able to recall simple treatments of a subject before mastering more complicated ones. For the objectives-centered instructor, memory is conditioned and possibly influenced by reinforcement and repetition. For the experience-centered instructor, memory is the internalization of environmental interaction and provides raw material for interpretation. For the opportunity-centered instructor, individual needs influence what is perceived and remembered in the learning process.

Learner motivation may also influence the effectiveness of the instructional process. Pedagogy assumes that learner motivation is not the responsibility of the instructor. Behavioralism assigns varying levels of importance to learner motivation, with most theorists believing that it is far less important than external rewards. Cognitivists, in contrast, see learner motivation as essential and as arising largely from expectations of valued rewards. Developmentalists largely agree with the cognitive view.

Conditions of learning refer to the circumstances under which learning occurs and/or the circumstances under which learning must be applied. Pedagogy assumes that learning is a process of self-discipline. No attempt is made to consider the conditions under which subject-matter will be applied; rather, it is assumed that knowledge in itself is sufficient to be applied to all matters that will confront the learner later on.

Behaviorists generally assert that during the planning of instruction it is crucial to specify conditions in which new knowledge and skills will be applied. This means classroom instruction must be carefully structured to replicate environmental conditions in which learned responses will ultimately be used. Cognitivists argue that principles, not behaviors, will

---

Learning Curves and Instruction

A learning curve is a representation of the extent and the means by which the rate of learning accelerates or decelerates with practice. Production managers have found, for example, that production rates are generally low immediately following the start-up of a new production line but will increase as workers learn what they need to do. Techniques exist for estimating such curves and their influence on the production process. For more detailed treatment, see Abernathy,[47] Andress;[48] Bass and Vaughan;[49] Gaither;[50] and Holdham.[51]

Such curves may vary in their configurations. In a negatively accelerated learning curve, learning occurs rapidly at first and then the rate slows. In a positively accelerated curve, just the opposite occurs: learning begins slowly and then accelerates. In an S-shaped curve, learning begins slowly and then tapers off. Negatively accelerated curves are typical when trainees are experienced, motivated, and material is easily learned. Positively accelerated curves are typical when the task to be learned is difficult and/or trainees lack experience or motivation. The S-shaped curve is typical when the task is difficult and is prone to change or when trainees are changed while learning is taking place.

transfer to job performance. Hence, learning conditions should allow for exploration of ideas and for reflection about action which is not possible in most daily activities. Developmentalists believe conditions of learning must be carefully geared to the unique personal needs of learners and that subsequent application depends on those needs.

The rate of learning refers to varying speeds at which learning may occur. Pedagogists assert that the teacher sets the rate of learning and measures student progress through testing. Behavioralists emphasize learning curves, utilizing charts that depict how long it takes on average for learners to master behaviors in order to perform them effectively (see box). Cognitivists assert that, since learning is a function of insight and memory, rates will differ by individual. For this reason testing is essential to assess how much has been learned at various points in time. Developmentalists think rates of learning will be influenced heavily by learner needs and the individual's stage of development in the life cycle.

To conclude, each major theory of instruction is based on a theory of learning. What the instructor does should be guided by how students learn—with the sole exception, of course, of pedagogy. Each theory of instruction makes certain assumptions about the nature of learning, the role of instructor, the role of learner, and human nature.

How Theories of Learning and Instructing Apply to Adult Learners

Before 1950, many educators assumed that theories of learning and instruction were as applicable to adults as to children. Since formal education in the United States has been focused largely on those between ages 6 and 21, most research studies before the mid-1960s centered on people in those age groups. Despite the best efforts of scholars, pedagogy has largely remained the dominant philosophical orientation of teachers in primary, secondary, and higher education. At the same time, behaviorism still dominates training practices in organizations, though the influence of pedagogy—especially through unspoken expectations of operating managers about desirable HRD practices—is quite often apparent in this context as well.

However, Knowles [21,25,42] has pointed out that teachers of adults began to question the validity of pedagogical assumptions in the early 1960s. Cyril Houle's 1961 study, *The Inquiring Mind*,[52] propelled the movement forward. Examining 22 people, Houle found that adult learners can be classified into three groups:

1. *The goal-centered,* who use learning experiences as means to their own ends.
2. *The activity-centered,* who participate in learning for purposes having little to do with its objectives or outcomes.
3. *The learning-centered,* who are simply interested in knowledge for its own sake.

Houle's student Allen Tough [43,44] continued the work of his teacher and found that:

• Adults initiate an average of eight personal learning projects each year.
• Adults almost always consult at least one other person in the course of such projects.
• Teachers tend to interfere with adult learning by imposing a pedagogical structure on an otherwise natural discovery-oriented, problem-solving process.
• Few learning projects are associated with formal schools or HRD departments.

Despite such research—and much more—there remains only a limited body of knowledge that can be used in teaching adults. Indeed, what is known can be summarized in a few major points. According to Zemke and Zemke,[53] adults:

1. Initiate their own learning projects in response to significant events that change their lives, such as marriage, divorce, parenthood, promotion, or job transfer.
2. Are more willing or motivated to learn as the number of significant events in their lives increases.
3. Tend to pursue learning experiences that are directly related to these significant events.
4. Will be especially open to learning before, during, and after a significant event is definite. Such a time is called a "teachable moment."

5. Prefer to acquire knowledge or skill that can be applied immediately in dealing with change created by a significant event.

6. Are motivated to preserve their self-esteem, a factor that should be considered when applying teaching techniques.

7. Prefer to focus on one major concept at a time. For this reason, they usually prefer learning experiences geared to one topic— not a survey of many topics.

8. Have less tolerance than children for information with no apparent, immediate value.

9. Tend to take fewer risks than children in learning. They integrate new learning with what they already know and are slow in mastering information that conflicts with prior experience.

10. Resist ideas that conflict with their values. This means that new ideas presented in a group setting should be geared to multiple value systems.

11. Prefer self-directed to instructor-guided learning.

12. Prefer application-oriented to theory-oriented course content.

13. Learn best through open-ended instruction that encourages a group of learners to share experiences.

14. Prefer a learning climate that is comfortable both physically and psychologically.

The nature of the learning task and the needs of the learners will provide clues to which learning or instructional theory will probably work best. The subject-centered approach works best when learners have no prior knowledge of a subject; the behavioral approach works best when learners are faced with acquiring a skill that can be measured or observed; the cognitive approach works best when you want to stimulate creativity and the re-evaluation of attitudes; and the developmental approach works best when the focus is on personal growth or career planning.[54]

In general, what is known about *instructing* adults seems consistent with what is known about *managing* them. The teacher of adults, like a manager, must:

• Clarify his or her own expectations, since they will have an impact on the perceived success of experiences.

- Assess individual needs and developmental stages for use in motivation and in instructional design.
- Use influence and modeling, not coercive power and threats of punishment, to achieve success.
- Match instructional approaches to the situation, much as effective leaders match their styles of supervision to the situation.

While the instructor's role varies in learning experiences, adults should generally be allowed considerable participation in all aspects of the design, delivery, and evaluation of instruction. For more on this subject see: Aslanian and Brickell,[55] Bigge;[56] Campbell;[57] Cross;[58] Long;[59] McLagan;[60] Sherer;[61] and Wlodkowski.[62]

References

1. Turner, J. *The Structure of Sociological Theory*, rev. ed. Homewood, IL: Dorsey Press, 1978.
2. Keat, R., and J. Urry. *Social Theory as Science*. London: Routledge and Kegan Paul, 1975.
3. Bernstein, R. *The Restructuring of Social and Political Theory*. Philadelphia: University of Pennsylvania Press, 1978.
4. Blalock, H. *Theory Construction: From Verbal to Mathematical Formulations*. Englewood Cliffs, NJ: Prentice-Hall, 1969.
5. Dubin, R. *Theory Building*. New York: The Free Press, 1969.
6. Gibbs, J. *Sociological Theory Construction*. Hinsdale, IL: The Dryden Press, 1972.
7. Hage, G. *Techniques and Problems of Theory Construction in Sociology*. New York: Wiley, 1972.
8. Mullins, N. *The Art of Theory: Construction and Use*. New York: Harper & Row, 1971.
9. Reynolds, P. *A Primer in Theory Construction*. New York: Bobbs-Merrill, 1971.
10. Shutz, A. "Concept and Theory Formation in Social Sciences." *Journal of Philosophy* 51 (1954): pp. 257–273.
11. Stinchcombe, A. *Constructing Social Theories*. New York: Teachers College, 1968.
12. Zetterberg, H. *On Theory and Verification in Sociology*, 3rd ed. Totowa, NJ: Bedminster Press, 1965.

13. Popper, K. *The Logic of Scientific Discovery.* New York: Harper & Row, 1959.

14. Sjoberg, G., and R. Nett. *A Methodology for Social Research.* New York: Harper & Row, 1968.

15. Rothwell, W. *Management Training in Support of Organizational Strategic Planning in Twelve Illinois Organizations.* Unpublished doctoral dissertation. University of Illinois, 1985.

16. Bunge, M. *Method, Model, and Matter.* Dordrecht, Holland: D. Reidel, 1973.

17. Buzzell, R. *Mathematical Models and Marketing Management.* Boston: Harvard University, 1964.

18. Casstevens, E. "An Approach to Communication Model Building." *Journal of Business Communication* 16 (1977) 3: pp. 31–40.

19. Love, C., and J. March. *An Introduction to Models in the Social Sciences.* New York: Harper & Row, 1975.

20. Zemke, R., and T. Kramlinger. *Figuring Things Out: A Trainer's Guide to Needs and Task Analysis.* Reading, MA: Addison-Wesley, 1984.

21. Knowles, M. *The Adult Learner: A Neglected Species,* 3rd ed. Houston: Gulf, 1984.

22. McLagan, P. "Competency Models." *Training and Development Journal* (December, 1980): pp. 22–26.

23. Zemke, R., and T. Kramlinger. *Figuring Things Out: A Trainer's Guide to Needs and Task Analysis.* Reading, MA: Addison-Wesley, 1982.

24. Miller, D., and S. Barnett, eds. *The How-To Handbook on Doing Research in Human Resource Development.* Alexandria, VA: American Society for Training and Development, 1986.

25. Knowles, M. *The Modern Practice of Adult Education,* rev. ed. Chicago: Follett, 1980.

26. Kazdin, A. *History of Behavior Modification.* Baltimore: University Park Press, 1978.

27. Guthrie, E. *The Psychology of Learning.* New York: Harper & Row, 1935.

28. Hull, C. *A Behavior System.* New Haven, CT: Yale University Press, 1952.

29. Lefrancois, G. *Psychological Theories and Human Learning,* 2nd ed. Monterey, CA: Brooks/Cole, 1982.

30. Spence, K. *Behavior Theory and Learning.* Englewood Cliffs, NJ: Prentice-Hall, 1960.

31. Skinner, B. *Science and Human Behavior.* New York: Macmillan, 1953.

32. Lewin, K. *Resolving Social Conflicts.* New York: Harper, 1948.

33. Lewin, K. *Field Theory in Social Science.* New York: Harper, 1951.

34. Bruner, J. "The Act of Discovery." *Harvard Education Review* 31 (1961): pp. 21–32.

35. Bruner, J. *Towards a Theory of Instruction*. Cambridge, MA: Harvard University Press, 1966.

36. Piaget, J. *Play, Dreams and Imitations in Childhood*. New York: Norton, 1951.

37. Piaget, J. "Intellectual Development from Adolescence to Adulthood." *Human Development* 15 (1972): pp. 1–12.

38. Athey, I., and D. Rubadeau., eds. *Educational Implications of Piaget's Theory*. Waltham, MA: Ginn-Blaisdell, 1970.

39. Ginsberg, H. and S. Oper. *Piaget's Theory of Intellectual Development*, 2nd ed. Englewood Cliffs, NJ: Prentice-Hall, 1978.

40. Havighurst, R. *Developmental Tasks and Education*, 2nd ed. New York: McKay, 1970.

41. Rogers, C. *Freedom to Learn*. Columbus, OH: Merrill, 1969.

42. Knowles, M., & Associates. *Andragogy in Action*. San Francisco: Jossey-Bass, 1984.

43. Tough, A. *The Adult's Learning Projects*. Toronto: Ontario Institute for Studies in Education, 1971.

44. Tough, A. *The Adult's Learning Projects*, 2nd ed. Toronto: Ontario Institute for Studies in Education, 1979.

45. Hilgard, E., and G. Bower. *Theories of Learning*, 4th ed. Englewood Cliffs, NJ: Prentice-Hall, 1975.

46. Ibid.

47. Abernathy, W. "The Limits of the Learning Curve." *Harvard Business Review* 52 (1974): pp. 109–119.

48. Andress, F. "The Learning Curve as a Production Tool." *Harvard Business Review* (January-February, 1954): pp. 87–95.

49. Bass, B., and J. Vaughan. *Training in Industry: The Management of Learning*. Monterey, CA: Brooks/Cole, 1966.

50. Gaither, N. *Production and Operations Management*. Hinsdale, IL: The Dryden Press, 1980.

51. Holdham, J. "Learning Curves—Their Applications in Industry." *Production and Inventory Management* 11 (1970) 4: pp. 40–55.

52. Houle, C. *The Inquiring Mind*. Madison, WI: University of Wisconsin Press, 1961.

53. Zemke, R., and S. Zemke. "Thirty Things We Know for Sure About Adult Learning." *Training* 18 (1981) 6: pp. 45–52.

54. Ibid.

55. Aslanian, C., and H. Brickell. *Americans in Transition: Life Changes as Reasons for Adult Learning.* New York: College Entrance Examination Board, 1980.

56. Bigge, M. *Learning Theories for Teachers,* 4th ed. New York: Harper & Row, 1982.

57. Campbell, D. *Adult Education as a Field of Study and Practice.* Vancouver, BC: Center for Continuing Education, 1977.

58. Cross, K. *Adults as Learners.* San Francisco: Jossey-Bass, 1981.

59. Long, H. *Adult Learning: Research and Practice.* New York: Cambridge Publishers, 1983.

60. McLagan, P. *Helping Others Learn.* Reading, MA: Addison-Wesley, 1978.

61. Sherer, J. "How People Learn." *Training and Development Journal* 38 (1984) 1: pp. 64–67.

62. Wlodkowski, R. *Enhancing Adult Motivation to Learn.* San Francisco: Jossey-Bass, 1985.

For More Information

Daft, R. "Learning the Craft of Organizational Research." *Academy of Management Review* (October, 1983): pp. 539–546.

Hill, W. *Learning: A Survey of Psychological Interpretations,* 4th ed. New York: Harper and Row, 1984.

Spence, K., J. Spence, G. Bower, and J. Spence. *The Psychology of Learning and Motivation.* 14 Vols. New York: Academic Press, 1967–1980.

Wham, C., and P. Gibbs. "Real OD Practitioners Don't Follow Models." In *Targeting Change: Organizational Development,* C. Jackson, ed. Alexandria, VA: American Society for Training and Development, 1986.

Designing and developing the HRD curriculum.

This chapter summarizes methods for designing and developing an HRD curriculum. As we have noted, HRD refers to "organized learning experiences sponsored by an employer and designed and/or conducted in the work setting for the purpose of improving work performance while emphasizing the betterment of the human condition through the integration of organizational goals and individual needs." Consider the importance of the first word—*organized*—in this definition. Planning for HRD requires the practitioner to: 1) manage the function or department; and 2) manage all learning experiences sponsored or coordinated by the HRD function. The first task was covered in Chapter 10; the second—the organizational curriculum—will be discussed in this chapter. ■

What Is a Curriculum?

Although many definitions have been suggested, *curriculum* usually means a plan for instruction or learning. The time span of a curriculum can range from a few minutes or less to several years—or even over the entire lifetime of an individual or institution. Curriculum issues include:

1. Goals and objectives of instruction.
2. Values underlying them.
3. Methods of selecting, organizing, and delivering content.
4. Processes to facilitate learning.
5. Methods of evaluating intentions, methods, outcomes and curriculum itself.
6. Instructor selection.
7. Identification of learners.
8. Management of the setting in which the curriculum is implemented.

For detailed guides on curriculum development, see: Howson,[1] McNeil,[2] and Wiles & Bondi.[3]

Curriculum design involves careful planning of the curriculum before taking action, while *curriculum development* includes the gradual evolution of a plan from initial conception through implementation.

Components of an Organizational Curriculum

The term *program* is frequently used synonomously with *curriculum*. However, in this book *curriculum* refers to a long-term, strategic instructional plan for all formal learning events sponsored by the HRD department. In contrast, *program* means a single course or other planned learning experience with a definite beginning and end. A program *offering* is a single presentation of a program that is given many times. To cite a simple example: a one-shot workshop on supervision is an *offering* or *program offering;* a workshop on supervision with similar subject matter given repeatedly to different people is a *program;* a series of related programs on supervision in which the whole is greater than its parts (programs) is a rudimentary *curriculum*.

We will limit the term *organizational curriculum* to mean all formal, planned learning activities of the HRD department or those coordinated by the department. It includes all programs offered in the classroom, planned job rotations, external seminars, college courses, individualized study, materials, and other delivery methods integrated into a coherent whole greater than the sum of their respective parts.

The organizational curriculum serves to guide the long-term direction of developmental, educational and training activities. With this curriculum, decision-makers can help an organization adapt to changing external conditions and/or maintain efficient and effective internal work methods. It serves as both a policy and control tool with which managers can guide learning and a vehicle for helping individuals to cope with existing roles and prepare for others.

A *limited-scope curriculum* is part of the total organizational curriculum. It is geared to job progression ladders or job classes which help to organize the sequence and subject matter. For example, the nursing curriculum is only part of a hospital's organizational curriculum. Other parts are geared to other job classes. Each limited-scope curriculum is, in turn, comprised of a series of training programs. Each program is comparable to operational plans of first-line supervisors, while each limited-scope curriculum is comparable to intermediate plans of middle managers. Figure 13.1 illustrates the relationship between programs, limited-scope curricula, and the organizational curriculum.

Key Steps in Designing an Organizational Curriculum

Designing an organizational curriculum can be thought of as an eight-step process:

1. *Establishing purpose and goals.* What is the purpose of the curriculum? (Keep in mind that meeting long-term learning needs should be emphasized.)

2. *Determining a means of organization.* How will the curriculum be organized?

3. *Categorizing the organization.* How will the curriculum be subdivided into limited-scope curricula? Will the curriculum be designed to gear training to each job class, or will some other categorizing method be used?

4. *Assessing needs.* What should be included in the limited-scope curricula? (Again, emphasize long-term needs.)

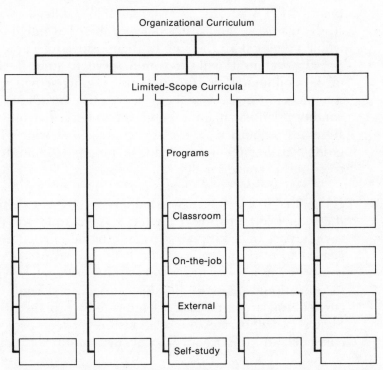

Figure 13.1 The relationship between the organizational curriculum, limited-scope curricula, and programs

5. *Determining delivery methods.* How will needs be met? What kind of programs will be included?

6. *Determining sequence.* In what order should programs be delivered? For what groups of learners?

7. *Implementing the curriculum.* What kind of structure, policies, and instructional leadership will be needed?

8. *Evaluating the curriculum over time.* (Emphasize the curriculum as a whole, not discrete programs.) [4]

These steps are illustrated in Figure 13.2.

Establishing purpose and goals is handled in much the same way as it is in long-term planning for the department. HRD practitioners, working together with other decision-makers, address such questions as:

1. Why does an organizational curriculum exist?

2. What should it include? Exclude?

3. What is the relationship between formal learning activities and organizational plans? HR (staffing) plans? HRD department plans? Plans of other departments?

4. What learners will be served? Over what time span? To what general and specific ends?

By answering these questions, decision-makers will determine how to engineer or encourage long-term organization development through organized learning activities. The way the questions are answered will reflect the values of decision-makers by showing what they consider important.

Determining the means of organization is the second step in the design process. This involves deciding on what basis the curriculum will be structured. There are, of course, various ways to do it:

- By individual.
- By work group.
- By job class or job progression ladder.
- By department or division.
- By location (job site).
- By project.
- By some combination of any or all of the above.

A curriculum organized by individual will use learning contracts for each person. If organized by work group, courses and other experiences will be separately established for many small groups across the organization. A curriculum structured by job class or job progression ladder will match programs to position titles, and a structure by department or location will match programs to the organization chart. A project structure will organize learning experiences by project type, needs, and duration.

The third step, categorizing the or-

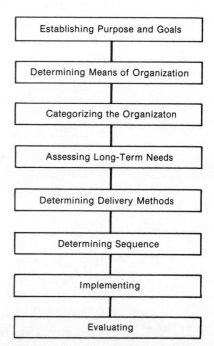

Figure 13.2 A model of organizational curriculum design

ganization, is merely a continuation of the second. At this point decision-makers sketch out the types of limited-scope curricula. For example, what will be the size of the management training component? What will be the other components? Some typical ones include: sales training, professional training, technical training, skilled training. Employees are placed in the appropriate category and a curriculum is designed for each group.

The fourth step, assessing needs, begins to address the kinds of programs that will be included in each limited-scope curriculum. At this point, it is worthwhile to consider the organization's strategic plan and any known individual career plans. In this step, general titles can be assigned to programs.

The focus of this step should be on long-term needs—such as orienting new employees, preparing employees for promotion or more advanced work in their fields, or updating employee skills. These needs should be considered long-term because everyone has them to some extent. Curriculum needs assessment is thus centered around predictable needs stemming primarily from job entry or future job movement. In contrast, program needs are more specific, being geared to the present and to a specific group.

In the fifth step, decision-makers determine delivery methods. What approaches will be used to meet needs? Examples include:

- Planned job rotations of individuals.
- Classroom courses.
- Self-study experiences.
- Seminars, workshops and other events offered by external vendors, colleges, professional societies, and other sources.
- Structured on-the-job experiences.

Each approach has its own advantages and disadvantages, which should be carefully examined during the curriculum design process.

The sixth step addresses the question: In what sequence should experiences be offered? Depending on the learners, some experiences are prerequisites to others. They should be identified and scheduled accordingly, within limited-scope curricula.

In sequencing programs for a limited-scope curriculum, three categories of programs should be considered:

1. *Those related to topic areas.* Some examples: management, computer science, and engineering.

2. *Those related to job class.* Employees in lower-level job classes on a job progression ladder take specific programs appropriate to that level; other programs are specified for higher levels.

3. *Those related to individual progress.* Programs are geared to maintenance (what are the policies and procedures of the organization?), job (what are the duties?) and promotion (what skills are needed for the next higher job?).

These categories overlap and are not mutually exclusive.

Four major designs can be used to sequence programs in a limited-scope curriculum: the *horizontal,* the *vertical,* the *diagonal,* and the *spiral.*[5] The vertical design is perhaps most familiar (see Figure 13.3). A new-

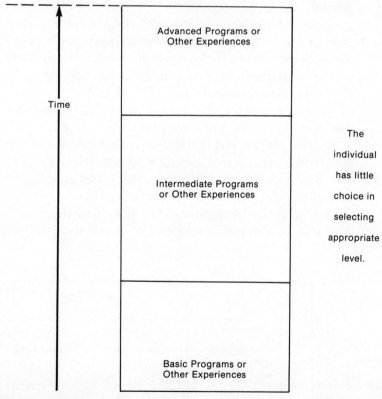

Time

Advanced Programs or Other Experiences

Intermediate Programs or Other Experiences

Basic Programs or Other Experiences

The individual has little choice in selecting appropriate level.

Figure 13.3   The vertical design

comer begins with basic programs and gradually moves up. Programs may be described as basic, intermediate, and advanced.

The horizontal design is somewhat different. (See Figure 13.4.) The learner simultaneously receives (or has the opportunity to receive) exposure to all three levels. For example, a basic program on general management can be followed by an advanced treatment of some specialized topic. Another example: a maintenance-geared program such as employee orientation is followed by a promotion-geared program such as one on the principles of supervision. The individual has some discretion in choosing programs, but little discretion in choosing the content of the program.

The diagonal design is a compromise between horizontal and vertical (see Figure 13.5). The learner can choose some but not all programs or experiences. For example, orientation (maintenance-geared) is required, but the individual can choose an elective that is job-geared or promotion-geared.

Finally, the spiral design is organized on the principle of repetition. (See Figure 13.6). Individuals are exposed over time to the same concepts, topics, or ideas but in increasingly sophisticated forms. For example, a group of learners may take a series of interrelated programs, such as Principles of Supervision I, II, III, and IV.

In the seventh step, the organizational curriculum is implemented through programs and limited-scope curricula. These experiences can be specifically tailored to the unique individual and work-related requirements of the learners. Decision-makers assess needs before each program offering, select appropriate instructors, and establish rewards and policies to support the curriculum purpose and goals.

Evaluation is sometimes thought of as the final stage, although in reality it is a continuous process. Evaluation takes place during and

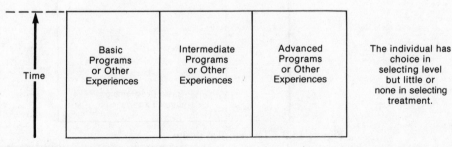

Figure 13.4   The horizontal design

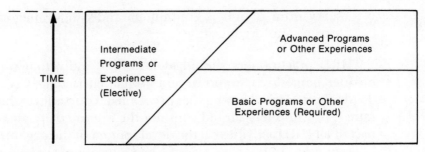

Figure 13.5 The diagonal design

after each program offering. Information is then fed upward to help improve limited-scope curricula. Periodically the organizational and limited-scope curricula are reviewed in their entirety for their aggregate long-term impact. This evaluation focuses on the overall results of the curriculum, rather than on individuals, programs, or offerings.

Though the model implies that an organizational curriculum is designed from the top down, there are alternatives:

- Instructional plans can begin as short blocks of instruction that are gradually put together to form programs first, then limited-scope curricula, and finally an organizational curriculum. With this approach, curriculum design proceeds from bottom (lesson or unit) up.
- The organizational curriculum is established but is considered apart from required experiences for individuals or work groups. The curriculum stands alone while learners pick and choose programs like people selecting food in a cafeteria. If this approach is used,

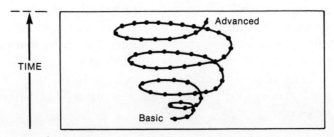

Figure 13.6 The spiral design

curriculum design is continuous and can be negotiated between learner and organization.

HRD practitioners should look beyond individual programs to the broader limited-scope and organizational curricula. It is not enough to do the short-term planning that program or course-level thinking implies; rather, practitioners should consider the intermediate and long-term impact of all HRD activities on the development of the organization through its employees. In this way, training and educational programs can become long-term change efforts.

For more on curriculum theory and practice, see Beauchamp;[6] Bobbitt;[7] Giroux and Purpel;[8] Goodlad;[9] Pratt;[10] Taba;[11] Tyler;[12] and Unruh and Unruh.[13] Several of these are classic treatments of the subject—notably those by Bobbitt and Tyler.

Basing the Organizational Curriculum on Major Learning Theories

An organizational curriculum can be based on any one or all of the four major theories of learning and instructing. This means it can be subject-centered, objectives-centered, experience-centered, and/or opportunity-centered—and so can the limited-scope curricula and the programs. To further complicate the process, within each major approach several distinct methods can be used. Choice of approach and method depends on the purpose and goal of the curriculum, values of decision-makers, and needs of learners.

The subject-centered curriculum grows out of assumptions of pedagogy. Planning is simple: instructors, not learners, make decisions about subject matter. Programs are classified as required or elective; they are typically organized in logical sequence from basic to advanced. Instructors actively control the flow of information from themselves to learners. Learners master increasingly complicated treatments of an idea or discipline. Learners are passive sponges of information whose experiences prior to instruction are considered largely unimportant.

The objectives-centered curriculum, on the other hand, is based on the learning and instructional assumptions of behaviorism. Planning focuses on:

1. Observable, measurable behavior.

2. Arrangement of instructional experiences devised from careful analysis of job tasks.

Instructors serve as behavior engineers who orchestrate effective job performance through learning experiences and other work improvement methods.[14] Learners are actively involved because they must demonstrate through behavior that they can apply skills in conformance with predetermined standards in circumstances similar to those encountered on the job.

The experience-centered curriculum is based on the assumptions of cognitivism. Planning focuses on identifying patterns larger than single tasks, such as cognitive maps or models of an entire process. Instruction proceeds from whole to part so that learners see interrelationships and configurations connecting them.

This type of curriculum is based on phenomenology, the belief that reality exists only as perceived and interpreted through the mind of the observer. For this reason it is possible to define the curriculum as:

- Approved by decision-makers or set forth in formal policies and manuals.
- Perceived by instructors.
- Observed by those watching instruction as it is delivered.
- Experienced by participants.
- Applied by trainees on the job.
- Perceived by supervisors of trainees on the job.[15]

The opportunity-centered curriculum is based on the assumptions of developmentalism. Instructional planning gives learners the responsibility of identifying their own needs. Experiences are best designed to coincide with significant events in the lives of learners, including stages of socialization in the organization. The learning process stresses mutual sharing, and instructors facilitate learning rather than direct it.[16]

In this section, we will point out the major advantages and disadvantages of each of these four approaches to curriculum design—and discuss methods for utilizing each approach.

The Subject-Centered Approach

Historically, the subject-centered approach has dominated, despite the best efforts of educational and HRD writers to promote other approaches.[17] High school and college students naturally associate curriculum with a series of courses that must be taken to graduate. Predictably, managers carry over this notion into organizational settings and associate training with courses needed by an employee to satisfy probationary requirements or, in some professions, mandatory continuing education requirements.[18]

Developing a subject-centered curriculum is relatively simple. The HRD practitioner:

1. Asks line managers what topics should be offered to each level of employee by job class or by the individual's stage in the socialization process.
2. Arranges program in some logical fashion, usually from basic to intermediate and advanced.
3. Offers the programs on a regular basis.

These steps are illustrated in Figure 13.7.

Asking managers about what should be taught is called *needs assessment*. In a small organization, it might be done in meetings; in larger organizations, a survey of employees and managers may be needed. As an alternative, the HRD practitioner can examine job descriptions and develop a series of program titles to correspond to each major job activity area. A separate, more specific needs assessment should be conducted before any program is offered, because specific individuals and groups will vary in their learning needs (see Chapters 14 and 15).

The subject-centered approach has three major advantages: it is easy, inexpensive, and fast.

Offsetting this are some serious disadvantages:

1. The curriculum only appears to match instructional offerings to learner needs. Specific individual needs can differ sharply, but this is not taken into account by the subject-centered approach, which considers only general needs by job class or group.
2. Planning focuses on topics or subjects, rather than on the ability to apply skills on the job.

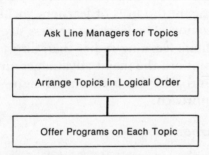

Figure 13.7   Steps in designing a subject-centered curriculum

3. Learners—and sometimes managers outside the HRD department—do not always participate in selecting subjects or setting priorities—and they may not accept a curriculum thrust on them.

The second disadvantage is perhaps the most serious, because the instructional offerings may not correspond to the needs of the job.

The Objectives-Centered Approach

Developing an objectives-centered curriculum is a complex process. Two methods can be used: the *decision-based* and the *competency-based*. The first focuses on correcting performance problems while the second focuses on exploiting opportunities for performance improvement. The distinction is sharper than it might appear. Decision-based methods attempt to discover barriers or impediments to performance; competency-based methods attempt to define good performance and then facilitate or improve it.

Decision-Based Method. To design a decision-based curriculum (or program), the HRD practitioner:

1. Conducts a performance audit to identify deficiencies by organizational unit, job class, or individual.
2. Delimits the deficiencies to make them specific, measurable, and observable.
3. Gathers information about deficiencies.
4. Assesses needs relative to deficiencies.
5. Writes instructional objectives intended to rectify deficiencies.
6. Groups objectives into lessons, units, and courses.
7. Tests the willingness of organizational decision-makers to deal with deficiencies.
8. Offers instruction intended to improve performance and remove deficiencies.
9. Evaluates how well improvement efforts transfer to job performance.

These steps are depicted in Figure 13.8.

The first step—a performance audit—is more comprehensive than many forms of training needs assessment. Based on a model of human performance, it analyzes such factors as:

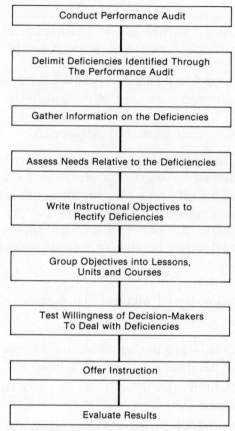

Figure 13.8 Steps in designing a decision-based curriculum

- *Job context.* Do people know when to perform?
- *Employee skills.* Do people possess the abilities needed to perform?
- *Behavior.* Do people know what they are to perform and possess necessary tools and/or resources?
- *Results.* Are people rewarded appropriately for good performance? Do rewards matter to them?
- *Feedback.* Are people informed about whether performance was adequate? [19]

Selecting an appropriate performance improvement approach depends on the nature of a deficiency. Since training is one of the most expensive approaches, it is warranted only when its costs are outweighed by potential benefits.

Major advantages of the decision-based method include:

1. An emphasis on analysis to uncover the underlying causes of problems. Improvement efforts then focus on these causes rather than on mere symptoms or side effects.

2. An emphasis on a range of improvement efforts. The HRD practitioner becomes more than a snake oil merchant peddling the same medicine—training—for every ill. Alternative improvement strategies are considered, including preparation of job aids, on-the-job coaching, and even work redesign.

3. An emphasis on cost-benefit analysis. The HRD practitioner selects the improvement strategy that will do the best job at the cheapest cost.

4. An emphasis on pressing problems. HRD practitioners focus on getting results where they are most needed in terms of impact on individual and organizational performance. Since adults are problem-centered in their approach to learning, decision-based interventions usually gain strong support from those most concerned about a problem.

Of course, there are also disadvantages to this method:

1. Analysis can be costly and time consuming.

2. Some people may not recognize that the role of HRD practitioner encompasses more than just standing in front of a class.

3. Managers may have formed their own notions about the cause of performance problems—and may resent the "meddling" of HRD practitioners who know less than they do about technical aspects of the work.

4. Correcting deficiencies is inherently oriented toward the past or present, not the future. As job conditions change, performance is altered, and so are deficiencies. For this reason, some thought needs to be given to likely future job conditions.[20]

Even with the disadvantages of the decision-based method it is clearly superior to a subject-centered approach because it focuses on improving performance, not just transmitting information.

Competency-Based Method. There are two types of competency-based methods: *instructional systems design* (ISD) and *behavioral skills-outputs* (BSO). ISD is often but not exclusively used for jobs possessing clearly identifiable results, such as the manual trades. BSO is more often applied to professional and managerial jobs.

ISD is a thoroughly integrated method. To apply it, HRD practitioners need to:

1. Do background research on the organization and its job categories.

2. Develop a plan to guide the instructional design, delivery, and evaluation effort. It should set forth work to be done, time schedules for completion, and resources needed.

3. a) Conduct task and job analyses to determine the nature of the work, conditions in which it will be performed, and criteria/standards by which to assess individual performance.
   b) Develop a plan for selecting and using media to support the training.
   c) Examine any training programs already existing that may be similar and can help in the design process.

4. Develop behavioral objectives (i.e., what learners will be able *to do* following instruction).

5. Select media to support training on each objective.

6. Determine how to group objectives and sequence instruction effectively.

7. Develop a complete training syllabus (i.e., list of learning or instructional tasks) that identifies the nature of all learning experiences to be offered to trainees.

8. Obtain organizational support for the syllabus, by giving managers a chance to review and alter it.

9. a) Group parts of the syllabus into courses, lessons, or units.
   b) Identify what resources will be needed to deliver and evaluate instruction at each level.

10. a) Select or write instructional materials (based on the syllabus) to achieve behavioral objectives.
    b) Give managers or subject experts an opportunity to review instructional materials before they are used.

11. Revise instructional materials based on the expert review.

12. a) Offer instruction to a pilot group of trainees to see how well it works in practice.

   b) Develop a system for assessing how well the instruction improves job or task performance.

13. a) Revise instructional materials based on experience with the pilot group.

   b) Develop a plan for implementing instruction, including policies on scheduling of trainees, testing methods, train-the-trainer materials, and use of facilities.

14. a) Prepare train-the-trainer material.

   b) Prepare student workbook(s).

   c) Prepare specifications for any special training equipment needed, such as simulators or computerized instructional systems.

15. Brief line managers on the curriculum, including programs and other learning experiences.

16. a) Prepare and schedule facilities.

   b) Conduct train-the-trainer sessions.

   c) Test student workbook(s).

17. Train employees.

18. a) Evaluate instruction as it is offered.

   b) Collect information on how well the training is applied on the job.

   c) Review and revise material as necessary.

These steps are depicted in Figure 13.9. There are also other models of ISD in Carkhuff[21] and Dick & Carey.[22]

The major advantages of ISD include:

1. *Completeness.* The approach focuses on every step of instructional design and delivery. It is useful for planning instructional projects regardless of their size or scope.

2. *The instruction is evaluated before, during, and after widespread use.* Materials are improved before learners are exposed to them, so that results can be reasonably predicted. Wasted time and effort are minimized, though testing itself is time-consuming and expensive.

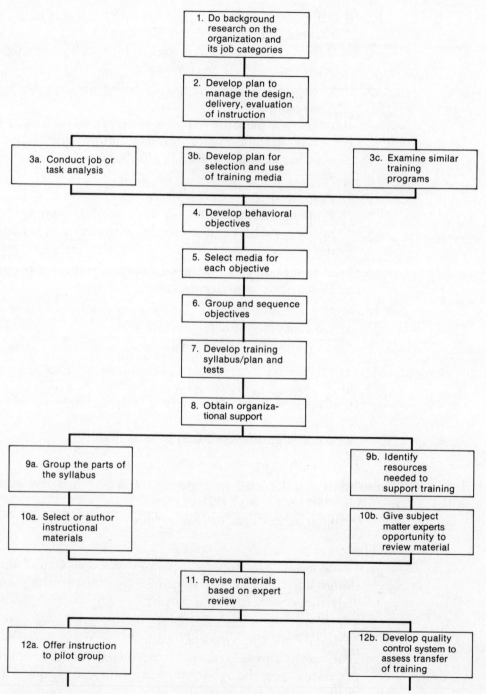

Figure 13.9 Steps in designing a curriculum using ISD

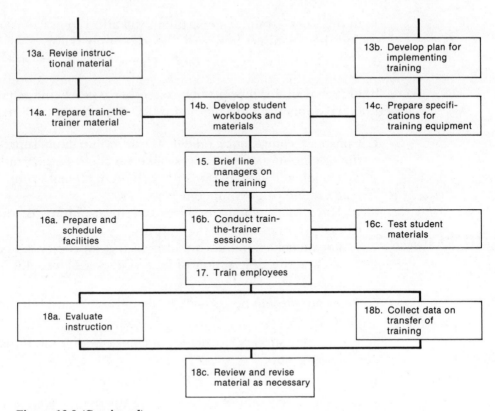

Figure 13.9 (Continued)

3. *Appropriate behavior or performance is emphasized.* Instead of focusing on what is wrong, ISD concentrates on gearing performance to norms based on job and task analysis.

There are also disadvantages:

1. *Present performance is emphasized.* ISD can be used during the design of new products or machinery so that employees are trained by the time the product is marketed or the machinery is ready for use. However, it does not necessarily consider such matters as the likelihood of future job changes.

2. *The emphasis is exclusively on individual behavior.* When new products or machinery are introduced, little thought is given to how changes

in the work group or department will affect interactions of people and thereby affect how well they can apply skills.

3. *ISD is time-consuming and costly.* This is its major disadvantage.

BSO (behavioral skills-outputs) is another type of competency-based method. To apply the BSO method, HRD practitioners will need to:

1. Construct competency models for all occupations represented in the organization. This process involves the following tasks:
   a. Do job and task analyses of each occupational group.
   b. Examine prior competency studies.
   c. Have role incumbents identify critical outputs of their work.
   d. Set priorities among the outputs.
   e. Create behavioral anchors for each competency. (A behavioral anchor is a description of behavior. See Figure 4.6 for examples.)

2. Ascertain present performance or competency levels for each occupational group.

3. Ascertain desired performance or competency levels for each occupational group.

4. Eliminate problems that HRD efforts will not solve.

5. Develop behavioral objectives by occupation or job class for each competency.

6. Sequence instruction by grouping objectives and then install the curriculum.

7. Evaluate the influence of HRD efforts on job performance over time.

These steps are depicted by the chart in Figure 13.10. There are alternative models of BSO in Blank,[23] Boyatzis,[24] Ingalls,[25] Klemp,[26] McClelland,[27] and Zemke.[28]

The advantages of BSO include:

1. *Emphasis on work outputs.* Since professional and managerial jobs often involve unobservable mental activity, this feature of BSO makes it uniquely suited for dealing with these jobs.

2. *Emphasis on performance improvement.* Unlike most other curriculum methods, BSO focuses specifically on desired performance.

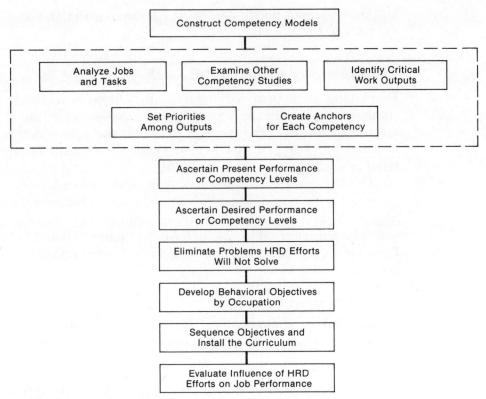

Figure 13.10 Steps in designing a curriculum using BSO

Disadvantages include:

1. *Emphasis on the present.* BSO is based on information about present performance and present activities of exemplary performers. It does not necessarily consider how performance will have to change to cope with future and perhaps unknown job conditions (although this can be done if HRD practitioners make the attempt).

2. *High cost and specialized skills.* Developing a competency model is no simple matter.

Despite these drawbacks, the BSO method is growing more popular and can be adapted easily to instruments for employee selection, job analysis, and appraisal. Indeed, its wide applicability makes it extremely useful for identifying career paths and corresponding training, education, and development needs. *Models for Excellence* is perhaps the best known example of the BSO method.

The Experience-Centered Approach

Developing an experience-centered curriculum is relatively easy when compared with the complexities of objectives-centered methods. There are three types: (1) the *creativity-based*, (2) the *action-based*, and (3) the *concept-based*. The first two overlap somewhat with the opportunity-centered approach.

The Creativity-Based Method. This method focuses on evoking new ideas rather than on building specific skills or transferring specific information. Most organizations are more familiar with convergent thought, which is characterized by a search for one solution based on marshalling facts. Divergent—or creative—thought is characterized by such activities as:

1. Generating new ideas.
2. Thinking about multiple ideas simultaneously.
3. Generating unusual ideas.
4. Shifting the context of ideas so as to explore comparisons.
5. Seeing beyond obvious solutions to possible long-term outcomes and consequences of action taken to address problems.

Divergent thinking offers perhaps the greatest potential for working smarter, not harder.

To develop a creativity-based curriculum, the HRD practitioner needs to:

1. Identify key problems confronting the organization through any or all of the following methods:
   a. Performance audits
   b. Quality circles
   c. Attitude surveys
   d. Organizational strategic planning objectives
   e. Meetings with managers
2. Break down each problem into several categories of components.
3. Base a program or part of a program on each category or component.

4. Implement the curriculum.

5. Gather information about the quality of solutions, including
   a. How many were subsequently used
   b. Outcomes of the solutions

This model is illustrated in Figure 13.11. A creativity-based curriculum is focused less on individual and more on organizational performance. Advantages of this method include:

1. *Emphasis on problem-solving.* Like the decision-based method, the focus is on key problems or issues confronting the organization. But unlike the decision-based method the creativity-based method tries to generate totally new, perhaps quite radical, solutions.

2. *Emphasis on preserving the creative impetus.* By exploring creative and nontraditional ideas over time, the organization institutionalizes innovation and helps to keep it alive.

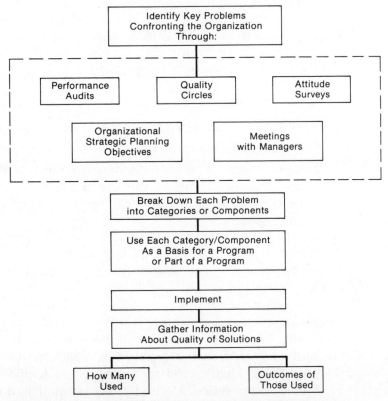

Figure 13.11 Steps in designing a creativity-based curriculum

Disadvantages of the method include the high cost of group problem-solving, the often inordinate length of time between generation of ideas and their subsequent exploration, and the possibility that participants in the process may not have sufficient information to make meaningful contributions on specific problems.

The Action-Based Method. This method of curriculum development is very similar to the creative-based. HRD practitioners:

1. Identify key problems or potential opportunities confronting individuals, groups, or the organization.
2. Feed this information back to those affected by the problems or opportunities.
3. Facilitate participative problem-solving to identify the knowledge, skills, or attitudes needed to cope with present problems or take advantage of future opportunities.
4. Facilitate action planning to:
   a. Establish learning objectives and activities for the organization over the long term (3–5 years).
   b. Establish learning objectives and activities for departments and work groups over the intermediate term (1–3 years).
   c. Establish learning objectives and activities for job classes and individuals over the short term (up to 1 year).
5. Schedule activities and find resources to carry them out.
6. Implement the curriculum through a sequence of programs.
7. Evaluate the curriculum by devising ways for individuals, groups, and representatives of the organization to receive feedback on outcomes so that they can devise their own improvement strategies.[29]

This method is illustrated in Figure 13.12. It is an Organization Development approach to curriculum development, based heavily on the action research model of Lewin.[30]

The advantages of this approach are similar to those for the creativity-based. An additional advantage is that this method places more emphasis on participative decision-making in the selection of problems and methods of dealing with them. Disadvantages include the high cost and long time needed to identify and act on those problems.

The Concept-Based Method. This method is quite different from the two others treated in this section. Based on the thinking of Jerome

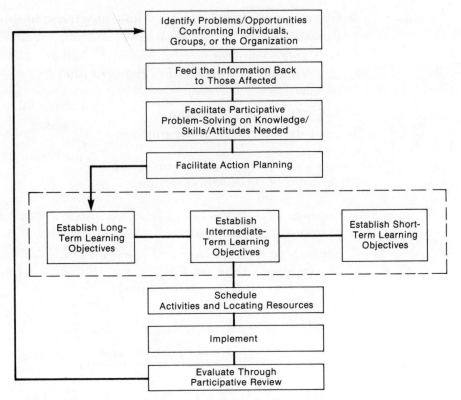

Figure 13.12   Steps in designing an action-based curriculum

Bruner,[31] a concept is defined as a category by which an individual organizes and interprets experience. A concept has a name, a definition, identifiable characteristics, and can be readily linked to examples.

To develop a concept-based curriculum, HRD practitioners will need to:

1. Identify key or critical concepts associated with successful job performance through such means as:
   a. Asking job incumbents
   b. Asking supervisors
   c. Observing successful and unsuccessful performers
2. Rank concepts according to priority.
3. Establish a "learning hierarchy" so that basic concepts are introduced before more complicated ones.

4. Group parts of the hierarchy into programs, lessons, and units.
5. Provide in each lesson and unit:
   a. A rule (definition)
   b. Definition of the concept's characteristics
   c. Examples
6. Implement the curriculum.
7. Evaluate the curriculum periodically.

These steps are illustrated in Figure 13.13.
Advantages of this method include:

1. *Emphasis on work concepts.* There is economy in learning key rules to improve performance.
2. *Emphasis on the most important facets of a task, job, or role.* Focusing on key areas of the work to the exclusion of less important areas makes maximum payoff more likely.

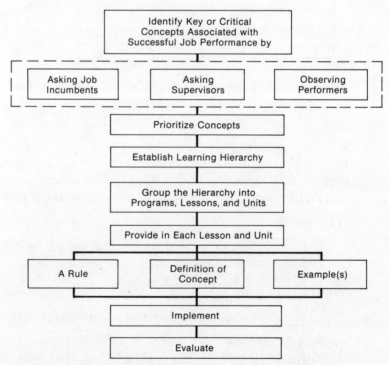

Figure 13.13 Steps in designing a concept-based curriculum

Disadvantages include the time needed to translate critical activities into concepts and the past (rather than future) orientation of the approach. Concepts will change as work conditions do, and this method makes little attempt to predict future concepts.

The Opportunity-Centered Approach

There are essentially three methods of developing an opportunity-centered curriculum: (1) the individualized-informal; (2) the individualized-contractual; and (3) the group-oriented. All are based on the assumptions of developmentalism, though they vary in how those assumptions are applied to instructional planning.

In the first two methods, individuals make their own decisions about learning needs and priorities. They:

1. Identify their own goals, objectives, and desired learning initiatives—perhaps linked to career aspirations.

2. Identify methods for achieving their own goals and objectives.

3. Develop an individualized curriculum of learning projects over the long term.

4. Meet their needs through
   a. Formal learning events sponsored by the organization and HRD department
   b. Informal learning projects on and off the job
   c. College courses and workshops
   d. Professional conferences
   e. Self-study and correspondence courses
   f. Vendor-offered instruction outside and inside the organization

5. Evaluate outcomes based on personal goals and objectives.

These steps are illustrated in Figure 13.14.

If the curriculum is individualized-informal, people establish their own goals without necessarily consulting others.[32,33] Learning plans are not usually formalized in writing. If the curriculum is individualized-contractual, people negotiate goals, objectives, and corresponding activities with superiors, counselors, and/or HRD practitioners. Learning plans are formalized in writing. Sometimes they are geared explicitly to career plans and forwarded to the HRD department so it can use them (1) in identifying and scheduling instructional offerings, and (2) for information about the collective aspirations of employees generally.

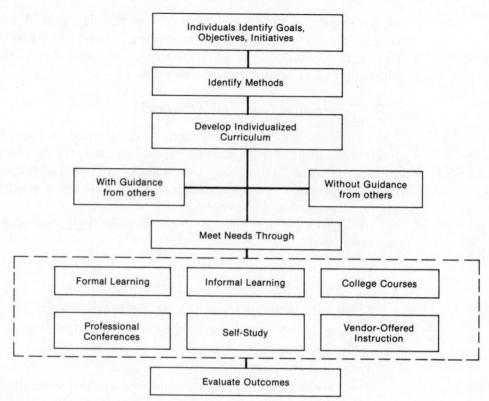

Figure 13.14   Steps in designing an individualized curriculum

Advantages of these methods include:

1. *Emphasis on the individual.* Since individual differences vary widely, it is important to take them into account. This method does best in this respect.

2. *Emphasis on career needs.* This method allows individuals to select their learning activities according to their significant life concerns and career objectives—and the result is usually high motivation to achieve.

On the other hand, there is a major disadvantage: people may be encouraged to meet their personal needs to the possible exclusion of organizational needs. By helping people advance in their careers, the organization may risk higher turnover and loss of investment in human potential.

To develop a group-oriented curriculum, the HRD practitioner needs to:

1. Formulate broad, general questions pertinent to job incumbents at each level and in each job class of the organization.
2. Establish programs to address each broad question.
3. Formulate more specific questions for each program or component of a program.
4. Offer each program and
   a. Allow learners to contribute their own questions
   b. Allow learners to refine questions, add them, or drop them
5. Organize each program for maximum participant interaction in trying to answer the questions finally agreed upon.
6. Evaluate each program in terms of individual perceptions.

This model is illustrated in Figure 13.15.

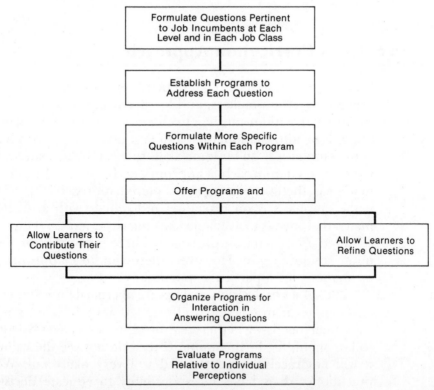

Figure 13.15 Steps in designing a group-oriented curriculum

This method is based on the Socratic approach of asking questions. Instructors serve as facilitators; learners share insights. Learning occurs through discovery, group interaction, and experience-sharing.

Advantages include:

1. *Emphasis on group interaction and team building.* Individuals learn from peers and experience group dynamics as well as formal learning.

2. *Emphasis on creative thought.* Individuals learn to draw on and reflect their own insights.

3. *Emphasis on making members of the learner group, not instructors, responsible for success of the learning event.*

The major disadvantage of this method is the difficulty of planning precise outcomes. The value of the group experience depends entirely on the experience level of participants and their willingness to interact.

How to Select a Curriculum Approach

What approach to use? That depends on curriculum purpose and goals, values of decision-makers, and learner needs.

Any curriculum can be effective for at least one purpose. If the emphasis is on information, then a subject-centered approach is appropriate. If the emphasis is on building skills that can be measured, then an objectives-centered approach is appropriate. If the emphasis is on generating new ideas, then the experience-centered approach is appropriate. Finally, if the emphasis is on providing individuals with a means by which to match their needs to available learning experiences, then an opportunity-centered approach is appropriate. There is no right or wrong approach in an absolute sense. However, there can be inappropriate approaches or methods for a particular purpose.

The values of decision-makers are of crucial importance for sustaining any long-term instructional effort.[34] If they back a venture because it suits their needs—whether real or only perceived—adequate resources will or should be forthcoming. If they do not see the value of a venture, it will not receive support—and will very likely fail. While the HRD practitioner does have a responsibility to educate decision-makers on options available, he or she will have to ask:

- What key groups of decision-makers are or will be affected by a program or the curriculum?
- What results does each group hope most to gain? Over what time span?
- What, if anything, does each group fear about the instructional effort?
- What curriculum approach is each group likely to prefer? Why?

By addressing these questions, the practitioner can gain important clues for choosing an appropriate curriculum approach, identifying needs, establishing initial and continuing support for the HRD effort, and ensuring effective transfer of learning back to the job. Different groups—such as top management, middle and lower management, and trainees—may each have their own goals, and these goals may conflict. Whose goals should take priority under the circumstances?

Finally, any instructional effort is sure to fail if it does not address learner needs. The basic questions are:

- What needs?
- What learners?
- In whose view?

Individuals may differ on their needs—and their perceptions should be considered in assessing needs and choosing the appropriate curriculum.

Summing Up: The First Volume

The first volume of this set has focused primarily on the "big picture," the macro-level of HRD. Here is a summary of some major points:

We defined HRD as "organized learning experiences sponsored by an employer and/or conducted in the work setting for the purpose of improving work performance while emphasizing the betterment of the human condition through integration of organizational goals and individual needs." The HRD field owes a debt to

1. The Human Capital school of economics, which emphasizes the productive value of human creativity.

2. Third Wave psychology, which emphasizes the human potential for growth.

3. The Systems school of management, which has provided tools for describing and analyzing organizations.

4. The Human Resources school of management, which has provided norms for thinking about people.

5. Organization Development, a sister discipline to HRD, which has provided tools for facilitating intergroup and intragroup change.

6. Organizational Communication, which has provided tools for facilitating communication—a process that is basic to learning in organizational contexts.

7. Adult Education and Job Training, which have provided tools for conducting instructional experiences.

HRD is a philosophy that deals with training, education, and development. Training is a present-oriented individual change process geared to improving knowledge and skills that can be used immediately on the job. Education is a future-oriented individual change process geared to stimulating new insights and preparing a person for career movement. Development encompasses the collective outcomes of a series of planned learning experiences over the long term.

HRD efforts are influenced by:

1. The broad environment outside organizations.

2. The organizational environment, consisting of
   a. External conditions
   b. Internal conditions

3. Work groups.

4. Individual differences.

Job performance depends on the opportunity to perform, individual skills and talents, the nature of the performance required, outcomes associated with performance, and feedback on outcomes.

HRD efforts are appropriate when (1) the opportunity to perform can be identified, (2) people lack skills and talents, (3) the nature of required performance can be identified but individuals do not know how to do so, (4) performance outcomes are meaningful, and (5) people receive feedback on outcomes but are unable to use it because they lack knowledge or skill.

Values are important as yardsticks for decision-making and thus affect performance. Both individuals and organizations have values, and people in the same profession or occupation often share many values. HRD meets most of the criteria that distinguish a profession from a mere discipline or field of study—but to be effective, HRD practitioners should clarify their own values and develop a personal philosophy to guide decision-making.

A role is behavior associated with a job or position. It is influenced by the environment, the organization, other people, individual values, and the work group. The HRD practitioner has 15 general roles. Each role is associated with certain competencies (behaviors) and outputs (work products).

To plan for entering the HRD field, learn more about it and then identify personal strengths and weaknesses relevant to personal career goals. Strengths help get the first job. Weaknesses can be corrected by gaining relevant experience, participating in formal or informal instruction, or other methods. Once in the field, an individual has 12 possible career paths.

It is important to recognize that HRD is not an end in itself; rather, it is a means to help organizations and individuals realize their plans. HRD should thus contribute to organizational strategic planning, human resources planning, and individual career planning. One way is to establish long-range plans for the HRD department itself and manage it accordingly. Another is to encourage the creation of a long-range curriculum plan that helps guide the overall development of the organization through the development of individual employees. This curriculum is in turn comprised of limited-scope curricula geared to specific job progression ladders or career paths. These limited-scope plans are further subdivided into short-term instructional programs, each possessing a definite beginning and end.

The first volume has thus described these critical issues and relationships:

- The HRD field and other fields.
- The individual as focus of change and factors or contexts affecting the individual.
- The HRD practitioner and his or her values, philosophy, actual or potential roles, and career plans.
- The external environment, the organization, and HRD efforts.

- HRD initiatives and other HR initiatives.
- Individual career planning and the HRD practitioner.
- The HRD department and its organizational environment.
- Ways of conceptualizing individual change (learning) efforts and instructional planning.
- Long-term, intermediate-term, and short-term instructional plans and the HRD effort or department.

The next volume focuses on the specifics of what HRD practitioners do, including:

1. Identifying instructional needs.
2. Developing instruction to meet those needs.
3. Implementing instruction through appropriate logistics and delivery methods.
4. Evaluating how well instruction will probably work, is working, or has worked to meet needs.
5. Ensuring that individual change is transferred back to the job.
6. Identifying possible future trends that will affect the HRD field and the roles of practitioners.

References

1. Howson, A. *Curriculum Development and Curriculum Research.* Philadelphia, PA: Taylor & Francis, 1983.
2. McNeil, J. *Curriculum: A Comprehensive Introduction.* New York: Little Brown, 1984.
3. Wiles, J., and J. Bondi. *Curriculum Development: A Guide to Practice,* 2nd ed. Columbus, OH: Merrill, 1984.
4. Galosy, J. "Curriculum Design for Management Training." *Training and Development Journal* 37 (1983) 1: pp. 48–53.
5. Torres, G., and M. Stanton. *Curriculum Process in Nursing: A Guide to Curriculum Development.* Englewood Cliffs, NJ: Prentice-Hall, 1982.
6. Beauchamp, G. *Curriculum Theory,* 4th ed. Itasca, IL: R. E. Peacock, 1981.
7. Bobbitt, F. *The Curriculum.* Boston: Houghton-Mifflin, 1918.

8. Giroux, H., and D. Purpel, eds. *The Hidden Curriculum and Moral Education.* Berkeley: McCutchan, 1983.

9. Goodlad, J. *Curriculum Inquiry.* New York: McGraw-Hill, 1979.

10. Pratt, D. *Curriculum: Design and Development.* New York: Harcourt, Brace and Jovanovich, 1980.

11. Taba, H. *Curriculum Development: Theory and Practice.* New York: Harcourt, Brace and World, 1962.

12. Tyler, R. *Basic Principles of Curriculum and Instruction.* Chicago: University of Chicago Press, 1949.

13. Unruh, G., and A. Unruh. *Curriculum Development: Problems, Processes and Progress.* Berkeley, CA: McCutchan, 1984.

14. Bailey, R. *Human Performance Engineering.* Englewood Cliffs, NJ: Prentice-Hall, 1982.

15. Caswell, H., and D. Campbell. *Curriculum Development.* New York: American Book Company, 1935.

16. Knowles, M. *The Adult Learner: A Neglected Species,* 3rd ed. Houston: Gulf, 1984.

17. Saylor, J., W. Alexander, and A. Lewis. *Curriculum Planning for Better Teaching and Learning,* 4th ed. New York: Holt, Rinehart and Winston, 1981.

18. Rothwell, W. "Curriculum Design: An Overview." *Personnel Administrator* 28 (1983) 11: pp. 53–54, 56–57.

19. Rummler, G. "The Performance Audit." In *Training and Development Handbook,* 2nd ed., R. Craig, ed. New York: McGraw-Hill, 1976.

20. Rothwell, W. "Strategic Needs Assessment." *Performance and Instruction Journal* 23 (1984) 5: pp. 19–20.

21. Carkhuff, R. et al. *The New ISD* (2 vols.). Amherst, MA: Human Resource Development Press, 1984.

22. Dick, W., and L. Carey. *The Systematic Design of Instruction,* 2nd ed. Glenview, IL: Scott Foresman, 1985.

23. Blank, W. *Handbook for Developing Competency-Based Training Programs.* Englewood Cliffs, NJ: Prentice-Hall, 1982.

24. Boyatzis, R. *The Competent Manager: A Model for Effective Performance.* New York: Wiley, 1982.

25. Ingalls, J. "Out With Job Descriptions: Write Competency Models." *Training* 16 (1979) 4: pp. 32--38.

26. Klemp, G. *Job Competency Assessment.* Boston: McBer, 1978.

27. McClelland, D. *A Guide to Job Competency Assessment.* Boston: McBer, 1976.

28. Zemke, R. "Job Competencies: Can They Help You Design Better Training?" *Training* 19 (1982) 5: pp. 28–31.

29. Rothwell, W. "Strategic Curriculum Design for Management Training." *Journal of Management Development* 3 (1984) 3: pp. 39–52.

30. Lewin, K. *Field Theory in Social Science.* New York: Harper, 1951.

31. Bank, A., M. Henerson, and L. Eu. *A Practical Guide to Program Planning.* New York: Teacher's College, Columbia University, 1981.

32. Houle, C. *The Design of Education.* San Francisco: Jossey-Bass, 1972.

33. Tough, A. *Learning Without a Teacher.* Toronto: Ontario Institute for Studies in Education, 1967.

34. Macdonald, J. "Value Bases and Issues for Curriculum." In *Curriculum Theory,* A. Molnar and J. Zahorik, eds. Alexandria, VA: Association for Supervision and Curriculum Development, 1977.

Glossary

Ability. The present capacity to engage in behavior.

Adult-Learning Understanding. Knowing how adults acquire and use knowledge, skills, attitudes. Understanding individual differences in learning.

Aptitude. An undeveloped or underdeveloped capacity to engage in behavior.

Authority. The amount of decision-making power that is delegated.

A/V Skill. Selecting and using audio/visual hardware and software.

Behaviorism. A theory of learning that focuses on observable, measurable change. Synonymous with "behavioralism."

Broad (External) Environment. Anything outside an organization.

BSO. Behavioral skills-output, a specific method of curriculum design.

Career. A series of jobs that are related in some way.

Career Counseling. A process of helping individuals plan their careers.

Career Development. A structured process of interaction between a representative of the organization and the individual.

Career-Development Knowledge. Understanding the personal and organizational issues and practices relevant to individual careers.

Career Management. A subcomponent of career development. It is a systematic, ongoing process to facilitate individual career planning.

Career Paths. Formal, detailed descriptions of interrelationships between jobs in an organization, expressed in terms of the training, education, experience, and behaviors required for movement between jobs.

Career Planning. A subcomponent of career development that is undertaken by an individual. It is a conscious, deliberate process of identifying and exploring career opportunities, setting goals, establishing direction, and choosing the means by which to attain the goals.

Career-Progression Ladder. Synonymous with a *job progression ladder.*

Career Strength. That which contributes to realization of a career goal or preference.

Career Weakness. That which impedes realization of a career goal or preference.

Cognitivism. A theory of learning concerned with the internal person and with insight or discovery.

Cohesiveness. The force that pulls a group together.

Competency-Identification Skill. Identifying the knowledge and skill requirements of jobs, tasks, and roles.

Computer Competence. Understanding and being able to use computers.

Concept-Development Cluster. Consists of three roles of the HRD practitioner concerned most with planning HRD activities. These roles are *Program Designer, Instructional Writer* and *Theoretician.*

Cost-Benefit Analysis Skill. Assessing alternatives in terms of their financial, psychological, and strategic advantages and disadvantages.

Counseling Skill. Helping individuals recognize and understand personal needs, values, problems, alternatives, and goals.

Culture. The unspoken pattern of values that guides behavior in work groups and organizations. It regulates behavior and thereby influences individual performance.

Curriculum. In normal usage, a plan for instruction or learning. The term is used in this book to refer to planned learning experiences.

Curriculum Design. The engineering of instruction, implying the formulation of a plan through careful forethought.

Curriculum Development. The gradual evolution of an instructional plan from conception through implementation.

Data-Reduction Skill. Scanning, synthesizing, and drawing conclusions from data.

Delegation Skill. Assigning task responsibility and authority to others.

Departmentalization. Grouping jobs together in an organizational design.

Development. One of several ways to stimulate individual change. It is long-term, sometimes spanning three years or more. Systematically rotating an employee through a series of jobs with some purpose in mind is a process of development.

Developmental Theory of Career Planning. The view that individuals pass through stages of development.

Developmentalism. A theory of learning that emphasizes the importance of individual life cycle stages in learning.

Dimensional Theory of Career Planning. The theory that asserts that career planning is a matter of analyzing individual personality, analyzing occupations, and matching them.

Division of Labor. How the duties, responsibilities, and tasks of an organization or department are allocated.

Divisional Structure. An organizational design in which a layer of management is added below the functional structure to oversee activities by location or product type.

Economic Theory of Career Planning. The theory that assumes people select occupations in which they can maximize their income.

Education. In the work setting, it is one of several methods to stimulate individual change. Its focus is intermediate-term and on preparing people for promotion, transfer, or other anticipated future progress.

Entrepreneurial Structure. An organizational design in which there is only one manager with decision-making authority.

Environmental Analysis. The process which (1) identifies the characteristics of the environment most critical to the organization and (2) predicts how those characteristics are likely to change.

Environmental Variables. Differences between individuals resulting from family, culture, and social class.

Evaluator. The HRD role of identifying the extent of a program's or product's impact.

Existential Theory of Career Planning. A theory that says career decisions result from individual choice alone. People must accept responsibility for "frightful freedom" and for giving meaning to a world that otherwise lacks it.

Experience-Centered Instruction. A theory of instruction based on *cognitivism*. It focuses on what learners experience during instruction and on evoking new insights.

Facilities Skill. Planning and coordinating logistics in an efficient and cost-effective manner.

Feedback Skill. Communicating opinions, observations, and conclusions in such a way that they are understood.

Functional Structure. An organizational design in which managers or supervisors are given responsibility for particular kinds of activities like personnel or marketing.

Futuring Skill. Projecting trends and visualizing possible and probable futures and their implications.

Group Facilitator. The HRD role of managing group discussions and group process so that individuals learn and feel the experience is positive.

Group-Process Skill. Influencing groups to both accomplish tasks and fulfill the needs of their members.

HR. Human resources.

HRD. See *Human Resources Development.*

HRP. See *Human Resources Planning.*

HRD Department. The department which has the chief responsibility for directing and/or coordinating HRD efforts in an organization. The term is used synonymously with the Training Department.

HRD Effort. A general term that can refer to any HRD activity at any level—curriculum, program, unit, or lesson.

HRD Function. Refers to any activities related to HRD that occur in an organizational setting, regardless of whether conducted by an HRD department or by those outside of the department.

HRD Practitioner. Literally, one who practices HRD. The term can be used broadly to mean anyone who is associated in any way with the training, education, or development of people. In this book it is frequently used in a more restrictive sense to mean one who designs, delivers, and evaluates instruction as a full-time job in an organization.

Human Resources Development. Organized learning experiences sponsored by an employer and designed and/or conducted in the work setting for the purpose of improving work performance while emphasizing the betterment of the human condition through the integration of organizational goals and individual needs.

Human Resources Planning. The process of trying to ensure that the right people with the right skills are on hand at the right time so as to implement organizational strategy. HRP integrates and coordinates hiring, promoting, training, and other activities.

In-House. Literally, that which takes place inside an organization. It is distinct from external, that which takes place outside an organization.

Individual-Development Counselor. The HRD role of helping an individual assess personal competencies, values, and goals and identify and plan development and career actions.

Industry Understanding. Knowing the key concepts and variables that define an industry or sector (e.g., critical issues, economic vulnerabilities, measurements, distribution channels, inputs, outputs, information sources).

Instructional Experience. A general term referring to participation in a program or to the program itself.

Instructional Writer. The role of preparing written learning and instructional materials.

Intellectual Versatility. Recognizing, exploring, and using a broad range of ideas and practices. Thinking logically and creatively without undue influence from personal biases.

Interface Cluster. Consists of four roles that are concerned more with the relationship between the HRD department and its environment than with the internal operations of the department. These roles are *marketer, group facilitator, instructor* and *transfer agent.*

Internal Appraisal. That step in organizational strategic planning that assesses how well the organization is achieving its purpose. It basically consists of analyzing organizational strengths and weaknesses.

Intragroup. Within a group.

Intraorganization. Within an organization.

ISD. Instructional systems design, a specific method of curriculum design.

Job-Progression Ladder. Career paths in which progressively higher positions in the organizational hierarchy are explicitly linked and the education and experience needed to progress are explicitly stated.

Leadership Cluster. Consists of two related roles of the HRD practitioner, that of *strategist* and *manager of training and development.*

Learning. A change in perceptions, attitudes, and behaviors of an individual or a group or organization.

Lesson. Part of an instructional unit, usually expanded to clarify how to carry out an activity.

Library Skill. Gathering information from printed and other recorded sources; identifying and using information specialists, reference services, and other aids.

Life-Cycle Theory. The view that individuals, groups, departments, and organizations progress through stages of development, each of which is characterized by a central crisis that must be resolved before progression to the next stage.

Life Planning. A process of establishing goals and directions for one's entire life. Career planning is a subcomponent of life planning.

Limited-Scope Curriculum. A portion of an organizational curriculum geared to those in a specific job progression ladder, job class, or occupation.

Manager of Training and Development. The HRD role of planning, organizing, staffing, and controlling training and development operations or training and development projects and of linking training and development operations with other organization units. (*Models for excellence*, 1983, p. 79).

Managing HRD at the Strategic Level. The process of developing a long-range plan for the HRD department that takes into account present strengths/weaknesses and likely future opportunities/threats that might affect it.

Marketer. The HRD role of selling Training and Development viewpoints, learning packages, and programs and services to target audiences outside one's own work unit.

Matrix Structure. An organizational design in which project managers (see *Project Structure*) are placed at the same level or status as divisional managers (see *Divisional Structure*).

Media Specialist. The HRD role of using audio, visual, computer, and other hardware-based technologies for training and development—and producing software for these technologies.

Model. A simplified representation of an object, process, or phenomenon.

Motivation. That which acts to impel behavior.

Motivational Variables. Differences between individuals resulting from the values they associate with various types of rewards.

Model-Building Skill. Developing theoretical and practical frameworks which describe complex ideas in understandable, usable ways.

Needs Analyst. The HRD role of defining gaps between ideal and actual performance and specifying the cause of the gaps.

Negotiation Skill. Securing win-win agreements while successfully representing a special interest in a decision situation.

Norm. A rule of conduct. Explicit norms stem from formal policy or procedure; implicit norms arise informally between individuals.

Objectives-Preparation Skill. Preparing clear statements to describe desired outputs.

Objectives-Centered Instruction. A theory of instruction based on *behaviorism*. It focuses on observable and measurable outcomes of instruction.

Operating Objectives. Statements of measurable results desired from the HRD department.

Opportunity-Centered Instruction. A theory of instruction based on *developmentalism*. It focuses on matching individual needs to appropriate instructional experiences, particularly for helping people adapt to change resulting from their life cycles.

Organization-Behavior Understanding. Seeing organizations as dynamic, political, economic, and social systems with multiple goals; using this larger perspective as a framework for understanding and influencing events and change.

Organization Development. A long-term change effort directed to an entire organization or some part of it, using techniques from the applied behavioral sciences.

Organization Understanding. Knowing the strategy, structure, power networks, financial position, and systems of a specific organization. (*Models for Excellence*, 1983, p. 36).

Organizational Culture. See *Culture*.

Organizational Curriculum. All formal, planned learning activities that are either conducted or coordinated by the HRD department. It includes all programs offered in the classroom, planned job rotations, external seminars, college courses, individualized study materials, and other delivery methods integrated into a coherent whole. It is the long-term learning plan for the entire organization.

Organizational Design. The process of establishing and maintaining the allocation of work duties and reporting relationships. Synonymous with structure.

Organizational Environment. That part of the broad external environment which influences the functioning of an organization directly. Any supplier, distributor, or stockholder is part of the organizational environment.

Organizational Goal. A desired end state or condition that does not lend itself to measurement.

Organizational Objective. A desired end state or condition, derived from a goal, that does lend itself to measurement.

Organizational Purpose. The reason that an organization exists, its mission.

Organizational Strategic Planning. See *Strategic Planning*.

Pedagogy. An informal philosophy of teaching that focuses on what the instructor does rather than on what participants learn. It emphasizes the transmission of information.

Perception. The way people interpret what they sense.

Performance. In the simplest sense, the outcomes of behavior.

Performance-Observation Skills. Tracking and describing behaviors and their effects.

Personal Philosophy. In a professional context, an individual's beliefs about how a profession should be viewed and about the appropriate approaches and methods of practice.

Personality. Acquired patterns or habits of behavior.

Personnel/HR-Field Understanding. Understanding issues and practices in other HR areas (*Organization Development,* Organization Job Design, *Human Resources Planning,* Selection and Staffing, Personnel Research and Information Systems, Compensation and Benefits, Employee Assistance, Union/ Labor Relations).

Physiological Variables. Differences in the physical and mental abilities of individuals.

Policy. A broad description of preferred actions intended to ensure coordination within a department or between departments. It is activated through *procedures.*

Presentation Skill. Verbally presenting information in such a way that the intended purpose is achieved.

Procedures. Related to policies, they provide detailed guidance on how a task is to be done or how activities should be handled in a manner consistent with policy.

Profession. A field or discipline with core elements distinct from other fields or disciplines; a field that has passed through particular stages of development; an occupation requiring governmental licensure.

Program. An instructional experience with a definite beginning and ending. A subcomponent of a *limited-scope curriculum* and an *organizational curriculum, it is synonymous with course, seminar, or workshop. It is composed of units* and *lessons.*

Program Administrator. The role of ensuring that the facilities, equipment, materials, participants, and other components of a learning event are present and that program logistics run smoothly.

Program Designer. The HRD role of preparing objectives, defining content, and selecting and sequencing activities for a specific *program.*

Program Policy. A description of how the HRD department determines when to reimburse for training, who is eligible for it, and other major issues. The policy makes clear the purpose of the HRD department and for what it is accountable.

Project Structure. An organizational design in which managers are placed in charge of a team of people temporarily for the duration of an assignment or project.

Psychological Theory of Career Planning. This theory says that early childhood has a profound impact on subsequent career choice. Work is really a sublimation of infantile impulse, and occupations can be described in terms of the needs they help satisfy.

Psychological Variables. Differences between individuals resulting from perception, attitude, personality, learning, and motivation.

Questioning Skill. Gathering information from individuals and groups and stimulating their insight through interviews, questionnaires, and other probing methods.

Rational Theory of Career Planning. A theory that assumes that people consciously select their careers. Occupational choice depends equally on a sense of personal identity and information about labor market demand.

Records-Management Skill. Storing data in easily retrievable form.

Relationship Versatility. Adjusting behavior in order to establish relationships across a broad range of people and groups.

Research Cluster. Consists of three roles of the HRD practitioner concerned with determining the need for formal, organized learning activities or the value of such activities in removing performance deficiencies. These roles are *evaluator, needs analyst,* and *task analyst.*

Research Skill. Selecting, developing, and using methodologies and statistical and data collection techniques for a formal inquiry.

Role. A set of behaviors expected of someone by virtue of his or her job duties and status.

Satisfaction. Feelings about both outcomes and methods used in achieving them.

Skill. Task-specific ability.

Social-Learning Theory. The view that people learn by observing and imitating the behavior of others.

Sociological Theory of Career Planning. A theory that says family, religion, and school are crucially important in early career planning decisions. People learn from those with whom they come in contact.

Socialization. The process of learning how to enact a role in a unique setting or work culture. It consists of three stages: role anticipation, role development, and role stabilization. During socialization, individuals gradually internalize the values of those around them.

Span of Control. The number and types of jobs that report to a supervisor.

Springboard. A job so highly visible outside an organization that it frequently leads to

moves into a higher-level position in a different firm.

Standards. Short, concise statements of broad import that serve as directives for action.

Status. Rank within a group.

Strategic Plan. The result of the organizational strategic planning process. A formal plan is written; an informal plan is unwritten and is carried around in the minds of the highest-level decision-makers.

Strategic Planning. The process by which an organization determines how it will achieve its purpose over the long term, given expected opportunities and problems presented by the external environment and the strengths and weaknesses of the organization itself. Perhaps most easily understood as a mode of competition.

Strategist. The HRD role of developing long-range plans for what the training and development structure, organization, direction, policies, programs, services, and practices will be in order to accomplish the training and development mission.

Structure. The formal means of organization; the grouping of departments, divisions, work groups, jobs, and individuals.

Subject-Centered Instruction. An instructional approach based on *pedagogy.* It focuses on what will be taught and, from the learner's standpoint, acquisition of information.

Suspension Bridge. A career ladder that links otherwise unrelated jobs in an organization in terms of the education and experience needed to move between them.

Task Analyst. The HRD role of identifying activities, tasks, sub-tasks, and human resource and support requirements necessary to accomplish specific results in a job or organization.

Theoretician. The HRD role of developing

and testing theories of learning, training, and development.

Theory. A plausible principle or group of principles offered to predict and explain facts, observations, or events.

Training. One of several methods to stimulate individual change. Its focus is short-term and is directed solely at furnishing the knowledge or skill that individuals need to carry out present work duties efficiently and effectively.

Training Department. See *HRD Department.*

Training-and-Development-Field Understanding. Knowing the technological, social, economic, professional, and regulatory issues in the field; understanding the role T&D plays in helping individuals learn for current and future jobs.

Training-and-Development-Techniques Understanding. Knowing the techniques and methods used in training and understanding their appropriate uses.

Transfer Agent. The HRD role of helping individuals apply learning after the learning experience.

Unit. Part of an instructional program.

Values. Perhaps best understood as a persistent belief that one way of behaving or one goal is preferable to an opposite way of behaving or another goal.

Visualizing the Future. An important step that precedes strategic planning. It involves developing a vision of what an organization should be at some point in the future.

Work Group. Organizationally-created associations of people. Everybody who works in the same location and reports to the same supervisor is part of an easily identifiable work group.

Writing Skill. Preparing written material that follows generally accepted rules of style and form, is appropriate for the audience, is creative, and accomplishes its intended purposes.